ATHEISM IN CHRISTIANITY

The Religion of the Exodus and the Kingdom

ERNST BLOCH

Translated by J. T. Swann

HERDER AND HERDER

1972
HERDER AND HERDER NEW YORK
232 Madison Avenue, New York 10034

ISBN: 665-00012-x
Library of Congress Catalog Card Number: 72–165 497

CONTENTS

5

To think is to step over, to overstep.

The best thing about religion is that it makes for heretics.

Religion is re-ligio, binding back. It binds its adherents back, first and foremost, to a mythical God of the Beginning, a Creator-God. So, rightly understood, adherence to the Exodus-figure called "I will be what I will be," and to the Christianity of the Son of Man and of the Eschaton, is no longer religion.

Only an atheist can be a good Christian; only a Christian can be a good atheist.

What is decisive: to transcend without transcendence.

Dies septimus nos ipsi erimus.

(Augustine)

ATHEISM IN CHRISTIANITY

ROUND THE CORNER

1. Against the Goad

Remorse alone does not bring maturity, above all when the conscience that pricks still does so childishly, still according to custom, but in a slightly different way. The voice still comes from outside, from above—"the One above," so often suspiciously at ease. Thou shalt be still: this downward, exclusively downward cry from above, against too many demands from below, looks exactly like the well-disguised, indeed apparently good slogan that one should not covet one's neighbor's goods, or that even the Jews are now men once more. And it has the same purpose.

There is a sort that will always want to think things over, or—what is often the same—hold back altogether, so long as a substitute father-ego outside does not persuade the generally quite submissive conscience any differently. But remorse, as really breaking new soil, must do more than just trade in the regulating *On-dit*—and with it for the most part no more than the lord and master of the day. Far better, therefore, for the real conscience to listen to the voice of those who suffer need; need they can only remove by removing those who do not suffer, but live from that need. And this above all demands maturity; demands mind, not meekness.

13

The mind feels it harder at times to speak candidly than to feel true. But there has very often been a way of speaking in metaphors, a forced speech, easy to grasp but harder to come to grips with. The good soldier Schweik has turned up in every age; and, what is so noteworthy, so instructive, not without echoes of the Bible in his mouth; for one should not muzzle the ox that treads the corn, however necessary the drivers may find it to do so, both inwardly and outwardly. Especially when the ox has ceased to be an ox.

2. A Glance at Slave-Talk

He who crouches will say only what They-up-there want to hear. That too is slave-talk, where the worm wriggles and the dog's tail wags, as has always been the case. It is straightforwardly submissive slave-talk, concealing nothing. But there is another sort which is far more noticeable. That is the slave-talk found in the studied lines of the underground text, where its form gives food for thought.

This slave-talk is dangerous to the ruling classes, and has therefore always been masked from them. It has never been expressly examined as it deserves; it has never been subjected to form-criticism, although that would be very instructive for Bible-criticism too. For it differs from texts which have merely been changed or added later from above: it wears its mask, rather, from below, and wears it freely, as a first form of alienation, a characteristic change of ground.

This special sort of "clothing" reaches from Aesop's Fables to Montesquieu's *Lettres Persanes* (1721), where the France of Louis XV wears a Persian mask. It is there too when a portrait of Caligula can bring the name of Hitler to every tongue. That is good slave-talk, even cunning in an admissible sense: it allows freedom to be more than merely whispered in a subjugated and over-ordered world.

This sort of slave-talk has even inspired a writing of its own. One that is not just bare-faced satire, but which, like Schweik, has a quality of sly irony that does not need more learned turns of rhetoric or knowledge—a quality it manifests through many different ages. One might well ask whether some parts of the Bible should not have had a lesson for these circles; the many instances, for example, when the people murmured to themselves. And in fact certain passages did teach, not only in the course of permitted Bible-readings, but also in the sermons of the Poor-people's-priests. They taught their lesson, from the poor widow with the empty oil-jug to the priestlings of Baal and Mammon, in whom men saw reflected the clergy of the day. And even if the attentive listener, now no longer bowed to the ground, did not himself associate the name of Balaam with all sorts of cross-grained blessings which should really have been curses (Num. 22), the tangle was willingly seized upon by slave-talk and turned round and re-directed against the local lords, in order, while singing their praises, to kick against their goad. Men often spoke in parables, saying one thing and meaning another; praising the prince and praising the gallows to prove it.

Later on, of course, when the type of pressure changed, the outsider could no longer understand this art of cursing while one blessed. And *Gulliver's Travels* could then become a children's book, despite the scornful way in which its alienation is camouflaged. It could become harmless, *hors de concours*. For the slaves change.

SCANDAL AND FOLLY

3. No Longer So Submissive

Left to himself no man likes to suffer. Unless he does not really suffer at all, but takes cringing pleasure in it, even enjoying the blows as inevitable if his soul is to well-up again; then the look of suffering is not only mollified but thankful. And it is just this thanking that seems so hypocritical. But— leader, enslave us! This cry, this tune has become suspect at last. It has appeared in several places, but the man who acquiesced without a murmur was more of a dog than a new-born man. One does not want even the loftiest boot in one's face any more, on the excuse that far from degrading one it makes one better. The real better-ones always found that just too much, just too stupid.

4. From Sighing to Murmuring

Nor is that exactly a pious attitude. One does not bend the knee to every so-called blessing from on high. That sort of gesture and feeling points back to the relics of old-time

16

slavery. Need teaches us, for this reason too, not to pray any more; that it is for the most part so obviously brought about by our fellows.

The name and address of those who have caused it and kept it going has in the meantime become fairly well known. Their dwelling-place is recognized, however they put on a new disguise or seek false anonymity. And it is a very earthly one: very much a place of flesh and blood which has been seen through and is, therefore, in our power if we want it so—not simply above us. So this state of affairs could quite clearly be prevented—could even be used—by us, and by us alone.

Even when something good occurred, only a few men really stood upright. we give thanks for your gracious gifts . . . Who still says that now? The words might have been sung at his cradle by winged creatures from Eden . . . The hen drinks no drop of water without a glance to heaven—however many human hens there are; the stupid children's verse is no longer a complete parable for them. Men might still give thanks for salvation, especially when they no longer know where to turn for counsel, or when the air is thick. But an Up-there that is deaf—that, for most of the men who travel this road, is as good as none at all. The king's mounted messengers come very seldom, and, anyway, kings are no longer current coinage. So even when there has not been much enlightenment, old feelings have stopped, or are just paid lip-service. The experience of the father-ego is tacitly as good as dead, so its transposition high above is dead as well. In most states now there is no throne; all the more so, then, no transposed, celestial One to fill the gaps in human needs and explanations. Except as a stop-gap.

The Church has too readily and too long kept slaves with their nose to the ground. For Paul as well as for Luther all government is from God be it ever so bad. The opium of the people, it was called; but those who move in better circles know, unless they have trimmed their sails to quite another wind, that in real truth its name should be: the end of an illusion. That is true here, even if no more than here: any

17

shallow business-man could cause believed-in magic to be more astonishing than the real thing. The chieftain is ex. The Up-there, after so much social and scientific tree-felling, has been cleared entirely. Superiors, the Superior itself, exist, for the vast horde of employees who have come to their senses, only here below: that is quite enough for them to kneel to.

So, for the prescribed daily round and the stale routine, a state of semi-disillusionment is more useful than ever. And the mist, no longer believed in, can rightly be forgotten—so far as that is necessary.

5. Renunciation and the Semi-Disillusioned

NOT HOME AND DRY

Freedom implies release from something. That makes for emptiness—though it can be a purifying emptiness, open to real honesty. But the immediate, important issue is: What is this release for? Where does it lead? And no less important here, now that we have really done with all that is counterfeit: Has anything of genuine worth been lost? In the haste and, too often, superficiality, in the badly-wrought disenchantment of a man who has brought only half his mind to bear. And the other half—should he have one—may well not be of the best, in the case of man descended from the apes, or a man who can confuse St. Francis with Tartuffe (should he in fact have heard of either). There is an absolute withdrawal here, a poor-quality thing, over-direct, leaving an emptiness that cannot, in the long run, retain its purity in the way the Enlightenment wanted. No half-baked Enlightenment can make it here. Not that it re-establishes the old hypocrisies; but what it can do is to sow stupidity in other, non-priest-ridden ways—namely, Philistinism *(corruptio optimi pessima),* followed up later, in threatening gloom, with dreadful ersatz like the "Blood and Soil" movement of the Nazis.

When a dim, disturbed peasant-girl in Lourdes says she has

18

seen Mary, that is easy to explain, but it is also easy, and more than banal, to assert that the man in the Sputnik has seen no trace of the living God. Even conventional piety can, at this level, say it already knew God was invisible. In short, today's pseudo-enlightenment fits today's hypocrisy; the one is trash, the other rubbish; neither is *ad rem.* The narrow, dreary, not-at-any-price, above all at a reduced one, corresponds well to hackneyed lip-service, and *vice versa;* only seemingly do they disturb each other. The fact remains, however, and nothing can detract from it, that thinking men, as such, were refusing to be priest-ridden any more. Long before simple, devout feelings had grown rusty, long before the real Enlightenment, pamphlets against the clergy and their lies were going the rounds among the peasants, complaining about the miserable swindling and deception of the poor. The real complaint was about the way the Scriptures were twisted to serve the exploiters and drudge-merchants, but these pamphlets also show the common man's will to speak for himself: he has finished with being struck across the mouth.

The peasants, however, were defeated, and their place was taken by the rationalistic bourgeoisie: in their Enlightenment the will to come of age became an all-consuming mission. In the eighteenth century, rejection of the earthly lord went hand in hand with rejection of an other-wordly Olympus. So when the citizens of France first dared to use their minds, they not only put to flight the this-worldly figure of the master and Lord, but at the same time reduced his other-worldly image to the status of a spook. It is, of course, true that the subsequent bourgeois period by no means saw the abolition of the lord: new, economic masters came, for the world of master and serf could not at the time be swept away entirely. So the religion of the On high had to be kept for the people: the old myth of lordship from on-high which, in Christianity, sanctioned, or at least explained, the unjust distribution of this world's goods with the just distribution of those of the next. For Christianity had become the state religion—a position for which it was not entirely unfitted.

Be comforted! That was the soothing formula for every murmur. Salvation lay for the Lutheran in the poor soul and her God; for the Papist in the Beyond. But it has also become clear, most recently among the German Fascists (certainly not a biblical crowd), that neo-paganism does nothing to revoke the real slave-ethics, the real master-outlook. Not even with Haeckel and Bölsche and "My church is the forest" behind it. When the law of the strong, and of natural selection, took the place of the word of love, it became apparent that giving up the Bible is not always enlightened: Nero's torches can burn all the brighter for it. Quite apart from these latter-day fruits, the enlightened Philistine of an earlier age, before Haeckel, Bölsche and the forest-church, had shown that not only faith can blind. Little tracts like "The Truth About Monasteries and the Stupefaction of the People" and "Moses or Darwin?," the products of half-educated and therefore only semi-disillusioned men, contributed little to lucidity or breadth of thought among the free-thinkers of the day. But most instructive of all in this anti-biblical world was how easy men found it to jump all the hurdles later on—this was no stock of Jesse . . . And it was not even as if there were any clarity in their position; indeed a touch of religious conscience still remained—of conscience, therefore, that was still mentally active, and active against the sacred fount of German strength, especially when it so clearly claimed to come from Antichrist. It would not all have been so easy if Francis of Assisi had been in the background, instead of the whore of Babylon.

Of course no simply-speaking anti-religious, preferably anti-Christian disillusionment was proof against really rotten illusions: against witchcraft that dispensed with all Ten Commandments, and even with the avenging thunderbolt. And it is also true, and more relevant here than ever, that it was the Church that gave the world the widest-reaching instrument of cruelty; and the Church is the institution least founded on enlightenment. She forbade cremation because of the resurrection of the body, but even in that field she did pioneering work: the funeral pyres of the Inquisition made her a model of progress even in witch-burning.

There is only this point, that Church and Bible are not one and the same. The Bible has always been the Church's bad conscience. Tolstoy, speaking against her, called not on Haeckel but on the words of Jesus. The Enlightenment, therefore, will be all the more radical when it does not pour equal scorn on the Bible's all-pervading, healthy insight into man. It is for this very reason (one not remote from the Enlightenment) that the Bible can speak to all men, and be understood across so many lands and right on through the ages.

6. The Strange Ubiquity of the Bible and Its Language

Why is it, then, that this remote language is never boring—or is so, in most cases, only at second hand? There are still valid reasons for the Bible's great popularity in the past. In Protestant countries it was even responsible for teaching its followers to read. It was called, simply, the Book, and no other book had so many editions down through the centuries; no other book made its way like this to the still and the quiet in the land. It did not matter to them that the stories there were so often intricate and contradictory, according to the various sources from which they were composed—no more did it matter to the age-old stories themselves. Even an obscure term like "Son of Man" would affect the simple undistracted reader, and mean more to him than the fancy language of loftier circles. Nor did the deep, personally-involving element in Scripture suffer distortion even in the Bible regions where no man commonly trod, or could tread any more. It is language as speaking-to.

This personal call, found nowhere else, has kept the Bible popular. Right through the ages and across the lands, as though

21

her life coursed in their veins; with Nimrod round the corner, with Jesus as guest. At all times borne along by her pictures and speech, so uniquely native to all lands, striking home over the great distance of space, and more than space. There is no other example: nothing has been absorbed like the Bible, despite its alien stock. For it speaks to so many people as though it had grown up with them. Nor is that just because children are taught the Scriptures so young. Tom Thumb and Hansel and Gretel come equally soon, and Barbarossa is certainly as well-known as King Solomon. And yet the earlier figure had for a long time the greater hold on people's fantasy, especially among the simple; and the stories told of him were precisely the biblical ones.

The examples multiply: Rebecca at the well, "I am Joseph, your brother," the Christ-child in the manger: all are recounted in the tersest of pictorial terms: all are archetypes. The chief contributory factor to their wide dissemination was, from the social point of view, the predominantly plebeian, and then peasant environment of which the writings speak, and in which, after conquest, they themselves came into being. They differ in this from most non-biblical sources of the military or inner-priestly worlds, even from Lao-Tse and from the teachings of Buddha, which cannot be taken out of their own country. And Scripture's language, too, is democratic. That is why Luther, when he was translating it, observed the peasant people's speech around him: so that the text would speak with their voice, and not just speak about them. And then the scenes themselves: in the old German pictures the stable at Bethlehem lies deep in snow; it is taken for granted, just as the Negroes take for granted that the Christ-child is black, and a black Moses thunders at the slave-owners in the Negro spiritual, Let my people go! That can be done with the Bible. No doubt a distinctively archetypal element is present, here too, as it is in the scene of Rebecca at the well, and of Joseph recognizing his brothers—a highly condensed master-image, not restricted to the Bible. For one sees the same primordial human feelings at work in the Nausicaa scene of the Odyssey or, so far as re-union is concerned, in Electra's meeting with Orestes, in Sophocles' play. But, for all that, is it conceivable that the Odyssey or Sophocles should find their way into the tiniest of cottages, and entirely without revision? The Bible-texts still drive smoothly home; in comparison with them, these works are, in their unmodernized form, superfluous. And when we stop to consider some of the other ancient religious documents, is it really possible to think of Lao-Tse's Tao, or the teachings of Buddha, or even the Epic of Gilgamesh as *tua fabula* in the same way as of the Bible—this book that is read by a peasant-girl of a winter evening in her mountain cabin? Is there any other case where the remote history of a small nation in a distant country only needed to be written-up to enjoy such ubiquity, and that as much for its form as for its content? Here was more than the board and lodging the classics offered us: far more, for wherever the Bible became established, it also became homely, to an astonishing degree.

It was, of course, the peasants in revolt who took the Bible, because of its democratic message, and in the first place, therefore, because of its universal language, to be *their* book. Not only because of the soft tones of love they heard there, but rather because of the anger—anger against the Ahabs and the Nimrods ("the mighty hunter," as Thomas Münzer said, "who first bestowed on man the heritage of Mine and Thine")—and because of the Exodus from slavery in Egypt. *Let my people go!* rang out to all the oppressed, "without difference or distinction of race or faith"—as Thomas Münzer said.

But there is another, negative side to this picture, too, a foil to the positive truth about the Bible, the positive biblical truth. It is this, and it is a striking fact: that the Church of the ruling-classes, and of the peasants' enemy, Luther, also took their stand on the Bible, and on a Bible that was not alien to their spirit. But it was a different Bible; in it there was no murmuring, except that of Corah and his company, who were destroyed. "Suffering and the Cross, suffering and the Cross is the Christian lot!" cried Luther to the rebellious peasants: he

23

could use the language of the Bible, and he did so, too, with Paul at his right-hand. For, leaving aside the inflammatory book of the Peasant Wars, one could surely, at the other end of the scale, always reckon too with the Bible's adaptability to select master-ideologies: it could sing the song of consolation, it could glorify dependence, as we have seen. It could and did make powerful matches which in no way appealed to the people and their "spirituals": quite the contrary, by Jove—by that Yahweh-figure so often still akin to Jupiter and the divine Caesar.

The point, however, to be made against all pseudo-enlightenment which sees religion as a spent force caught between the alternatives Moses or Darwin (and also to be made against all misty ambivalence) is this: the counter-blow against the oppressor is biblical, too, and that is precisely why it has always been suppressed or distorted, from the serpent on. It was the counter-blow that gave the Bible its popularity and its appeal. In the final analysis there is some similarity here to fairy tales which, for all their origins in a distant Arabian or Indian home, were, "like the Bible," able to melt almost without residue into a new environment.

The similarity admittedly also reaches to those regions where man is descended from the apes: for both the Bible and fairy tales are "hoaxes for children and nurse-maids." But the common factor, in the sense intended here, is rather their *closeness* to children and to ordinary folk. That is where the power-corrupt clergy failed. The biblical texts succeeded at the first attempt; and not only the naïve ones are accessible.

7. Whose Bible?

The Bible speaks with special directness to the ordinary and unimportant. It alone can claim to be audible to everyone. As for the way the clerics have used it, that can largely be judged and condemned by the text itself. For the Scriptures were always there to serve as the priests' bad conscience, not just in the case of pastoral letters under the Nazis: the funeral-pyres of an earlier age (which Calvin also helped to stoke) were not exactly Christian either. The preachers of the Peasant Wars, on the other hand, whether in England, Italy, France or Germany, took their whole stand on the Bible, on its truly popular tone. But the clerics were deaf to the cry of "Away with the Ahabs and Jezebels!" and spoke far more on Ahab and Jezebel's behalf, lauding them to heaven by the grace of God. Not that they found no room for prophetic wrath: that came in when they talked down to the people, along with much that was more germane to their masters' cause. And this attitude of theirs was not mere blasphemy or flagrant hypocrisy, for they could quote in their support many texts submissive to authority—interpolated by authority in fact. The Bible, then, is by no means a pure and undiluted solution of *De te fabula narratur,* of the ubiquity we have mentioned, valid for every social class. True, it cuts right across the nations, but, in its accepted form, it by no means cuts right across social classes. On the contrary, there is something very two-faced about it; something that is often a scandal to the poor and not always a folly to the rich.

Münzer could turn the Bible against Ahab and Jezebel, and even against Nimrod, in a way that would not have been possible with any other religious text. But Luther could take the same text and read it as a work not only of inwardness but also of "aboveness," of authority. And he did so with such ruthlessness and strength of language that some of the things he said sound as though they came from Moloch. The very ubiquity that led him to take notice of the people's speech was here repudiated as "Mr. Omnes," as the mob that should be "shot to pieces," with not a hint of "Let my people go!" And nowadays, when the biblical text is such a splendid thing, with such inner depths and authenticity, when it is demythologized at all costs, even at the cost of the fire, is it not true that the spark in it which flared up from below is also paralyzed, and can change nothing any more? Or there again, the On-high, the Up-there is thought of as the "Utterly-other," and the submissive, well-conducted citizen must leave it well alone. Conversely, this numinous "Utterly-other" can then act in a very mythical, repressive way, as if the Scriptures took no notice of the people's speech, but rather struck them across the mouth; but more of that later. The Bible is, then, by no means zealous only for the cause of My little ones, of the murmurers and malcontents; quite the opposite.

But over and against all this stand sentiments no other religious book contains: suffering that will suffer no longer; buoyant expectation of Exodus and restoration transformation—not in some Psalms of lowliness, but very definitely in Job, and elsewhere too. Piety here, from first to last, belongs to the restless alone; and the particular brand of Utopian loyalty which keeps him restless is the only thing that is, in the long run, deep.

PROMETHEUS A MYTH TOO

8. From Murmuring to Contention

When something is threatened, it withdraws into itself. Dread, above all things, makes us draw into ourselves, makes us pale and lonely. Dread is vague; unlike fear it has no single clear-cut object. Its fog is all the more crippling for that; it can be so dense, so full of horror, that the ego sinks helplessly away. And it draws back into an inwardness devoid of ego, a lonely, contact-less realm, where all one expects is the next blow. That holds good wherever one starts from, even with pure inwardness, with sheer, blind feeling. That sort of ducking the blows has a different ego from the one which drowns there.

The man possessed by fear, however, still possesses himself. There is an external object there, against which he can pluck up courage. With his ego still (unlike with dread) undissipated, he is still able at least to assert himself against it, however down-trodden or weak-kneed he might be. And from fear can come murmuring: the sound which first distinguishes a man from the blinkered herd. It may still be an entirely inward sound: a hidden fist, so to speak, whose only mark is on an acoustic register. It may for a long time remain buried within fear, ignorant even of the exterior threat, of the thunder above that has brought the fear forth. But for all that, this murmuring, which the Scriptures also call contention, can be the place where real backbone first begins to grow, and to stand upright. With a head on it which has begun to conceive the hope that the *last* word about what man can do, and what will be done to him, has not yet been spoken.

Already, then, this first beginning has two sides: a meek one which wags its tail on high, and a defiant one that kicks against the goad. Murmuring can certainly be cheeky or stupid, but it is always more human than tail-wagging. And so often it has been prophetically right—less stupid, then, than the lords and masters would have liked.

9. *"The Lord Has Said that He Would Dwell in Thick Darkness"*

Doubt begins where life becomes intolerable. That sort of head-shaking is far older and commoner than any which comes from thought. Doubt precedes thought every time when too much is asked of us—when things are a bit steep and the outlook is black.

Spare the rod and spoil the child is a proverb that takes some swallowing. The anger that wields the rod must be seen as thoroughly self-justified if it can only appeal to high superiority. Otherwise the On-high would begin to lose its footing in the face of the real *thinking* doubt that now comes to join mistrust—that comes when its time has come: the time to reject the giant's claim to rule over us and take us in. If he is seen then as an anti-human giant, he is already judged.

When Joseph embraced the brethren who had thrown him into the pit, he cut a different figure from the jealous God who does not forget unto the fourth generation. And, despite the similarity, even the vacillating, and hardly any more self-righteous figure whom Abraham could persuade into sparing

28

Sodom if ten just men lived there—even this figure is different from the jealous God. That is why this story has always appealed to heretics rather than courtiers. Job, for instance, would never have been so ready to sacrifice his son. For him, piety was not to be confused with conformity to law and order.

10. Contrary Principles in the Bible: Creation and Apocalypse

("And behold, it was very good"—"Behold, I make all things new.")

He who speaks down from on high must certainly have something beneath him. As if his people were children—preferably his own—to be kept in tutelage.

The idea was not confined to early biblical sources. The Lord was the *numen* of the tribe; no less, but no more. Along with him there were, even early on in the Bible, other gods, Baalim, but they were weaker than him. Elijah mocked Baal completely: perhaps he was asleep, or away on a journey, so he could not accept the sacrifices made to him.

Only, even here it is not quite certain whether what he mocked was merely a *figment of the imagination* of these Baal-priests, or a real competitive god who was powerless only when compared with Yahweh. But when the tribal god Yahweh began to be worshipped not just henotheistically as a god, but monotheistically as the *only* one, he rose in people's minds from a purely local, tribal god to the Lord of all mankind, even the Lord and Creator of all the world. And it was above all his position as *creator* (a position the deities of other nations, like Zeus or Marduk, did not hold) that blocked the way, in the Psalter's words, to the pot arguing with the potter.

Instead, the Creator says at the end of his six days' work (and before that, too, after the third and fourth and fifth days, when life was formed): "And behold, it was very good." This

29

does not quite agree with his regret in Noah's day, when the wickedness of man was great in the earth, that he had made the race at all. But then, of course, the Fall came in between, with the serpent as scapegoat for the fact that not all the Lord had made was very good, or rather should still be called good when not all that happened was according to his will. So, through the serpent, freedom came into the world. But the curse which has lain on the world since man's first disobedience and expulsion from Paradise, was in fact taken as a cast-iron excuse for the Creator (who also made the serpent); the misery of this world was, from now on, no concern of his.

Not all religions share this conception of God as the actual maker of the world; and in fact very few would be so definite in their unqualified approval of the product. For them the greatest of the gods devotes himself to noble leisure, after the manner of the earthly aristocracy; war and government are the activities one can imagine Zeus or Marduk or Ammon-Re undertaking—there is nothing of the demiurge, the mud-pie-maker, about them. The demiurge conceptions of Genesis probably come from the Middle Kingdom, where the local sculptor-god, Ptah, became in a similar fashion the god of the entire kingdom of Egypt. Demiurge work is no longer frowned upon; it just makes the creature all the more dependent on its maker. But the Lord-and-master element which characterized all the other gods, not just Re or Marduk, is in no way diminished by all this. Indeed, when the solar emblems of ancient Egypt and astro-mythical Babylon disappeared, a Demiurge rose up in compensation to stand higher than the sun, for it too he had created. He made the earth his footstool, as the psalmist says, and he who is above the world was enthroned high in heaven above, as the One-and-only, the Invisible who lies beyond all that can be seen.

That is why misery fits so badly into this world made by such an all-creating God, the most omnipotent of all god-hypostases; and yet how rapidly misery gained ground. In the Lord's own people, too, and in Canaan: almost none of the promises were kept. Instead there came the Assyrians, Medes and Persians, the Babylonian captivity, Antiochus Epiphanes and the Romans, the destruction of the Temple, the razing of Jersusalem, and then, finally, the dispersion among the nations. And the ancient world itself, in its entirety, with all its rejection of the world and of creation, found its way right to the heart of the Creator-God's own people, the nation of *Behold, it was very good* . . . This cry gave way to *Paue! Paue!* (Be still! Be still!) Stoic trust in Heimarmenē, Fate, finally turned diabolical, and there was no helping hand then for the Demiurge, no *post-factum* construction of a sinful Fall. It was evil spirits that lived under the heavens now, in a world which had not fallen, but was *ab ovo* the product of an evil World-soul. From then on, the Bible has its own sort of dualism— though it was certainly incipient before then: the dualism that lies in the concepts of creation and salvation. It was latent in the Bible, and repressed, ever since the appearance of the serpent in Paradise (no worm in the apple, but rather the apple of Knowledge itself). And similarly the Messiah-dream gathers weight precisely because it is not inspired from up-above-us by a Creator-God and Lord, but is filled with the hope that lies before-us; and this comes from the *Exodus,* the departure out of mammoth Egypt, which is in its turn the shoddy product and symbol of the world that has come to be.

So the principle that leads into this here-and-present world cannot also be the principle that leads out of it: that leads into a better world, the one true world, which in Christianity was later called *"mellon aion"*—the aeon free from rule and misery.

The real question here is whether man should be considered great or small. If mankind has "fallen," if he is half, or indeed wholly corrupt, then he can of his own accord do only evil: he can only err. Ever since the serpent's poisonous bite, his endeavors are evil, right from the days of his youth. In Lutheran eyes the corruption is so total that he just cannot *not* sin. For Catholics his efforts are still morally so weak that he must in the end exclaim, "Lord, lift the load yourself!" And that is where the scapegoat comes in, and Lucifer, and the demons which broke into Ptah-Yahweh's wonderful work of art. Because of them the load must be lifted—and the Creator of all things can then make his entry as the Redeemer of all.

Lord, lift it up yourself—this finally discredits those movements of creatures and of thought which in their totality go to make up "history": the story of human, man-made happenings. For Augustine history has indeed a very definite function; it was he who first singled out the category as a dramatic series of events, with acts and a *dénouement*. No longer is it the simple ebb and flow of eternally repeated incidents, as even Greek historians for the most part thought of it: in the light of the Bible it is something ultimate—the struggle between the evil rich and the Kingdom of God, which gains the final victory. But not even in Augustine's thought is any real human activity at work, for all the primacy he gives to will as a powerful and active principle even in man. All there is is the plain and simple following of God's will, and obedience to his saving deeds in history; and the plain and simple preparation (through the Church) for the Last Days, for the Judgment and the Kingdom. It was Augustine who gave us the dramatic concept of history and applied it to the Last Days of the Apocalypse, and to Christ as the turning point of time; but, for all that, there is, even in his thought, a clean break between history and the coming of the Kingdom. And with this break there goes a theistic absolutism of enormous proportions, thoroughly and decisively a-historical, despite his conception of history as the pilgrimage made by the City of God on earth.

Of course Augustine does not go so far as Karl Barth; for Barth sees as untrue each and every aspect of God's deeds which shows itself in history: God's action on man can only be like a "bomb-crater," it can never be historical. Nevertheless the jealous *Creator*-God does not, even with Augustine, leave the salvation of his world (salvation *out of* his world) to any spark of light which might spring up from inside human history itself: Abraham, Jesus, the whole of *salvation history* is

32

determined from above; otherwise it would all be, to Augustine, nothing but a helpless, vain wandering and pilgrimage. The enduring personal union of the Creator-divinity with a Savior-divinity, and the exoneration, now intensified, of the Creator-divinity and his work through the scapegoat provided by the demonic powers and Satan, all made for the exclusion of Prometheus at this end of things as well. Right in the *apocalyptic* order the old Creator-god displays and proves his own prowess in the *clean break* this order makes, for it has no need of human works or history.

However, this break in time is not a break in the *content* of the apocalyptic order: that would be irreconcilable with the equation Creator-Savior, with "Behold, it was very good" and "Behold, I make all things new." And it would be irreconcilable, for that matter, with the Mountain of Moriah, where the Lord sees differently; not to mention that quite antithetical, self-opposing God-principle which does away not only with marauding demons, but with the whole of Genesis pre-history as well, with the words (which *do* now show a real break in content): "Behold, I create new heavens and a new earth; and the former things shall not be remembered" (Is. 65. 17); "for the former things have passed away" (Rev. 21. 4). Here, however, some elements of primitive theism have been retained. Because of the Fall, when the demonic powers broke in on man, and because of the simple circular movement from there to creation, as the "primal state" before the Fall and the demonic intrusion, the new life which bursts in on man so radically has been in many ways back-dated. To man it can only come now as rebirth; to the world only as "transfigured" nature, that is, nature restored to its old state in Paradise. True, one cannot say here, as one can in the Platonic philosophy of anamnesis and of the *ordo sempiternus idearum, "Nil novi sub idea";* but certainly a *restitutio in integrum* has been added to the mixture, a turning-back in and through obedience; and again this is because man turns to the Demiurge as Saviour.

But the six days of creation and Paradise ("a park where only beasts could stay, not men"—Hegel) are not eventually

33

restored; not even in the Apocalypse—not even in its utmost
dreams, where all that remains good in and from the world is a
heavenly Jerusalem. And where even this figment of religious
fantasy is "coming down"—comes, therefore, from above;
though it is also prepared for men—"as a bride adorned for her
husband" (Rev. 21. 2). It was not without reason that Luther
called this last book of the Bible "every mobster's bag of
tricks": for its Eschaton is neither an inward thing, nor, even in
its wildly mythical character, an inaccessible taboo; nor does it
even preserve the links with the father-figure, the figure of
authority over nation and world. On the contrary, it contains
the strongest feelings of dissatisfaction found in any *re-ligio,*
any binding-back: and its adventist element is entirely free
from any *ordo sempiternus rerum.*

11. Discernment of Myths

GETTING AWAY FROM TALL STORIES

If you want to lull someone off to sleep, you don't talk loudly.
Many things seem refreshing when they merely dull the senses
in another way, while claiming to purge them. Let's get away
from the old fairy tales—that's fine; but all that happens is that
the primitive, uncultured specters are thrown out, but the
directives and announcements from on high remain to haunt us
as they always did. They just withdraw a bit and operate on the
inner perceptions, where they can avoid being stigmatized as
"mythical"—unlike Jesus' cures, for instance (where he is
swimming against the stream); and, for that matter, unlike his
alleged will to be crucified (where he is humbly submitting to
the idea of decree): both of these are now deemed mythical.
For both of them—the conceivable laying-on of hands and the
inconceivable empty tomb—are incompatible with modern
notions of an existential inner life. We should, then, be able to
make distinctions in the old stories themselves: distinctions
which, on closer analysis, have to do with myth. Do the
mythical fables treat of fabulous human deeds, or do they just

34

gloss over and embellish the pressure behind these deeds? For not all that comes down to us as fable is equally remote.

The first thing is to be able to discern the tone of these primitive stories. Although both are equally unscientific, the fairy tale has a recognizable tone quite different from that of the saga, with its mythical element. The fairy tale, too, may tell of wonderful deeds, but the listener can see through them—no sword hangs over him. That, in the second place, is due to the different social strata which fairy tales, on the one hand, and saga and myth, on the other, have imaged. For fairy tales are concerned with the people, sagas with their rulers; fairy tales tell of children and poverty, sagas of witches and Goliaths. There is all the difference in the world between the brave little tailor who goes out to seek his fortune, and the giant who bars his path—*he* stands for the great lords who breathe eternal fire and brimstone over eternal underlings. For all its happy ending, Grimm's "Giant's Plaything" is, with its serfs, a saga; Andersen's "Ugly Duckling," on the other hand, with its spirit of transformation and liberation, is the most beautiful of fairy tales. It is clear, of course, that both fairy tales and sagas are full of pre-scientific ideas; but how differently these ideas are used: what a different aim and purpose the fairy tales have, with their courageous, cunning heroes, compared with the myths, whose mighty lords instill fear on every hand. There are certainly mixed forms, too: even "Little Red Ridinghood" was originally a saga about the stars high above mankind, although the popular fairy tale has changed its function out of all recognition, so that now, in contrast to most myths, nothing more is asked of our mind than that we should use it. To speak in a modern way, most fairy tales have something Chaplinesque about them. They are not "mini-myths" as the reactionary interpretation would have it; nor are they myths with the magic crudely extracted. The fairy tale is a genre that has tried to avoid falling into the feudalism of the saga and the despotism of the myth, and has managed to save the mythical element in a different form—a form which suits its own proper spirit.

35

The mythical in a different form: that means, in the *third place*, then, that a distinction must be made within the genre of myth itself, for all its pre-scientific nature: a distinction between the *gigantic, dominating* element and those factors which, to say the least, would be more proper to a palace rebellion. And it was precisely the fairy tale that induced sensitivity for this irregular but highly important feature of some myths—the serpent myth in Paradise, for example. Everything that is Promethean is at home here, even a fairy-tale element *sui generis* within the mythical. And for the first time, it allows the Zeus-element of myth to stand out in sharp relief, however much Zeus may throw a cloud-blanket across his heavenly home, and however much Greek drama, where man discovers his superiority to the gods, may be preoccupied with the Prometheus legend.

If all of this were to be treated equally as myth, and so thrown out lock, stock and barrel, the Bible's many non-conformists would become meaningless, too; and their position is far from being obscure. On the contrary, they are light-bearers. This holds good right from the time of the serpent, that arch-myth of a "different" sort: the sort which is in fact more uncongenial to the cloud-blanket of the heteronomous than many present-day demythologizers, with their *Existenz,* would like to think. It holds good even though it is commonly said of this serpent and its thoroughly pre-scientific myth, that it is, so to speak, the larva of the goddess Reason.

This, in the *fourth and final place*, makes for a critical attitude, and not a pre-scientific one, towards anti-mythical suspicion itself, let alone towards some of the mythical, and above all, astro-mythical ideas included in the *ancient view of nature.* Fear and ignorance undoubtedly played their part here, a part very easy to see through; and the nonsense that could produce a sacred cow and horned moons and Elijah's fiery chariot is not even pre-scientific. But, to compensate for this, there is an entirely *qualitative* way of looking at things, which does not eliminate the *qualitative* aspects of nature. This reaches far beyond the level of primitive myth, even beyond Schiller's *"Götter Griechenlands."* It lives in "feelings" of beauty and nobility in nature, in nature-images and sayings of a pictorial, poetic kind, whose old-fashioned tone continues to raise a problem in its juxtaposition with a physics which has grown entirely away from questions of quality. Marx even says (though less radically than Bultmann), at the end of the Introduction to *A Contribution to the Critique of Political Economy:* "It is well known that Greek mythology was not only the arsenal of Greek art but its very ground." But science does not lack a supreme sort of mythical memory, either, wherever "qualities" and "forms" still stand within its ken. Its memory is not of blind faith, of course, nor of supposed revelations from on high, but of a world in which qualities, and even objective beauty, were not necessarily beyond discussion from the very start. Kepler—with his age-old *"Hen kai pan"*—had an extremely aesthetic, musical cosmology with very definite echoes of Pythagorean myth: one might have thought he was no longer operating in an exact sector of nature at all. And going even further, the Romantic philosophy of nature stemming from Paracelsus and Böhme and reaching its climax with Schelling (or, in a different way, with Baader, and also to some extent with Hegel), behaved as if the mythical picture of nature with its primitive analogies had not yet lost its relevance. Which was often highly suspicious, though sometimes it scented the fire, like Faust in the cave.

Even in this last point, then, the fairy tale showed itself again in some of these myths of the "different" sort—not standing yet with Prometheus, but still standing with Orpheus, whispering the spell "Fount, pain, quality." The question here is not of giving the death-blow to fantasy as such, but of destroying and saving the myth in a single dialectical process, by shedding light upon it. What is really swept away is real superstition; nor is this given any time to save itself in the *Hic Rhodus, hic salta* of some merely outwardly demythologized theo-dicy or theo-logy.

37

A particularly sober and discerning mind is called for, when the pace has been so hot. Sober in its refusal to see things just in black and white: its refusal to call every fairy tale an old wives' tale: its openness to shades of difference even in the obscurity of myth. One does in fact find discriminating attitudes in this matter: attitudes which make not the slightest concession to the obscurantist, but which even occasionally unearth in the myths some trait of Luci-fer (the Light-bearer: in a proper etymology). Along with much else which, so far as nature is concerned, is still undecided; still, as Goethe said, "filled with mystery by light of day." Hence: "The key-concept of religion is still the Kingdom: in astral religions a kingdom of crystal; in the Bible (with total eruption of its underlying intention) a kingdom of glory" *(The Principle of Hope)*. In short, even the religious land of olden days, however smooth-running "reduction" may have made it, cannot be mapped and measured in any forget-me-not corners it may still have, without a special sort of fantasy, which is, then, not yet dead.

BULTMANN'S FRONT PARLOR OF RELIGION: "MODERN MAN"

For that reason it is not enough for there just to be a sort of blind and narrow brooding which bears only on that "precious, quiet room" and what it still, so very "actually . . . " appeals to—as if there was not quite as much bad air in this modern sort of cure of the soul as there was thin air in merely outward-directed myths.

In short, for a long time now *Bultmann* has, in his turn, begun to show discernment—after he had, in 1941, linked up demythologization, as modern, scientific awareness, with Heideggerian existentialism, as the basic modern situation of each man's My-own. And this My-own, with its sense of being spoken to in the Bible in what is claimed to be a purely individualistic manner, free from the impersonally social "one . . . " and the wordly "it is," is the private straw this Christian remnant clings to. The bodily, the social, the cosmic: it can all, for them, be discarded from religion as worldly, as the world: the soul need not bother about it, need neither act nor even understand: Scripture speaks from existence to existence, and in no other way, least of all "about" anything. Or if it does speak "about" something, it does so only in a pre-scientific, mythical way, and consequently its words are, in Bultmann's view, to the scientist nonsense, and to the Christian worldly confusion (and not self-knowledge). The purely "situational" depths of faith can have no part with "objective" consciousness of any sort, precisely because that is profane— and all the more so if it is tainted with myth. The religious man is like the modern man in that none of Scripture's mythical "statements" (until one reaches its really unworldly "revelations") can concern him. "Revelation does not convey knowledge about the world: it addresses man" . . . "What, then is revealed? Nothing, if the question about revelation refers to doctrines; but everything inasmuch as man's eyes are opened to himself, and he can understand himself again" . . . "Revelation can be described as that opening-up of hidden things which is, simply speaking, necessary for man and decisive, if he is ever to attain the state of 'healing' and salvation, if he is ever to reach his proper self" (*Glauben und Verstehen*, III, 1960, pp. 30, 29, 2). "In faith the closed context presented (or rather produced) by objectivizing thought is abolished" (*Kerygma und Mythos*, II, 1952, p. 198). But, in the final analysis, Bultmann continues to mean by "closed context" that of the myth, as if there were no rebellious or eschatological myths as well. And, blithely ignorant of the gun-powder they are handling, his school sees all myths, irrespective of their tenor, as nothing but stale worldly talk about the "unworldly," nothing but a peculiarly grotesque "objectified representation of non-objective transcendence." So there is, for this type of demythologizing, scarcely any essential difference between the unclean spirits which enter the swine and the "objectified" doctrine about the Last

Things—or rather about an apocalypse that is not just private, but cosmically final. And the New Testament is full of this sort of thing; it is fairly bursting with the "new" aeon, which certainly does not restrict itself to speaking from one My-own, one existence, to another: the crisis here is of the world, not just of the soul.

Bultmann's theories do not, it is true, weed out this eschatology in its entirety—whether it is purely myth or not. What they do is to take it out of the danger-area of cosmic history, and away from the figure of Christ, whose position within that area is so very explosive, and put it back in the realm of the lonely soul and its solid middle-class God. —Using Kierkegaard in the process, and installing themselves in his arc between "the moment and eternity"; no longer just with "dialectical theology" and its tension between moment and eternity, but with so-called "present" eschatology. This being so, revelation is taken all the more as awakening self-knowledge in its proper form, rather than as concealing within its covers some great goal of history and of the world; though *qua* Kierkegaard, it is true, this does take place in the *topos*, even if not in the darkness and in the unconstruable question of the Moment. Which, as such, precisely because of its utter closeness, its most immanent immanence, appears to be *more than just human;* and is in fact the Immediate in all its driving force, the Immediate which is not yet even mediated to itself, and which exists *in everything.* This unpassed Moment, so far beneath all else, contains in fact the secret of existence—or, rather, *is* that secret plain and simple. And for that very reason its *Hic et nunc* is not only formative of individual Christians, but remains intact and undissipated in all existing being. The Moment at least resists the claims of the pastor of souls better than would be the case if the mere present tense called on by the preacher were already the same as eschatological presence. But the contrary in fact is true, for the cash-payment intended for and in this presence, the metaphysical verification of the saying "Cash can laugh," has a long path before it, and one that cannot be shortened "existentially" by sayings like "The Lord is my shepherd," and "I'm home and dry."

Again it is always supposed to be nothing but God's own activity that shows itself in the "qualified" Moment: that "liberates *from himself* the man who was previously *delivered up to his own works*, so that he can begin to learn the things of God." If one goes deeper, however, into this apparent transition from the order of alien, external myth into that of God's word and "kerygma," one finds a particularly tall story, a myth of the real old sort, which the whole "auto-hermeneutics" of Bultmann and his school, however far they may have taken things, still presupposes. It comes to light as the heteronomous arch-myth of the Fall, according to which man must first be delivered from himself, even now, when *Deus pro nobis* has appeared. Pride, sin and error still remain, where there is no obedience to the command from on high. Jesus' resignation right up to the point of being sacrificed is, then, in the opinion of his followers, still the nerve-center of his word to us— unless the kerygma of Christ itself purely and simply comes down from on high as well: " The word of Christ is a sovereign decree." And for this reason, no doubt, this resignation is, along with the resurrection of the body, taken to be beyond discussion; not beyond discussion in the way that nonsense is, but in the way that sense of a quite different sort is: not as contrary sense, but as disparate—and consequently—as real "*skandalon*" and "paradox."

With this, the demythologizer Bultmann comes close to what is in fact the opposite pole to his basic individualism and *pro-nobis*-hermeneutics: the pole of Rudolf Otto's total religious transcendence (the "utterly other"), which is also present *cum grano salis* in Karl Barth. And the path to this is precisely through the pathos the On-high still generates in Bultmann, with the heteronomous, mythical preponderance he gives to "judgment," "grace," and the transcendent which is withdrawn "beyond our disposition." The enduring, thought-provoking element in these rudimentary ideas of Bultmann's, the so very much more immanently operative factor of "presence," is, therefore, dearly bought. (Although really there is more of Kierkegaard in this idea, and even of Pascal's cult of the authenticity of the "subjective," of the *ordre du coeur,*" than of Bultmann's individualistic Heideggerianism. To say nothing of Jesus' highly revolutionary, *all-transforming* assertion "I came to cast fire upon the earth; and would that it were already kindled!"

Despite this, however, the thing that makes a strong impression in Bultmann's writing is the element of "nearness," above all of the "Moment"; this is the core of his *Kerygma and Myth,* so far, at least, as it is still able to show through a not-disinterested blindness to all that is not calm and quiet, along with a "patience of the Cross" that is quite common enough without even mentioning Jesus; and so far as apparent rejection of the "worldly" is not able, by preserving highly unchristian conditions in the world, to become a hiding place and even an alibi of what nowadays passes for Christian.

BARTH'S INNER CABINET AND SAFE STRONG-HOLD OF TRANSCENDENCE

Lukewarm talk is very good at washing away all that is left of one's own activity. A man will often feel more modern when he is zealously attacked than when he is zealously lulled to sleep. When he is told straight away who is the master and who the servant, instead of being spoken to in a completely demythologized way and then, immediately afterwards, put back in his place with a mass of ancient myths.

This lack of bluntness has been rectified by a theological system of complete heteronomy, one that presents a clear front again; indeed, it fairly throws itself at us—making once more an idol of the mythical On-high, and worshipping nothing else. For Rudolf Otto the important thing is the "Utterly-other"; for Karl Barth it is "transcendence pure and simple" (*The Epistle to the Romans).* This effectively tears down all forms of liberal or culture-oriented theology, but it also tears down all "hoministic"-existentialist theology, and all "activating"-eschatological theology too: *Deus minime Deus pro nobis.* Rudolf Otto first spoke in terms of a pious shudder of awe, but in the *Idea of the Holy* (English translation, 1928) he cut this off entirely from man and man's concerns. The divine can only ever be present now as the impenetrable frontier of man's being, thought and speech; it can never be an autonomous principle within him, or even one which receives him into itself. Otto's "feeling" for the holy is something taken primarily from the field of religious psychology and anthropology—it is not purely biblical. The awe-filled realm of the "trembling *Numen*" is very wide indeed, and all the wider for the ghosts and idols it has swept up in it. The result is that Otto has been accused of portraying the Holy "minus its moral factor," indeed entirely without mentioning the mildness and the light of Christ—a minus which should be reckoned rather to the mythical horror of his particular religious selection than to anything else: the horror of this transcendence that is more than just non-human. Otto is more consistent, but also more treacherous, than the other taboo-mongers of heteronomous myth, when he gives pride of place on the altar to primitive gods of anger, war and revenge (even Japanese ones), rather than to the Zeus of Otriculi, with his "man's cheeks, so beautifully round"; and to the Christ of Grünewald's Crucifixion rather than to "Come Lord Jesus, be our guest," or to Fra Angelico's Elysian heaven. *Theos agnostos,* the objectively unknown—not just humanly unknowable—God must, however, in the final analysis, play himself out in the realm of the Utterly-other. This is not all that irrational in Otto's interpretation, but on the contrary, quite understandable, when one looks at the way the Fascist "destruction of reason" came into vogue. In any case, the religious should be linked as closely as possible with the *trembling awe* of the myth, precisely because this sentiment is breathed down from above; and that holds for the Bible too. Even Christ's own mildness is wafted off into the night where pagan spirits walk, and given the name of *"mysterium fascinosum,"* visible in the mysterious distance alongside the *"mysterium tremendum"* of the ancient thunder-god—or, in other words, not visible at all. There is no connection here, however, with that utterly other Utterly-other of the stalwart anti-Fascist and trenchant Christologist *Karl Barth;* all that arises from Otto's system is the God-man gap again, even without the *fascinosum.*

Already in 1919, in the early days of *The Epistle to the Romans* (which even in its later editions never made the slightest concessions to "cultural Protestantism"), Barth set the sharpest possible boundary-line between man and the On-high, between time and eternity. And in doing so he built man up, contrary to his polemical and very un-wishy-washy intentions, out of a harmonious mixture, in which every element blunts and neutralizes the others. In Barth himself, this singular friend and foe of man and thorough-going reactionary, there is no talk of blunting; he just reduces man's activity, along with that of state and Church (for all of it is purely creaturely), to the smallest possible proportions in relation to the activity of God. The consequences of this are enormous; the ultimate degree of the heteronomous is reached: "The divine utters an unchanging No into the world." No room here for any Bultmannian "self-knowledge of the inner depths" reaching up into areas "beyond our reach," commensurably *à la mode.* No room for any fundamental ontology, whether neat or in a dialectical mixture, where no one knows any more who is guest and who is host, what is temporal and what eternal. No, Barth has torn down the correlation between this world and the next, starting from a theme lost since the days of the real, true Luther: the theme of revelation through God's primordial word. There is an infinite qualitative difference between man and God, between what a creature can do for himself and the only real autonomy, that of transcendence with no holds barred. "The true God dispenses with all objectivity, and is the origin of the crisis of all objectivity; he is the judge of the world's nothingness" *(The Epistle to the Romans, II).* The divine parousia lies in this crisis

44

and there alone; that is the starting point of Barth's radical statement: "God utters his eternal No into the world."

It is the starting point, too, of the idea of the shattering Moment as the one grim place where God and man cross paths—an idea in its turn derived from Kierkegaard. And Kierkegaard's basic tenet about the "blissful awareness of always being in the wrong before God" also has its origins here. There is no other way in which God, *even in Christ*, enters man, the world and history. And even in the Moment, indeed there most clearly of all, his entry takes on the form of a blow from above, with its "bomb crater" (an image taken not without reason from the field of artillery). Or, at the very most, God's entry is like a point of intersection: "In Christ, the plane of worldly reality is cut vertically through by the plane of divine reality" *(Gesammelte Vorträge,* I, p. 5). Even in the Moment, then, it is more a question of a violent encounter than of the sort of touching of two points which takes place when a tangent meets a circle. Here is the source of Barthian "nearness" to the *Deus totaliter absconditus,* to the hiddenness of God in Luther's sense—an idea which again produces competition with the idea of complete transcendence. But Luther, for all the absolutist nature of his God, makes a distinction between *Deus absconditus* (that is, God, in so far as he will not be known by us) and *Deus revelatus* (that is, God, in so far as he enters into communication with us through his word); a distinction which Barth, more Lutheran than Luther, refuses to acknowledge. Luther, too, keeps the "fear of the law" almost gnostically separate at times from the "love of the gospel," whereas Barth draws them much closer together again—always, even here, for the sake of a more strongly emphasized transcendence. For in every separation of law (even ritual law) from love (whether preached or practiced) there is an implicit counter-movement against the heteronomous; one that is not restricted to the gospels; one that stretches in an unbroken line from Amos and the three Isaiahs to him who is Lord over the sabbath: one that, even before the

45

great Gnostic antitheses of Marcion, and right up to the days of the great chiliast Joachim of Floris, the "Isaiah of the thirteenth century," continues to make clear the distinction between the era of law and that of love (and illumination). This movement acts consistently here, too, when Barth has to serve a writ even on the gospel to render service to his claims, in accordance with the bitter, painful words that it is the divine, and not the devil, that utters its unchanging No into the world; and in accordance with the plainly anti-spiritual, highly anti-Promethean words, "The reality of religion is man's disgust at his own self" *(The Epistle to the Romans)*.

Jesus himself is, for Barth, a Yes to the world (in the same sort of way in which Luther took refuge from God's wrath under the hen-like wing of Christ). For the world is still "God's creation," despite its totally fallen state; and, as unfallen, as God's work in Jesus Christ, it is God's Yes to the world, and to good deeds, to achievement, and to justification at the same time. This hazy faith, which serves only as "hollow space" for the eschatological, in the end ascribes even the Law itself to "un-faith." But the main point is that God's Yes to the world through Christ (and, after the external "covenant," through him alone) is by no means another carte-blanche for an *analogia entis* (now somewhat mollified) based in the God-world relationship, which now, as before, is one of contradiction. Even apart from faith which is the "form of the gospel" the law still has a lofty function in relation to God's one word: that of claim and decision and judgment of that word. Nevertheless, and for this very reason, *analogia fidei* alone holds sway in the world (that is, against the world); and its relation to the world is now admittedly of the most contradictory kind, for the Yes to the world is the Yes of eschatology which *ends* the world. Not, of course, that this eschatology can be understood as having any real relationship with the world; as being, for instance, the Utopian product of some Hegelian world-process, however discontinuous; or even, following Augustine, as being the final home-coming of the *civitas Dei* after its wanderings through history. Contrary, in fact, to all forms of immanently transcending mediation, "when you are *really* talking about the Last Days, you can at *all times* say: the end is close" (Barth, *Die Auferstehung der Toten,* p. 60; English translation, London, 1933).

War, then, is declared on every side, even on the realm of the end of time, which "escapes all time"; war on man-centered actualism and on the ideas of history and world—the war of the most highly thought-out myth of lordship. The taboo of God's other-worldliness and the sovereignty of his revelation minimize every achievement of man's spirit, every facet of his experience and thought in the fields of culture and philosophy and even religion. Barth not only gives new, untimely life to this taboo, but builds it up till it takes on the dimensions of a gorgon.

The spark soon fades when the region of the mind is shunned. Even Barth tends to retreat back into feeling and, indeed, remain there—the Up-there brings that with it. But with him this feeling is never soft; and above all it knows about itself, and about what the mind takes from it. Which accounts for the quite recognizable, but on the other hand unknowable nature of the other, so totally aloof and unattainable world (there are connections here with Kafka's *The Castle* and *The Trial*).

But then how can Barth make such definite pronouncements about this eternally Unknowable? On what grounds can he say that it utters an unchanging No into the World? He could of course quote Isaiah, so far as the hiatus between the human and divine is concerned (although Isaiah was full of his God): he could quote the angry words of Yahweh, "My thoughts are not your thoughts, neither are your ways my ways" (Is. 55. 8). But if in that text the great distance between heaven and earth is invoked, there soon comes a word of God that is no more disparate than the rain which comes from heaven to water and enrich the earth—no more disparate than the word which "shall not return to me empty" before it has filled itself out with mankind. Barth must have considered himself the one creature exempt from the boundaries of the creaturely knowledge he so radically asserted. Otherwise he would not have been able to give such definite and detailed information about a divinity who was *turned away from* man. The Kant of *Dreams of a Ghost-seer* would have called a "favorite of the heavens" the theologian who, *malgré lui*, could elaborate in its unattainable hiddenness the transcendence hidden from men. And then, so far as the enduring divine pathos for this most heteronomous of realms is concerned, what difference is there between its inescapable effects on earth and the activity of Moira, the blind goddess of fate, who, although she had high authority, holding even Zeus in her sway, was not held, by theistic standards, in very high regard? Or again, and this is a central point, what is the criterion, in this *ad absurdum* glorified heteronomy, for deciding between a divine order which utters *ad nauseam* its unchanging No into the world, and the *eidos* of Satan who is now, more than ever, the adversary? Of course Barth's myth of lordship, hypostasized to an instructive and excessive degree, is protected from this judgment upon itself, for it cannot in its lofty essence enter into the field of human vision or human thought or human history at all. But neither, therefore, can it enter the lists as Last Judgment over others, as last crisis at the end of history, in a last, eschatological opening-out of the world.

Finally, even Barth's idea of the divine is entirely lacking in history. So it entirely lacks all newness, all the pregnancy that can lie in process and differentiate it from the static. Consequently, the Barthian system—considered now entirely as an anti-Promethean mythological type—has no time at all for a "new aeon," no feasible place, whether in history or nature, for the Eschaton: the "Moment" is, here too, the only place for that. But not as a place to be prepared as of right for the impact, a place of realization for that which will itself realize all things. No, the emphasis given to the Moment is, simply speaking, a-historical: not Johannine in the sense of something that has here-and-now come near us, but Greek in the sense of something that has always been and will always be like that. Hence the indifference to the question of a historically final eschatology: "when you are really talking about the last days, you can at *all times* say, the end is close."—The right answer to this lies in Moltmann's words: "These differences between Greek and Judeo-Christian thought, between logos and promise, between the epiphany and the apocalypse of truth, have been laid bare to our generation in many fields and by various methods" (*Theology of Hope*, English translation 1967). And, as Moltmann goes on to say, calmly pre-supposing a similar method taken from *Das Prinzip Hoffnung*, these differences are, along with the spirit of Utopia, relevant in the nature-question too; indeed, that is precisely where they come alive. He goes on then, implicitly with *docta spes*, but explicitly enough when it comes to this all-too-present eschatology: "Universal suffering will rise up and burst asunder the all-sufficiency of the cosmos, just as eschatological joy will again sound its praises through a 'new heaven and a new earth.' In other words, apocalytic eschatology is indeed cosmological, but that is not the end of eschatology: it is the beginning of an eschatological cosmology, or an eschatological ontology, in which being will be historical and the cosmos will be open to the apocalyptic process . . . Even the New Testament has not closed the window opened out by the apocalyptic vision into the breadth of the cosmos and the freedom which lies beyond what is accepted as cosmic reality" *(loc. cit.)*. There may be signs here of an all too abstract up-dating of the apocalyptic vision; signs that are all too massively theological, still holding on to the safe stronghold and the so-called patience of the Cross. But every movement tending to leap on ahead does provide true opposition, not least of all to Barth's brand of historical nullity, to his static, alien transcendence. For his "patience" of the Cross has marked out the contrary position so clearly; a position without compromise, without theatricals; the position, truly, of the omnipotence of the gods. For that is what it quite evidently is, in the not irreligious, but metareligious end.

Despite his anti-rational cult of "feeling," however, Barth

has little in common with Schleiermacher, who is for the most part, so full of "cultural Protestantism." But Hegel wrote against Schleiermacher, excoriating the "patience" of the Cross, and, above all, that patience which, still a human quality, goes to the limit of bowing down before the heteronomous—before transcendent absolutism. For Schleiermacher, too, had defined religion as "the feeling of simple dependence on the absolute" ("the inexhaustible, unthinkable ground of the world"). Hegel was not just calling on man to give conscious account of himself when he said apropos of this sort of undiluted emotional servility: "The best of Christians would in that case be the dog . . ., but religion belongs to the free spirit, and to him alone" (*Werke*, 1832-45, Vol. IX, p. 296). This is, then, directly opposed to *Theos Agnostos*, where Barth's Lord, his hidden *Theos Kyrios*, has his home. Though, there again, that *need* not be his home.

In other words, the Utterly-other, the true *absconditum*, only becomes really profound, really free from taboo and monstrous superstition, when it is directed away from God and made to qualify the mystery of man, the *homo absconditus*. As with Bultmann's "present" eschatology, so here too with Barth's realm of "mystery," the price is too high—is, in fact, quite superfluous.

But all the same, however untenable the alienation with which it operated, Barth's system did manage to achieve distance, heteronomy, transcendence. It did rediscover with its *Deus absconditus* the problem of the *incognito*—a plus that even cultural Protestantism's cozy anthropology could not maintain. And, with that, *Deus absconditus* becomes a recognizable pointer to *homo absconditus*.

Here too, therefore, the hidden elements and archetypes of myth are re-directed; but not the hypostasized power-idols— these are doubly tabooed. The myths here are of a quite different sort. They are not the transcendent-hypostasizing, but the transcending, Utopia-forming kind, whose account has not yet finally been settled: they are the jail-breaking myths of the subversive human spirit. To throw myths out lock, stock and barrel, with no respect for persons, again appears, especially from this point of view, the characteristic of Bultmann's hardware store. But to single out myths of lordship and treat their Olympus as the judgment seat of an inscrutable but never-erring transcendence is typical of Barth's mosaic of Majesty (not of Job's, however—nor of the heaven of the Son of Man). That is why Marx could say, "Prometheus is the greatest saint in the philosophical calendar." He is in the mythological calendar too—that is, in the destruction and salvation of the myth by light: a fairy-tale explosion right out over and beyond the present day.

The (provisional) net result of all this is that the Promethean aspect (and consequently all that is of eschatological intent) is also present in myth; just as all that is mythical or mysterious must be present in Prometheus, the *novum et ultimum* of human activity and history, if it is to be anything more than obscurantist dallying with a transcendent Byzantium. Hallowed be thy name—that too is no community-prayer of subjects and sycophants, no heteronomous panegyric, but rather a dethronement of *Deus maximus,* non-*optimus,* at best quite non-existent.

SCHWEITZER AND THE ESCHATOLOGICAL APPEAL TO SCRIPTURE

For long enough the only thing to do was not to go beyond the usual. It was always sufficient in those days to let Jesus be the good man who gave us the task, and set us the example, of loving one another as he loved us. But the unpalatable truth that in following out this task men would offend not each other, but the established master-serf relationship—this scandalous truth was covered up, in the name of love, of course. The main thing was to preserve the mild brother-figure. One could get along with him, and the serfs could be kept in harness. One could, in fact, maintain one's grip on the idea of love—relaxed to allow of hypocrisy and other forms of lip-service—better than ever before. "Behold, I make all things new"—the rebellion in these words remained more than painful to the ears of a universally bureaucratized Christianity; it was glossed smoothly over by the liberals, castrated by the conservatives. "If you do it to the least of my brethren, you do it to me"—Münzer and company, who really wanted to establish this Kingdom of love (and do so now), for they were enthusiasts like Jesus, had the worst possible press in Christian theological circles, and at best no press at all.

It might, then, appear at first sight all the more remarkable that precisely this "now" in Jesus' preaching, its burning eschatological drive, could appear in the midst of a thoroughly bourgeois theology. Johannes Weiss and then Albert Schweitzer, certainly no revolutionaries, made what was at the time a disturbing exegetical discovery. From the days of John the Baptist ("The kingdom of God is close at hand") the man baptized by John for the Kingdom was bound to show himself not only as a revolutionary but also as a holy fool. According to Weiss (*Die Predigt Jesu vom Reich Gottes,* 1892), Jesus made his debut as the figure who "has nothing more in common with this world" but stands "with one foot already in the next"—he was, of course, already at that time not a "historical" but a "futuristic" figure. Weiss did, it is true, retrace his steps, and that not in a "futuristic" way, leaving the eschatological picture of Jesus and going back to the liberal one, where there were no enthusiasts. But then Schweitzer began to pull out the stops in the field of eschatology which lay behind the outward life, and in the preaching of Jesus, seeing him only secondarily as the moral teacher of the Sermon on the Mount, primarily, however, as the anointed herald of the Kingdom of Heaven which was close at hand. The apocalyptic Savior-myth (with its fundamental Exodus from Egypt) seemed to have been made flesh at last, in the person of Jesus, for his followers: "It is impossible with eschatology to read modern ideas into Jesus and receive them back from him, through the medium of New

Testament theology, in life-giving form" (Schweitzer, *Von Reimarus zu Wrede. Eine Geschichte der Leben-Jesu Forschung*, 1906, p. 322).

In the middle of this age of equipoise and still static physics, Schweitzer is thinking of the reverse side of the picture. He is thinking of the highly explosive coming of God's Kingdom, of the not only war-like but also cosmic catastrophe expected during Jesus' lifetime, or at the very latest, with his death. And a shudder went down the spine at the thought of apocalyptic horsemen from heaven, a shudder of delirious ecstasy at the thought of baptism in the glory of heaven which was going to burst immediately on the world, or if not immediately, then very soon. It was just this sort of highly un-bourgeois extreme that showed itself at this time in notes made about the outward life of Jesus and his disciples—a life which, to all appearances, had been so peaceful. And Schweitzer's notes read rather like jottings from around the year 1000, or even from around 1525, when the end of the world was really thought close at hand, instead of like hermeneutical reflections from the rectory. Their effect on New Testament studies was shattering. Even Karl Barth could say after this, "Christianity which is not wholly and entirely eschatology, and nothing but eschatology, has nothing whatsoever to do with Christ" *(The Epistle to the Romans).*

Here too, however, in the case of both Weiss and Schweitzer, the new discovery, precisely because it was so shocking to the bourgeois, flowed back into its opposite: into a more conventional liberalism, with a Jesus who was more acceptable to the remaining middle-of-the-road churchgoers. Schweitzer, pointing out just where expectation of the End falls overboard, spoke of this Jesus as an enthusiast. And certainly, as the last days did not in fact come when he had said they would, it was very easy afterwards to describe as an "error" and an illusion the way he had fixed their chronology. Instead, then, the brakes were put on; there was a fresh retreat into cultural Christianity and aid to developing countries: "What came out of all this is that the salvation-history outlook took over from early Christian eschatology" (Ernst Käsemann, *Exegetische Versuche,* I, 1964; English translation, London, 1964). And Moltmann, with the *docta spes* of his *Theology of Hope,* made the not unjust remark about Barth (who still wanted to keep eschatology in a form other than Schweitzer's) that here too it was a case of confusing "eschatological" with "otherworldly"; of thinking all the time in Greek terms of being rather than in biblical terms of *Futurum.*

Now, once again, another stream must flow, bearing onward the "rediscovered eschatological message of early Christianity" (with its prophetic origins), bearing it into a dimension of time that is future, of *topos* that is ultimate; a dimension which has little place in theology, but an all-pervading place, thanks to the myth of Promise, in the Bible.

You just can't get round these things. They are just not prepared to stay in the background. Murmuring is just there in the Scriptures—murmuring with intent: to go seeking. It asks no more of the reader than bare honesty, for it cannot be easily suppressed: nor (what sounds better) overlooked. Hope, not Have or Already-have, is the Bible's ownmost word; even the stuffy old "Comfort, comfort. . . ," fobbing people off when not actually taking them in, has never completely robbed it of its fire. The general set of the Bible is too demanding for that; the particular attitudes it develops are far too far removed. "If I forget you, O Jerusalem, let my right hand wither"—a verse like this from the Psalms cuts right through everything, even through the well-established shepherds who want to keep their flocks: it simply abolishes them. Nor is it meant just as a remembrance: unless it be of a Jerusalem somehow left outside: the Jerusalem of the Promise which, as such, cannot come to terms with the actual one. Cannot come to terms with misery that is doubly unbearable, not with mere pitiful well-being, and least of all with the non-arrival, non-attainment of the better aeon. And cannot, therefore, consist (or even be present) in the peace of the Christian soul, or in its examinations of conscience; still less in its charity bazaars. Otherwise there would have been no need for the so paradoxical, roundabout route of eschatology; nor for the persecutions afterwards, either.

Chesterton's remark is to the point here, when he said with thought-provoking lack of harmony, that the people who accused the Christians of having laid Rome in ruins with their firebrands were calumniators, but that they grasped the nature of Christianity far better than those moderns who conceive of the Christians as an ethical community whose members were slowly tortured to death because they taught that men had a duty towards their neighbours, or because their meekness made them easily despised (cf. *The Everlasting Man*). The Catholic convert Chesterton was far removed from revolt, but not from the really dangerous *skandalon* of early Christianity. And, reaching back over the intervening abyss, there is affinity here with the very different, but equally disturbing and scandalous verse of that other Englishman, the chiliastic mystic William Blake, when he wrote: "The spirit of turmoil shot down from the Saviour, and in the vineyards of red France appear'd the light of his fury" (*Europe, a prophecy*, 1794. —The first part of this quotation reads in the original: "But terrible Orc, when he beheld the morning in the east, shot from the heights of Enitharmon . . ."). Given a straight eschatological "understanding of the Scriptures," these outbursts (and Blake's is even Anabaptist) do undoubtedly come closer to the real transcending aura of early Christianity than all the various "Eschatons" of Bultmann, Barth and Schweitzer put together—even when you take account of the way they talk about Exodus. For it is hermeneutically impossible to restrict this talk to the New Testament when its archetype lies in the Exodus from Egypt, and even far earlier than that. The preaching of the prophets from Amos to Daniel already had apocalyptic undertones of its own which even Paul could not eliminate, and which should still be audible today: "The prophetic message must be termed eschatological whenever it *denies* what has *up to now* been the historical ground of salvation" (von Rad, *Theology of the Old Testament,* II, 1960). What is it, we might well ask, apart from the underlying conservative ethos, that gives most theologians, right from the days of Melancthon versus Münzer, the social mission to combat eschatology, or at least water it down? What is it that makes the fulfillment of this task easy even from the point of view of method? It is simply that their systems are bound together with Greek thought, which is being-oriented and anti-historical, instead of with the historical thought of the Bible, with its Promise and its *Novum*—with the *Futurum* as an open possibility for the definition of being, right up to the point of Yahweh himself. For the inscription on the temple of Apollo at Delphi reads "EI," "Thou Art"; but Yahweh appears before the people, and not only at the burning bush, under the title *"Eh'je ascher eh'je,"* "I will be what I will be." Hence, the singularly unsensual idea of God in the Bible, so foreign to the ancient concept of presence; hence too the difference between epiphany and apocalypse, and between the mere anamnesis of truth (re-membering, circular line) which stretches from Plato to Hegel, and the eschatology of truth as of something still open within itself, open with Not-yet-being.

The basic sense and direction of this biblical thought appears again in Hermann Cohen's eschatology, which has its roots in and takes its power from *Messianism;* although he shares the attitude that will always so "reasonably" surrender the eschatological in its struggle versus antiquity, for the sake of Future-being. "This is the great cultural riddle of Messianism: all the nations put the golden age in the primordial past; the Jews alone hope for man's development, hope in the future" (*Religion der Vernunft,* 1959, p. 337). These words stem from no Protestant theological faculty, nor from belief in a Messiah and an epiphany that have already come. What he says holds good right from the time of *Eh'je ascher eh'je,* though his omission of the gospels, equally Jewish in origin, and of the New Testament apocalyptic material (which Buber called "Superstitious shying away from the Nazarene event") divides Messianism as "the ethics of reason" from eschatology as alleged "mythical infection" in a way no Christian theologian would tolerate. That is the unnecessarily high price, far in excess of any Christian "demythologizing," paid here in order to keep the non-antiquity of the Bible (and therefore its eschatology) in high relief. It is also instructive that precisely this sort of anti-mythical feeling, grown up here into total antagonism, does in fact throw out of Messianism not only any Messianic person (the anti-Yahweh of Job), but all traces of the Total-*Futurum* of apocalyptic literature as well. And does so even though the person (in Messianism the rebel—an anticipation with a cosmic side, too: new heaven, new earth) belongs to that other face of the myth which in its turn belongs (all the more for this) to reason, and not to stupid old Adam.

So again at this end of things we see how the person of the rebel, along with the apocalyptic Promise-myth, is implicitly an important figure in biblical exegesis. And how these very myths, in their clarity, shed decisive light on others of their kind outside the Bible, too: on crypto-Messianic myths, which are by no means lacking in the "light of his fury," but which still, despite that, need the words spoken in the Bible, "Behold, I make all things new," if they are ever to come alive with fire. We can see this in the Bible versus Zeus, who brought a murderous deluge down on man, and dashed the light-bearer Prometheus against the cliffs, like a cross—the Lord-of-the-world, against whom the Promethean in man always rebelled, being better than its God. The Prometheus myth appears again, still far from standing properly on its feet, but for the first time fully understandable now that it has broken away from static Greek thought. And able now to break through into the *Futurum,* thanks to the power of the *Novum* which first came into its view (into the Utopian dimension of its view) through the Bible. This is reason enough why the *ultimatum* that lies within the *Novum,* within this *Eschaton pro nobis,* would not have suited the book of any exegesis which still bore Olympus close to its heart but would be all the nearer for that to

Christians of the new aeon, who considered that they alone were genuine.

12. Marxism and Religion

> Fear made the gods.
> LUCRETIUS
> Atheism is the humanism that comes from suppressing religion.
> MARX

CLERICALISM CAN'T BE FORGOTTEN

If the shoe pinches you throw it away. But the old saying goes: Need teaches you to pray. Is that also because those who live off prayer have cultivated need? The flock, not knowing where to turn, drew to itself pastors particularly ready to care and cultivate it. The class-conscious worker, as opposed to the well-muddled petty-bourgeois, has not for a long time been able to forget that. After all, he saw so many shepherds of his soul stand by the powers which exploited him. What a care-free complacency in power from wealth and wealth from power—what a shameless peace. With a papal blessing for the Francos of every area, and pious prayers rising for their victory; with eyes shut as if by arrangement whenever Jews or heretics were (ever more expertly) burnt. And when the going was tough most Lutheran preachers, too, sided with the power from which they so fervently and dutifully stemmed.

OPIUM OF THE PEOPLE, AND QUITE ENOUGH OF IT TOO?

Being doped is a pleasure you pay for. There was always opium there for the people—in the end it tainted their whole faith. If the Church had not always stood so watchfully behind the ruling powers, there would not have been such attacks against everything it stood for—although of course it may have been competing with them for first place among the rulers, as in the Middle Ages. Whenever it was a question of keeping the serfs, and then the paid slaves down, the dope-dealers came unfailingly to the help of the oppressors. It is for this reason, and not because of any scientific insight, that Marx could approve and reinforce Voltaire's *"Écrasez l'infâme,"* while feeling no need to intensify it. He did not intensify it because he saw the Church, along with the state, as the reflection of quite different, unrestrainable abuses rooted in economics, and therefore biting in at a deeper level. But he did support the bourgeois revolutionaries of his day, because the Temple then was as much the preserve of the money-changers as the Church's God was of the whole class-society. With the great and the lowly, with the prominent and the punished, with eternal praise from its servants and toadies even in the opium-heaven.

Marx did not just repeat that there is no God, or that God is just a clever invention of the priests. This last assertion, anyway, falsely assumes that all priests from the druids on already had the wisdom of Voltaire, and that they were as enlightened as an atheist of the eighteenth century, and only talked naïveté, for between the Encyclopaedists and him come Hegel and Feuerbach. Feuerbach above all, with his optative theory, and with the divided-self and alienation theories of religion, according to which religion's roots lie not in trickery but in impenetrable illusion. For man is divided against himself: at one moment he is a limited individual and at the next he is unlimited and divinized, set over and against himself as an alienated Self, as God. Both the division and the alienation must be repealed: "Nothing exists besides nature and man; the higher beings created by our fantasy are merely the fantastic reflections of our own essence."

It was precisely this process of reflection which led Marx in the end to understand, and see through, the highly ideological function of the Church in the more developed forms of

59

class-society. Just as it was Marx who analyzed historically the allegedly universal and invariable essence of man and of the religious spirit proposed by Feuerbach, varying and concretizing these elements to take account of men in different societies, and so of different forms of alienation of self. And in this way the critique of religion won back for Marx all the old force of the Enlightenment: the power, that is, to link up the heavenly haze with the ideology of deception again—not with the intentional, subjective, indefensible deception of olden times, but with the objective deception imposed automatically by society. Religion was now for the first time linked up historically with class-society. In the process a certain universality stemming from the Enlightenment still showed through, but only inasmuch as religion was almost equated with the Church. Consequently other, socially different, anti-ecclesiastical forms of belief, like the sects, still remained unnoticed. But it was, on the other hand, now possible to level a full critique at the one social form in which religion had flourished—that of the Church; and to think of the Church as an ideology. Hence Marx's critical remarks about the opium of the people: remarks based on economic analyses and more incisive, therefore, than the mere invective common in the eighteenth century.

These criteria demand to be remembered at more than just the level of vulgar Marxism, for when they were put to the test under Pius XII they manifested the quality of growing always more true. In fact they belong to the heights of Marxism; for if bourgeois and vulgar-Marxist atheism became trivial, Marxist atheism on the contrary not only purged the negation-process but also cleared the way for far-sightedness. Indeed, one can go so far as to say that even the tritest materialistic platitude can still, in the matter of religion, have implications against the alienation of self—via Marx and Feuerbach. While present-day bourgeois profundity, with its appeal to poetic angel or encompassing transcendence, according to taste, can only show as implicit something that is in any case very common: the apologia for private ownership.

It is above all fear that keeps men submissive. But even the thought that wishes can be fulfilled from on high makes man a beggar. So it was not impudence that first turned irreligious (for impudence is proper to beggars), but humaneness. And in this way materialism has always been endowed with a liberating role for man: it stood upright against the pressure from above, and set knowledge (the *sapere aude,* dare to use your mind) over against fate which, far from being seen through, was even glorified. An upright bearing, then, and the will to know sets the tenor of every great critique of religion; Thersites is not there, but Prometheus always is, with his torch. It is equally true here of course that stadia cannot be jumped over all of a sudden, as they can in the abstract. But nothing, especially with such tough forms of ideology, can be a substitute for *revolutio in capite et membris,* especially when "religious socialists" of yesterday and of today have always been content not to touch the Church of their rulers but just to paint it pale pink, instead of having a new country in mind, and no mere patch-work. In accordance with the more than merely political warning of the young Marx: "At such times half-grown spirits are of exactly the opposite opinion to fully fledged military leaders. They think that reducing combative strength is the way to make good their losses . . . whereas Themistocles, when Athens was threatened with ruin, prevailed upon the Athenians to leave it for good and found a new Athens on a different element—at sea."

But now, granted the importance of this radical attitude against the rulers' Church, and against the opium of the people which is found in her as in all institutionalized religion— granted this, there is nevertheless a "different element" present in her, too, and one that vulgar Marxism has by no means explored for the purposes of founding a "new Athens." This is relevant to Marx's opium-quotation and to the critique of religion; for that very true sentence about the opium of the people comes in the context of remarks which are equally true, but deeper than vulgar materialists would like to think. That is why these people generally quote the opium passage out of context. In the Introduction to the *Critique of Hegel's Philosophy of Right,* it actually reads: "Religion is the fantastic realization of human nature, inasmuch as human nature has no true reality . . . Religious misery is at once the *expression* of man's real misery and the *protest* against it. Religion is the sigh of the oppressed creature, the heart of a heartless world, and the soul of soulless conditions. It is the opium of the people. The suppression of religion as men's illusory happiness is the demand for their real happiness . . . The criticism of religion has plucked the imaginary flowers from their chains, not so that man may wear a dreary, unimaginative chain, but so that he may throw off his chains and pluck the living flowers . . . The critique of religion ends with the doctrine that the highest being for mankind is man: with the categorical imperative, therefore, to overthrow every state of affairs in which man is degraded, enslaved, abandoned and despised in his very being." That, then, is the full context; there is "sigh" there, and "protest" too, against the bad conditions of the day; it is clearly not just a question of putting to sleep.

The point is made, therefore, against all vulgarizing tendencies, that preaching was, in the German Peasant Wars, more than just a "minor religious mantle," as Kautsky later called it; and that this other sort of preaching came "likewise" from the Bible—almost as if religion were not merely *re-ligio,* binding-back. Though of course meanwhile the Church's lamps were lit pretty well exclusively for the burial of freedom, or for the promotion of whatever would prevent the freedom of the children of God, her children, from coming into the world. A Church that *nolens volens* no longer has all its restoration ideology intact will have to suffer some regrets and second thoughts on that score even before Marxism appears on the scene. The critique of religion in the spirit and context of Marx's thought liberates from undiscriminating taboos far more than Marxism does. One cannot of course expect miracles from a consideration of the opium-quotation in its entirety (instead of just half of it), but it might at least open the way, as they say, to conversations between believers purged of ideology and unbelievers purged of taboo. *"Écrasez l'infâme"*—that means: wipe out not only infamy, but also all stubborn, plodding half-measures.

THE TUNE WAS DIFFERENT BEFORE THE FEAST; MYSTICISM AS A LAY MOVEMENT; THE FIRE OF THE PEASANT WAR; SIMPLIFICATION

An honest man is one who has never consciously obscured anything. One who has never felt the urge to fish in muddy waters even when he fished, piously, up there. Mysticism, it is true, was at one time very popular; and the word comes from *"myein,"* to shut the eyes—but to do so, like the blind seer, with the intention of seeing ever more clearly. Convulsion, possession by spirits, foaming at the mouth, went by the name of Shamanism, not mysticism. Mysticism properly so-called, as it is found most clearly in Eckhart, was inaugurated at a high point of *reason;* it had its birth on one of the peaks of philosophy, and was brought into the world by the last great thinker of ancient times, Plotinus. To him it was *"haplosis,"* the intense simplification of the reasoning soul that occurs when it withdraws into its depths, which are the same in their essence as the primordial One. As in orgiastic ecstasy, so here too, consciousness plays no part; but here it is for the sake of a would-be still higher light, not in order to end up in convulsion, mental fog and blood.

Plotinus and Neo-Platonism are the fount, and indeed the content, of all later Christian mysticism; neither Denis the Areopagite nor Meister Eckhart added anything new—unless it be that in Eckhart the heretical, anti-ecclesiastical lay movement of the late Middle Ages became articulate in German; which is a decisive factor in any socialist evaluation. The unity between the realm of soul and the World-ground, the German "striving for first principles" and "running to the fount of purity" is all inherited from Neo-Platonism; but it was connected significantly with the by-passing of the sacramental

Church, and then of all authority. And that is why Eckhart's mysticism was condemned; the papal Bull just singles out one fact: that he "proposed to the common people things that were likely to obscure the true faith," and his teaching must be stamped out "so that it shall not any more poison the hearts of the simple." As in fact it continued to do in the revolutions of the next two centuries, along with its predecessor, the mysticism of Joachim of Floris, Abbot of Calabrese—among the Hussites, and with Thomas Münzer in the German Peasant War: events, indeed, not notable ideologically for the rule of clarity, but ones in which the mystic fog was at least not of service to the ruling class.

One may regret this fog, as for instance Kautsky does when he calls on Thomas Münzer, with full use of the petty-bourgeois diminutive, for "a few minor samples of apocalyptic mysticism." But it is hard to call reactionary the fog that enshrouded a Huss or a Münzer—to do so unconditionally, so to speak *a priori*. It is of course true that when the mystics place God within men they equally presuppose an Other-world (and indeed one that is even over-transcended within itself) which, with lofty paradox, they go on to unite with man. But the paradox is, in its turn, one that wipes away the whole business of Other-worldery, and does so for the sake of man, and in man. Neither death nor tribulation shall separate us, as Paul says, from what man finds in himself. Or as Eckhart says, complementing Paul, in his sermon on Everlasting Birth: "I am aware of something within me, shining within my reason. I know well that it is something, but what it is I cannot grasp." The feeling of light apparent in these words may, according to one's sympathies and those of one's age, seem either utter nonsense or the most solid sense; one can either understand it or feel quite alien and not understand it. But one thing is certain: Eckhart's sermon does not intend to snuff man out for the sake of an Other-world beyond him; it does not intend religion to be mere alienation of the self. Indeed *anima mea anima nostra* has seldom or never been so highly thought of.

The revolutionary Anabaptists, those disciples of Eckhart and Tauler, showed afterwards in practice exactly how highly and how uncomfortably for every tyrant. A subject who thought himself to be in personal union with the Lord of Lords provided, when things got serious, a very poor example indeed of serfhood.

Many centuries later, the paradox of this doubled-over transcendence was to light a very strange flame: the flame of Feuerbach, with his turning against religion. It is the earthy realist Gottfried Keller who, in the final part of *Green Henry*, has his free-thinking Count point out the parallels between the mystic Angelus Silesius, a late disciple of Eckhart, and the atheist Ludwig Feuerbach, with, as *tertium comparationis*, the way they lead God's lofty remoteness back down to the human subject—the anthropologization, therefore, of religion. Keller could equally well have directed attention to the post-mystical and pre-Feuerbachian element in the young Hegel, according to whom "the objectivity of the godhead has gone hand in hand with the corruption and enslavement of man"; and who went on to say: "Leaving aside early attempts, it has remained primarily the task of our day to vindicate, at least in theory, the treasures which have been thrown away on heaven" (*Die Positivität der christlichen Religion*, 1800).

So much, for the time being, on the subject of a religious, or rather bursting-in-on-the-religious mysticism which, as such, is surely not entirely reducible to mere levitation or to old wives' tales, as vulgar Marxism would have it.—Or even to fog, if that means that Eckhart would not have been a mystic if only he had written more clearly. Anyway this first insight into man's alienation of himself, namely, that human treasures have been bartered for the illusion of heaven, did not come about without some contribution from mysticism. And it is an insight whose home is not in any Church-centered transcendence, nor, in itself, in any purely abstract antagonism to religion, but in the whole Marx—the Marx who plucked "living flowers."

THE END OF STATIC METAPHYSICS: CONCRETE UTOPIA

When a name has become harmful it should not be used any more. It will conjure up false and confusing ideas, and make unnecessary work for those who have to clear them up. And new wine should not be put in old wineskins, even when they are, beyond any possible doubt, the very same good old wineskins of former times: their day has passed. The term "metaphysics," too, seems to have decayed, when you look at it historically. All it needed was for Fascist wide-boys like Rosenberg to start selling rot-gut under the label, and Fascist collaborators like Jung to start retailing Klages' eccentricities to the present day.

It goes without saying, however, that metaphysics of the genuine old variety cannot be likened to this; that is something it has not deserved. Its damage and its danger are of quite another sort. And yet the least one can say is that this metaphysics has become paralyzing, transfixing, indeed even underhand in the way it has established its Behind, its Up-there, and become a ready-made handhold—in the way it has bolted a static door in the face of the real *Meta*, the Tomorrow within the Today. For that is what was always aimed at when "true being" was detected beneath every disturbance—whether it was called *(omnia sub luna caduca)* Idea, Substance or, equally handy, Matter. The new philosophy, on the other hand, both despite and because of its real *Meta*, is by no standard just more old metaphysics. For its relationship to the Not-yet-manifest does not allow of the slightest hint of an *"ontos on"*; of an ontology, therefore, that being inwardly agreed and settled as the Behind-there, has already got everything completely settled and behind it. To be sure, it is also ontology of a sort (this field has not yet been cleared of Positivism nor of other forms of agnostic eunuchry), but only the ontology of Not-yet-being—Not-yet-essentially-being. Therefore it affords no real handhold: there can be no successful career-making here. Nor is it the metaphysics of some already Ab-solute. That sort of conclusive trump-card is entirely lacking—*qua* dialectics, *qua* matter with no historico-cosmic climacteric—from true dialectical materialism. It is lacking for this decisive reason, because the process of dialectical materialism is an open one, one that is alone encompassed with real possibility and not with already decided reality. The recognition has dawned at last that Utopia, Still-Utopia is the one essential thing by which being is defined in the order of essence; so it is the central theme of metaphysics itself. The ontology of Not-yet-being is from start to finish entirely different from what has gone before, inasmuch as *Existentia* and *Essentia* no longer wax and wane in direct proportion to each other, as is the case in almost the whole of the old fixed metaphysics. There the Metaphysical is present behind everything as the realest of the real, instead of at least evincing some *Futurum*, some latent tendency, which would accord with its mode of being (admittedly a difficult one).

A word must be said here about the so-called conquest of metaphysics adduced not only by Positivists and agnostic eunuchry but also, erroneously, by Heidegger—of all thinkers least concerned with process. Adduced by this champion of antiquarian (or imitated) babbling, this thinker of murmured theories is preoccupied with the "oblivion of being" (of the "being of yore"), and not in the least with stepping into the realm of the Being-of-possibility. Heidegger does indeed say unexpected, in a way that almost involves metaphysics in an "overcoming" within itself: "The conquest of metaphysics can at first be conceived only as coming from out of metaphysics itself, as a sort of surmounting of itself by itself" (*Die Überwindung der Metaphysik, Reden and Aufsätze*, 1954, p. 79). But then, rather less "at first," and, far more, "letting loose" his "conquest" precisely as one of the still-progressive moments of the old metaphysics, Heidegger goes on to conclude, redressing the balance and making the very "possible"

67

itself respectable by transfixing it: "The humble law of the earth maintains it in a state of sufficiency consisting in the rise and fall of all things within their allotted [!] sphere of possibility, which all things follow, but which none of them knows. The birch tree never oversteps its possibility. The bees live within the limits of their possibility. Only the will . . . drives the earth beyond the well-selected sphere of its own possibility into something that is no longer the possible and is therefore the impossible" (*loc. cit.*, p. 98). This sort of conquest of metaphysics obviously consists, then, in eliminating from it everything that could still turn out to be world-changing *Meta* (even in Plato, who travelled three times to Syracuse for the sake of this *Meta,* because he realized there was more here than the mere possibilities of birch trees and bees). Heidegger's alleged No-longer-metaphysics is the very worst of the trees of the ancients, right down to the days of Blood and Soil; it is the opposite of a "surmounting of itself by itself"—taken in the possible sense of an ontology of the Not-finalized, of Not-yet-being.

Heidegger really trivializes metaphysics, making of it the old, untenable theory of mere remembering; the theory of the merely circular process of appearances—of (what in Nietzsche is so unexpected) the eternal return of the Same. So when Friedrich Engels equates metaphysics not primarily with Other-worldery but with static thought, and rejects it for that reason, a considerable change in terminology has taken place—one, therefore, which exceeds the bourgeois understanding. Where there is dialectics, there is, in what has unfortunately become the common Marxist usage, no more metaphysics; whether in Heraclitus or Plato, or even Böhme—and none in Hegel's "dialectical pulse of life." But on the other hand even the truly un-other-wordly materialists of the French Enlightenment are known as Marxist metaphysicians, inasmuch as they actually remained within the static picture of the world. And indeed the rigidly mechanistic idea of the cosmos still held in Marxism itself is not unmetaphysical.

68

But the new wine does not belong like this in the old skins: the dialectically concrete Utopia and the Possibility— "Substratum"—of the *Novum* does not belong to the old metaphysics with the reasonableness (certainly a singular sort of reasonableness) of this simple binding-back, this bare *re-ligio.* Implicit in Marxism—as the leap from the Kingdom of Necessity to that of Freedom—there lies the whole so subversive and un-static heritage of the Bible: a heritage which, in the exodus from the static order, showed itself far more as pure protest, as the archetype of the Kingdom of Freedom itself. As the abolition of every On-high which has no place for man; as a transcending with revolt, and equally a revolt with transcending—but without transcendence. So far as it is, in the end, possible to read the Bible with the eyes of the Communist Manifesto. For then it sees to it that no atheist salt shall lose its savor, grasping the Implicit in Marxism with that *Meta* which prevents the salt itself from growing tasteless.

13. Bible Criticism as Detective Work

1. There is nothing that cannot be changed somehow, for better or worse. Least of all will a writer's sketch remain, on revision, as it was before. The difference between hack and craftsman shows through here, too, in that the craftsman knows how to cross out and chisel off, as if he were sculpting a statue. Of course quite a lot can also be spoiled that way, and it is easy to over-expand: hence the old Roman saying—Take your hand from the writing-slate. But usually crossings-out, and even expansions, leave the piece recognizable; it should be all the clearer for them. That is why one has the right to make so-called definitive editions—with particular reference to canonical claims. In this sort of revision, of course, the earlier texts are retained, as a kind of pre-proof. So comparison with them is possible, inasmuch as it helps; and few writers would shy from this. When the job is done properly, each change in the text should keep whatever was good and make it better and

clearer, not pervert it. All this must be prefaced to our argument in order to bring out the extent to which even an altered text differs from a distorted one.

It is obviously, of course, quite another matter when an author falls prey to other, later spirits ill-suited to him. Then his own voice can no longer be heard, but his legacy can be suppressed or falsified. Deceptive texts like this do exist; and the greater their influence, the more self-assured they are. All the more important, in that case, to dig for, and catch the sound of, the other voice underneath.

2. If, before that could happen, something had been passed on orally, it was generally all right. It had been driven home, had become habitual to its hearers, so *had* to remain true, word for word. —A truth which did not change till the written texts were re-copied, or till they were put together to form a new book. That is when the corrupt text first appears, giving no sense, often contradicting itself in the very next sentence, or on the next page. It can of course happen that sense of a sort, even of a more intelligible sort, does come out; not just arrant nonsense. But not a sense which feels as if it had been breathed into the text in its cradle. Then the corruption is harder to detect. It can generally in these cases be ascribed to chance: either to the mistake or sloppiness of some scribe, or to a misguided attempt to fill gaps in the text or to collect scattered material. All this is human, all-too-human error. —But, one might ask, is there not another element present in every text which is not itself as innocuous as its incompetent editor: the seductive purpose perhaps to be not forever innocuous? Indeed to be not forever incompetent, unless it be as a mask? On the contrary, to be highly competent, when it comes to long-concealed deceit?

It can be seen from many posthumous works, and from much that was composed from fragments or from oral tradition, that the society of the day had an incentive, not to say a mission, to indulge in text-trimming. There is none of this, naturally, in Grimm's fairy tales, nor in the collection, under

Pisistratus, of the Homeric songs. What advantage could he or his régime have drawn from suppression or re-emphasis? Though there is Thersites, whom the written Iliad portrays as a mere gossiper, a horrible blasphemer, who always found fault with the chieftains, and would always speak against war. —On the other hand, mythical elements no longer understood, or merged into one, are sufficient in the written Odyssey: hence Calypso, the "Hidden one," a goddess of death who promises eternal youth. And above all, in the Homeric epics the order of the songs and the linking-together of events has in many cases been very dubiously smoothed-over.

But what can one say about the activity of the "Homerids" when one becomes aware of the tangled-up chapter-order, and indeed the confusion of material, in several redactions of great works of philosophy—for instance in Aristotle's *Metaphysics?* There may well be enough negligent and inferior material in the more badly transmitted remnants of Homer and Aristotle to provide grounds for a new redaction. But the surprising thing is the extent to which textual criticism, even here, has not bothered to ask the question *Cui bono?* Even the most famous textual criticism of all, that of the Bible, has hardly given this question a thought. Despite the fact that the biblical text has more dilemmas than most, and more slanted interpolations which could not have come from mere sloppiness, and certainly from nothing inferior. A fact that has furnished Bible criticism (as the most famous of all philological activities) with particularly strong motives for asking: *Cui bono?* Especially with regard to the tense matters involved. Which means finally, that biblical criticism needs the broadening that will come from continually tracking down the interestingly different, rebelliously different readings in the available text. For nothing could completely efface or conceal the way things stood before the great redactions.

3. The suppressed outline of this earlier state of affairs can be made out all over the place, when it matters. But the untampered text had not for a long time been in circulation

among the rabbis: the Bible was solidly established. Its earliest manuscript did not go back beyond the sixth century A.D., and the Qumran discoveries not beyond the first century B.C. Nor did Qumran shed any really surprising light on other, older variants, for it follows on the whole the official Bible of Ezra and Nehemiah. And, being several centuries later than Ezra's official redaction, it can hardly still record evidence of sources which did not fit into a text that had long ago become canonical.

The contrary, however, is true of the time of Ezra and Nehemiah themselves: of Ezra above all—this "Church Commissioner for Jerusalem," newly returned about 450 B.C. from the Persian exile. Pre-canonical sources still existed then; sources which had been well preserved during the time of the so-called Babylonian Captivity. But Ezra the scribe now isolated from them, in a highly theocratic manner, the old "Book of Laws" dating from the time of Moses. He already had his work drafted when he came up to Jerusalem: the children of Israel told him to "bring the book of the law of Moses which the Lord had given to Israel. And Ezra the priest brought the law before the assembly" (Neh. 8. 1). Which resulted, in this well-established Jewish Church state, in the fact that the newly redacted Old Testament, with its "rejoicing in the Law," contained only a portion of that Israelite and Jewish literature which continued to live outside the Bible. This literature now led a significant, but dwindling, and typically non-conformist existence (in popular stories for example, and in the Haggadah), often alongside the Law and the clerically de-fused Prophets.

Characteristic of the direction taken by Ezra's reforms is the fact that the priests vacillated continually about the question of whether books like Job, and then Qohelet and the Song of Songs, were "Holy Scripture," or whether, in the equally ritualistic language of the schools, one would "defile one's hands" with them. And it is logical that Ezra's importance for the Old Testament, in the form it henceforth took, was always emphasized and elevated by rabbinical orthodoxy—despite all his predecessors since the days of the Kings, with their own "rejoicing in the Law" without, and even against, the Prophets. For only with Ezra and Nehemiah was there a really definitive attempt to reduce the biblical text to a strictly theocratic common denominator—in opposition to all prophetic notions about Exodus from Pharaoh, even in the concept of Yahweh. This is the point where the murmuring of the children of Israel disappeared finally from the official text; and in its place came a great mass of cultural interpolations, of atonement, and of the most submissive elevation of divine transcendence. And it is in view of this complete redaction- (or re-redaction-) process that the Bible can really generate a detective Bible criticism: one that at long last brings the *Cui bono?* question to bear on the pious (or rather less pious) distortion of so many decidedly subversive passages.

That then is what we shall denounce: distortion, not just corruption of the text: redaction by reaction. After all it was always the fragments in the Old Testament that were especially noticeable; the breaking-points in this long-drawn-out story and history book, which is, perhaps the most tense of all amalgam compositions.

The new cycle that came along and joined it was also only subsequently rounded into its present shape. Into the shape of a New Testament—no literal life of Jesus, but very often just preliminary preaching about it. And this became, belatedly, the subject of further Bible criticism; criticism not now concerned with the Law, but with the equally subsequent sacrificial-death theology of Paul, and with the influence this had on the portrait of Jesus. Here too, albeit in an entirely different manner, acceptance of life was taught in the form of a patience of the Cross which Jesus had never mentioned—and Paul himself had never seen or heard the living Jesus. The author of the Gospel according to Mark could, it is true, still avail himself of a no-longer extant collection of Jesus' sayings, but in all four of the gospels they have to a considerable extent been softened and bent to serve the interests of missionary work and the life of the newly-founded communities. Broken fragments are forever making that clear: for example, the difference between "baptism in Christ's death" and Jesus' rather less patient saying: "I came to cast fire upon the earth; and would that it were already kindled!" (Lk. 12. 49). Chronologically, too, gospel-criticism has to do with the influence of Paul's theology: his letters were written about 50 A.D., the first three gospels about 70, and the Gospel of John only about 100. Indeed the final decision about the scope and the basic form of the present-day New Testament took place only at the Synod of 382 under Pope Damasus. As a definitive decision, it was again institutional, and therefore in strong contrast with the sources, or rather source—and it was almost strange, the way the Revelation of John was kept as the one example of apocalypse.

Despite all this, however, the mainstream of Bible criticism has, since 1100 and even earlier, consistently directed its attention first and foremost to the Old Testament. Gospel criticism has followed much later, because of its *own particular* stumbling-block and its *own particular* ecclesiastically built-in, and re-built-in, labyrinth—not leaving everything to petrify, but putting everything indefinitely off. Old Testament philology, in fact (and not only philology), has always been critical and opposed to every arrangement, from Genesis down to Job; with its Promethean element within it, and with the prophet Isaiah, who would have a new heaven and a new earth created in the face of "Behold, it was very good," so that the former things should no longer be remembered. Here, above all there are not only linguistic differences and those which come from chronological confusion or from divergent parallel reports or unsolvable, substantial contradictions. There are also the most glaring interpolations—from Egypt, in the middle of everything, against the Exodus. That ought to be a lesson, first and foremost, to Bible *criticism,* when it takes its lead from social pressures which do not foster good redaction, and which provide it, for its detective-work, only with the sort of text that would never have roused the enthusiasm of a Thomas Münzer. This detective-work should have the most *positive* of aims: to see through and cut away the Exraean matter, and to identify and save the Bible's choked and buried "plebeian" element. It is only partly choked and buried, that is true. Otherwise the Bible would work in the same way as every other religious book of the upper classes and of deified despotism, instead of being irrepressibly the most revolutionary religious book of all—by virtue of its ever-expansive, explosive antithesis: *Son of Man—Land of Egypt.* Textual criticism concerned with this need by no means be neutral, like Homer criticism, for example. On the contrary *(nemo audit verbum nisi spiritu libertatis intus docente),* it provides philology with a goal.

4. Only small points were scented out at first. But, once on the trail, wider interests were aroused; and from them came the more startled and startling type of criticism. Chronological contradictions were the first things noticed; even purely material ones. For instance, when the Deluge first lasts 540 days, then 150; or when Abraham, who had declared himself before God too old to beget children, marries again after Sarah's death and begets several. Patriarchs from the most ancient Bedouin sagas talk like post-exilic, law-conscious Jews. Joseph's brothers, on the other hand, do not even know the prescriptions about food. And how many more hallowed discrepancies had to be broken open by Bible criticism. It is, then, all the more remarkable that this science had its tentative beginnings in the work of rabbinical commentators of the Middle Ages, under a very different Ezra, Ibn Ezra, around the middle of the twelfth century. He commented in vain on the revealing passages (Deut. 1. 1, 5; 3.8; 4.41-49), where Moses, who never set foot in Canaan, speaks "beyond the Jordan" to his people, laying down laws and conquering lands. Ibn Ezra's explanation was that at the time when Moses remembered these things and wrote them down, the Canaanites were still on

the other side of the Jordan. And he goes on: "Herein lies a mystery; if any man understands it, let him keep silent."

When it was at last set free, however, Bible criticism became one of the most exciting achievements of human acuteness. Not for nothing was it inaugurated—with a special reference to Ibn Ezra—by Spinoza. Nowhere is the utter independence of his mind more acutely in evidence—and the break with the most thoroughly established tradition of falsehood. His *Tractatus Theologico-Politicus* of 1670 (chapters 7-10) already concludes that in Genesis through 2 Kings there is a redaction made by the priest Ezra from various contradictory writings. Two of these lost documents are mentioned in the Bible itself: the "Book of the Wars of the Lord" (Num. 21. 14) and the "Book of Jashar" (Jos. 10. 13; 2 Sam. 1. 18)—this last being from the time of Solomon, about 1000 B.C. The first sketches towards an anatomy of the text were made by Jean Astruc, who discovered that two separate writers are distinguishable in the Pentateuch. He called them, following the names they used for God, the Jahvist (Yahwist) and the Elohist, and these names have remained unchanged (Astruc's *Conjecture sur les mémoires, dont il paroit que Moyse s'est servi pour composer le livre de la Genèse*, 1753, appeared anonymously). This founding-father of philological Bible criticism marked a regression from Spinoza, inasmuch as he made Moses and not the priestly class the redactor of the books named after him. Also important here is the fact that a Catholic theologian, Masius, one of the very oldest of Bible critics after Ibn Ezra, likewise pointed to Ezra and Nehemiah as the probable last and chief redactors of the Old Testament (in his *Commentary on the Book of Joshua*, 1574). Astruc's source-research, long unheeded, finally came out victorious in the nineteenth century. Wellhausen, the disagreeable heir of many predecessors, produced the sharpest analysis (*Geschichte Israels*, 1878, Vol. I), Gunkel the most mature and richly documented (*Genesis*, 1901), with Wellhausen adding his own personal bias and anti-Semitic attitude as a new source of error. Other sources splintered off in their turn from the Jahvist and Elohist; indeed the latest thing before the latest thing was to posit a non-Israelitic author from Southern Palestine, the so-called S-source, and to ascribe to him the Paradise and Tower of Babel narratives otherwise ascribed to the Jahvist (cf. Pfeiffer, *Introduction to the Old Testament,* 1941, pp. 159 ff.).

Leaving aside these hypotheses, and apart from songs and recognizable sagas, there are, then, four main, uncontroverted streams in the biblical *compositum:* Jahvist, Elohist, Deuteronomical, and priestly code. The Jahvist wrote down oral traditions in the ninth century, the Elohist in the eighth; both probably worked on behalf of prophetic schools. Deuteronomy comes from the seventh century and has many relationships with Jeremiah; its characteristic, compared with Numbers and Joshua, is the splendor of its period in its rich rhetorical style. Then the priestly document was added (the whole first chapter of Genesis—ostensibly the very beginning of the Bible). It originates in the Babylon of about 500 B.C., brought together by Ezra, the final redactor of the whole thing. Last of all a few archaic songs and some garbled remnants of primitive sagas are recognizable: the song of the ancient Bedouin, Lamech, for example (Gen. 4. 23); Deborah's song in Judges 5.2 ff.—certainly an ancient Triumph-song; Jacob's struggle with a god (Gen. 32. 24-31); and the primitive apparition *a tergo* of God in Exodus 33. 21-23, far older in tone and content than that of the burning thorn-bush in Exodus 3. 2-6.

Jahvist and Elohist documents were fused together for the first time in the seventh century, with numerous interpolations in the interests of the priestly caste; and the books of the Covenant and of Deuteronomy were added, with their detailed prescriptions about food, and their developed ritual. The account of this redaction can be found in 2 Kings 22. 8 and 23. 22 ff.: the high priest Hilkiah allegedly found the Book of the Law in the Temple, and King Josiah imposed it on the people as the *charta* of the new Jewish Church. The final, definitive and exclusive, hard-baked, ecclesiastical, canonical redaction, however, took place about the middle of the fifth century, under Ezra the priest, after his return from Babylon. Ezra the

77

priest came, as has been mentioned, from out of Babylon with the Law of God in his hand (Ezra 7. 14), and read it before the congregation in Jerusalem (Neh. 8. 1, 8); this should be remembered as the point of the whole story. —About this time too the lettering of the Bible was changed; quadratic script, a modification of the Aramaic, was chosen to replace the old Phoenician alphabet, and this also facilitated alterations. —The late Alexandrian version called the Septuagint is, of course, different in many respects from the present-day Massoretic text, chiefly in its shorter length.

That, then, is how the *compositum* called the "Pentateuch" arose, with its manifold interpolations and weldings-on in the prophetic books, notably Isaiah. And, in a similar way, light can be shed on the distorted and indeed unsolved state of an heretical book like Job, which only entered the canon at the price of similar interpolations and erasions. Apropos of this separate piece of redacting, the American Semitist D. B. Macdonald rightly remarked that if Goethe had died before he had finished *Faust,* leaving the first part edited but the second in disorder and without its *dénouement,* and then a mechanical editor had taken all this and bundled it together as well as he could, concluding it with the ending of the folk-story, there would be some sort of parallel with the present state of the Book of Job. There is only one element missing here—the most important one: the editor must be thought of not so much as "mechanical" but rather as a member of the Holy Office of the Inquisition, with the law-book *De Puritate Fidei* in his hand, proceeding against this heretical text by pruning where he cannot condemn, and by inoculating all it opposes.

Of course many parts of the Bible, the theologically and politically harmless ones like the duration of the Deluge or the virility of a patriarch, have only been harmlessly altered. But the Book of Job and, as will be seen later, the texts about Cain, and about Jacob's struggle with the "angel," and about the serpent of Paradise, and the Tower of Babel—all of them very pointed incidents—are not harmless at all; and no less harmful is the clerical revaluation, or rather denigration of these passages. No redaction, either, could smooth over the breaks in the biblical text, even the relatively harmless ones between the Jahvist and Elohist source, when the same subject-matter is being dealt with. Clear cases of this are the still recognizable remnants of ancestor-worship; the numerous relics of polytheism: for example, even the plural Elohim and the way God calls on his fellow gods (Gen. 1. 26; 11. 7); and the two creations of Adam, different in the first chapter of Genesis and in the second. Fragments of a creation-history deleted from the priestly code can be found, especially with reference to the "rebellious sea," in the Prophets (Is. 51. 10) and in Job (38. 8-11). The Jahvist remarks with surprise at the ritual separation of the Egyptians from the table of the foreign guests in Joseph's palace (Gen. 43. 32); he obviously did not know the Jewish law about foods, although it is meant to have been dictated by Moses. And, so far as the Temple-ritual in Exodus goes, Jeremiah himself (7. 22) has spoken the words which disclaim it: "For in the day that I brought them out of the land of Egypt, I did not speak to your fathers or command them concerning burnt offerings and sacrifices." This, and much else that is less rebellious, gives ample evidence of aporia, and Bible criticism prepares to shed light on these problems with all the force of philology, abolishing the traditional chronological order of the various pericopes, and above all unearthing key-elements which lay more or less deeply hidden under other material.

Much more important, however, and more troublesome, is the investigation of those remnants that have been *purposely veiled over by the priests, with their counter-revolutionary religious outlook.* They are only a few still recognizable islands now, but they tower up like the mountain peaks of some long-lost country out of a sea of honesty. The words of the Paradise-serpent can be counted among these Azores, and all the attempts, from Cain to the thought of a Messiah, to stand on one's own feet over against Yahweh, rejecting him utterly as the "doctor of Israel."

If Bible criticism is not in fact given this new slant and put to use, there can be no more philosophy of religion at all—least of all one shot-through with revolutionary and Utopian ideas.

5. The door is open. Heretical pressure has always helped see to that. The rebellious undertone, supressed in vain, stood the Peasant War in good stead—and not just the German one. Of course socio-economic agitation lies behind the ideological in-fighting, even in the Bible. It's just that the reports on this (the serpent come into the open, as it were) are even more repressed than the reflex mythical reaction to the On-high.

The political murmuring of the children of Israel and the rage "of the Lord" against it are, in Numbers 16 (almost nowhere else), described for the length of a chapter in greater detail than even the "rebellion of Korah and his company." And even in this rebellion a veil has been drawn over a popular movement, inasmuch as the only people mentioned are "leaders of the congregation . . . well-known men." They rose up against Moses and Aaron with a sort of priesthood of the laity. But they themselves can be seen for the priestly upper class they are: Levites attempting a premature palace revolution. That is all—except for the upshot and conclusion of the story, where the Priest-God, the God of priests and ruling classes, shows his reflexes in the face of a practical revolt by more than the mere suppression of red legends. This God of fear wipes out the whole company: he is no War-God now, but under the pen of Ezra and Nehemiah, simply the God, as it were, of white-guard terror: "But if . . . the ground opens its mouth, and swallows them up, with all that belongs to them, and they go down alive into Sheol, then you shall know that these men have despised the Lord . . . To be a reminder to the people of Israel, so that no one who is not a priest, who is not of the descendants of Aaron" (that is, of the High-priest), "should draw near to burn incense before the Lord, lest he become as Korah and as his company" (Num. 16. 30, 40). The least that can be said of this is that there is a faded echo here of political rebellion, and that the despotic cult-God of the priestly caste was, in ever increasing reinforcements and interpolations, set the task of denigrating it. The same concept of God was at work here as in that Paradise of pure obedience which, as Hegel said, was "a park where only beasts could stay, not men." And by the same token there is no sign here of that other concept of God, irrepressible even in the priestly redaction, which promises to lead the people out of Egypt, the land of slavery, and through the desert into the land of freedom. For no concept of God which has the *Futurum* as its mode-of-being (and this last concept is like that) can adjust to a religion that has been institutionalized down from above, and so finalized twice over. Whether it be the post-exilic cultic community back-dated to Moses' time, or a religion of transcendence so intense that it can only be approached via priests and cult: one where punishment consists in the high-and-mighty displeasure of a Transcendence which can only be treated with the most submissive attitude of repentance and atonement.

Taking the Bible as the handbook of such a regulated cultic community—and it was fitted-out for this job, although it remained chock-full of threatening volcanic crevasses—it had, of course, to be thought of as "inspired by God," and handled only apologetically, or at the most with allegorical and symbolic interpretation. With straightforward, credulous following of the text; not with discriminating attention to its true axis: that of our ever-growing penetration and self-insertion into the religious mystery before us. Defective criticism of the Bible's fracture-points did certainly produce commentaries which smoothed them over, sometimes profoundly allegorical ones, as in both Jewish and Christian exegesis of the Middle Ages and even later. But cases also occurred where simple ignorance of Bible criticism gave rise to fruitful misunderstandings of the aporia, and the most astonishing speculation became possible. As with Philco, who took literally, not as coming from two different sources, the twofold creation of Adam in Genesis, and consequently held to an earthly and a heavenly first man; the latter being able to provide a theory of the Son of

Man, the Messiah, the Logos in Jesus, which did not suffer from too much theocratic elevation. However, that sort of thing is a paradoxical exception to the rule that only critical attention to the fragments of *veiled* (and, in Exodus, *ineradicable*) *subversion* can bring to light the organon of the non-theocratic axis in the Bible.

It is clear that there is such an underground Bible, both *infra* and *contra* and *ultra* the heteronomous light of the theocratic firmament; criticism has made investigation of it possible, though it has hardly yet begun. The *homo absconditus*, from *Eritis sicut deus* to the Son of Man, who had no transcendent heavenly throne, but an eschatological Kingdom—that was the real *Biblia pauperum*, which had the intention, against Baal, of "overthrowing every state of affairs in which man appears as oppressed, despised and forgotten in his very being." And to that extent, in both the Old and New Testaments, this *Biblia pauperum* calls into being a religion of human Utopia, the Utopia of religion's non-illusory elements. Or, to use another Marxist formulation, setting the God-hypostasis firmly on our own feet: "God appears therefore as the hypostasized ideal of the as yet truly undeveloped essence of man; he appears as Utopian entelechy" (*The Principle of Hope*, 1959). So the banner should cry not "Demythologize!"—without distinguishing Prometheus or Baal from the "Kerygma"—but *"De-theocratize!"* Only that can do justice to the Bible's still saveable text. The Bible only has a future inasmuch as it can, with this future, transcend without transcendence. Without the Above-us, transposed, Zeus-like, high up-there, but with the "unveiled face," potentially in the Before-us, of our true Moment *(nunc stans).*

There, then, in the Bible itself, is the true *visio haeretica*, with (often suppressed) violent kicking against oppression, inspired by an unparalleled *expectation* of the real Utterly-other with which the world will one day be filled. Other concepts of God give vent to the mythology of the thundering Cronos, high above, but they generally contain no more then that. The Bible alone dwells centrally on the God of human hope and on expectation of the "perfect": "but when the perfect comes, the imperfect will pass away" (1 Cor. 13. 10). With this vision as sign-post, and therefore with a quite different sort of criticism—criticism *through* the Bible—it is possible to see more acutely than ever that there are in fact two Scriptures: a Scripture for the people and a Scripture against the people. And that these two rub ever more sharply together the more one reads beneath the Bible, which is itself still largely underground, but which cannot now be deflected by apologetics. So many passages bring home the self-same question: Where has man got to in the world of Nimrods? Where can he get to in the realms of hope?

EXODUS
IN THE CONCEPT
OF YAHWEH

14. An Unheard-of Saying of Jesus':
Departure-in-Full

What was, must be tested. It does not hold good of itself,
however familiar, for it lies behind us. It holds good only so far
as the Where-to continues to live before us in the thing itself. If
the link binding backwards is false, it must be cut. All the more
so if it was never true, but simply a shackle.

It is telling, that even the loyal Ruth did not go back the way
she came; she did not turn back, but followed the path of her
own free choice. And on this point Jesus' goodness itself
strikes off at a singularly sharp angle, away from tradition.
How small is his sense of belonging, even though he is the son
of an ancient house and family. He has passed beyond it,
broken with its power; no remnant of it still stands over him.
The old father-ego itself comes to an end; the new-born are
here with their fellows, leaving father and mother, following
Jesus. "And stretching out his hand towards his disciples, he
said, 'Here are my mother and my brethren!'" (Matt. 12. 49).

84

An untamed ego has burst through, has broken out of the sober nest with its authorities. Only the chosen disciples are his relatives—but closer still to all of them is the common element relating them in a no-longer oppressive bond.

The alien factor may of course be something quite different from mother and brethren, and it may have become alien long before Jesus. It all started quite boldly—started out from within itself; and it has "corrupted" youth.

15. Early Traces of the Break-Away; First Thoughts about the Serpent

The man who can speak for himself will not be fitted into other men's plans. New things always came from below, setting themselves up against established custom. The beginning above all is the time when the goad gets kicked against. Even in the touched-up Scriptures this kicking was not entirely eradicable, so people just called it names. And it stayed for that very reason, because anyway the punishment did not come, with its hoped-for intimidation.

The serpent sets the tone—seductive but also rousing. In none of its appearances is its image simple. It bears poison within itself, but on the Aesculapian staff, healing. It is the dragon of the abyss, but, at another moment, the lightning high-above. And long after it is meant to have brought sorrow on our first parents, the sight of the serpent-idol held aloft heals the children of Israel from leprosy. Nor did it tell lies, as befitted the most cunning of all the beasts of the field, at least not in the most important point of its promise. For it promised Adam he would be like God; and when Yahweh saw him afterwards he said, "Behold, the man is become like one of us, knowing good and evil" (Gen. 3. 22). What sort of sin is that, wanting to be like God and to know good and evil? So far is it from being unambiguous, indeed from being sin at all. that countless pious people from that time on would most likely have taken unwillingness to be like God as the original sin, if this text had allowed it. Is not knowledge of good and evil the very same as becoming a man?—as leaving the garden of beasts, where Adam and Eve still belonged? And what a disproportion between Yahweh's punishment (the expulsion, the death-blow) and a crime which, for the "image of God," as the Jahvist earlier calls him, cannot in the end be called a crime at all. Unless it was that this fault just suited the text very well (as it has all later whitewashers of the On-high), in that it brings in the first really black scapegoat. But precisely in this passage, the most outstanding passage in the whole of the "underground" Bible, the glint of freedom is ill-concealed. And all the less concealable in that the forbidden fruit which opens men's eyes is not deadly nightshade, but the fruit of the Tree of Knowledge, and that tree "was to be desired to make one wise" (Gen. 3. 6). Again and again in the underground Bible, the serpent stands for an underground movement which has light in its eyes, instead of hollow submissive slave-guilt.

This tone continues—still suppressed, it is true, but even gaining in importance thereby. Though early on, when the text is not only very archaic but also very disordered, the unseemly elements are not so clear. It is evident, however, *cum grano salis*, that the spirit of the serpent lives on in the twilight narrative of Jacob's fight with the man who blocks his way at the ford (Gen. 32), but who could not overpower him till Jacob's thigh was put out of joint in the fight, and even then Jacob held him fast. They wrestled till daybreak; and when the strange adversary wanted to break off the struggle because of the approach of dawn (an age-old sign of the nocturnal chthonian spirit), Jacob realized he was not dealing with any mere man. But even now he did not let his opponent go; they asked each other's names, for according to the ritual of magic, knowledge of a name gives power. The spirit refused his, except inasmuch as he referred to himself as a god—in the later text as God himself. There then follows the very un-humble, unreceptive prayer (or, rather, not a prayer at all, but a violent conjuration of the heavens, and one in which it is the man who is doing the violence): "I will not let you go, unless you bless me." Jacob's new name of Israel (he who strives with God) is also added here, in a strained attempt to provide an etymology for the name of the later tribe (it is confirmed by Yahweh in Genesis 35. 10).

The framework of this incident comes from the saga of a local river-god, a night-spirit who feared the dawn: in the text's later redaction he has had to be treated with monotheism. There is a noticeable similarity with the passage in Exodus 4. 24-26 where Yahweh intercepts Moses and tries to kill him. The Jahvist has transposed this Yahweh onto the Jacob-incident, and both he and the Elohist have made it agree with the Yahweh of the Paradise story, and with the cherubim of purity (who the Jahvist can't quite come to terms with). In this way the true context of the event becomes clear—revolt. Even struggling with a little local spirit who blocked the route would have been revolt, and revolt of a sort seldom found outside the Bible—revolt against demonic fear. In the event the struggle with Yahweh turned out well, with no punishment, and it enhances the sketch almost to the point of being a glimpse of something as distant as Job's own struggle. But it certainly looks back to the place, nearer the serpent's brood, where the *Tower of Babel* was built (Gen. 11. 1-9). And here there *was* punishment: vengeance of a sort which added only a minor detail to the expulsion from Eden.

The Deluge, that massive, almost total extermination of man, whose "wickedness was great in the earth," was a few centuries past and now man's wickedness was beginning to show itself from another angle, a constructive, progressive one: "Come, let us built ourselves a city, and a tower with its top in the heavens, and let us make a name for ourselves." The Haggadah, a popular, story-telling collection of traditions both parallel and subsequent to the Bible, often expressing the "voice of the people" in its freedom from priestly corrections and correctness—a real folk-tradition, not just an ornamenta-tion of folklore—presents this text, in a Midrash, in quite a different way: "God has no right to choose the upper world for himself and leave us the lower. So we are going to built a tower

87

with an idol at its summit, holding a sword, as if it wants to war with God" (Gen. R. 38, 7). It is almost a matter of indifference in this context that the material for the legend of the Tower really comes from Babylon—from the construction of the seven-storied High-temple of the astral myth, which stood, long-unfinished, at the time of the Jahvist (about 900), as an example among other things of the ancient archetype of the vengeance-blow of hubris. But the "Babel-thought" (as the young Goethe, standing before the cathedral in Strasbourg, called it, in honor of the builders of that temple), being the thought of *building* like God, connects immediately with the counsel of the serpent in Paradise: the counsel to become and to be like God. And for that very reason it is repulsed in theocratic style, with a confusion of tongues and scattering abroad throughout the lands.

In a highly subversive passage, the Haggadah goes so far as to insert the death of Moses into the Tower-archetype—in the context of its wrongfulness, certainly, but this time of a wrong done from on-high. The passage is quite different from its parallel in Deuteronomy 34, where life just breaks peacefully off: not for nothing has man eaten of the Tree of Knowledge, even though every tower has so far led to death and none to heaven. In the Haggadah-narrative Moses refuses to die; he holds Yahweh to his word: "In the Torah Thou hast written (Deut. 24. 15): thou shalt pay the poor man his wages on the same day, and the sun shall not go down upon it. Why dost Thou not give me the wages of my work?" Yahweh's answer is to remind Moses of his sins, among them the killing of the Egyptian taskmaster—as if this had not been the first blow of liberation from Egypt. Indeed another version of this other Tower-contra-the-On-high makes the blunt remark that Moses had to die so that men would not think him equal to God. The angel of Yahweh only with difficulty overpowered him, and the heavens, the earth and the stars began to weep at his death. In addition, the only reason why Yahweh buried him with his own hands was to prevent people from going on pilgrimage to his grave, honoring him instead of Yahweh. But, the legend concludes, the whole world is Moses' grave. No legend has indicated more clearly that the concept of Yahweh can be exchanged for a man; and even in myth this points to the fact that man has the same image as God.

The priests overlooked this myth, and it bore fruit later on in the category of the Messiah as a second God—the category of the Son of Man. Though the picture of Yahweh here was very different from the route-blocking, speech-confusing, face-extinguishing one of the Pauline text: "Do not lie to one another, seeing that you have put off the old nature with its practices and have put on the new nature, which is being renewed in knowledge after the image of its creator" (Col. 3. 9). That sort of thing can only hold good when the inner meaning of Jacob's struggle lies behind it, and the model of the Exodus. An Exodus which the fearful image of Yahweh experienced as a departure even from himself. The struggle alone, however, does not beatify; one also needs the help of that changeable sign which goes along with us on our way.

16. Breakthrough in the Theocratic Concept of Yahweh: First Thoughts About the Exodus-Light (Ex. 13.21)

But if something goes with us, it must in itself allow of different conceptions of itself. Even if only in reference to an Up-there in the face of which men behaved, as they did to their local lords-and-masters, like children who have been burnt. Saying always what pleased, making sacrifices to order—to appease. It was all done to humor the hidden marksman—so hidden was he, so doubly intangible, so withdrawn, letting fly the arrows of hunger and plague, or if well-pleased with the tithes, perhaps even giving out free bread.

Sacrifice is known to all cults; it is by no means purely biblical; but in the Bible it appears very early, and in no appeasing fashion either, in the Cain-saga (Gen. 4). Above all, here it does not go smoothly up to heaven. And, what is quite singular, quite exceptional, it is made to a different God than the one commonly thought of. With a revealing, only half-concealed break in the picture of this God. For it must not be forgotten that when Cain offered the fruit of the ground, Abel offered blood: the firstlings of his flock and of their fat portions. So when Yahweh had regard only for Abel's offering, he showed that his pleasure lay only in blood. But then the change comes, and it is Cain who becomes bloody, with the first murder. And the same Yahweh (who is later to entrust Abraham with the slaughter of his own son) now puts his curse on Cain. But then, as if he were no longer the same hard God who remembers unto the fourth generation, Yahweh not only modifies his curse, but withdraws it. Instead of an imperial ban on the outlaw, what comes, as though from a different source, is quite the opposite: "Not so! If anyone slays Cain, vengeance shall be taken on him sevenfold." And the so-called mark of Cain is, contrary to the common opinion, a mark of protection ("lest any who came upon him should kill him"). Nor was that enough: the man first represented as an accursed fratricide was blessed richly in his seed; for out of him came Jubalcain, "the father of all those who play the lyre and pipe," and Tubalcain, "the forger of all instruments of bronze and iron." There is too in the traditional text, which is so much concerned with the murder, a highly suggestive gap—one noticed already by the Massoretes. It is caused by an omission in verse 8: "Cain said to Abel his brother . . . And when they were in the field, Cain rose up against his brother Abel, and killed him." The man who had offered only the fruit of the ground, and for this reason reaped a harvest of wrath from the blood-drinking Yahweh, does not fit in with the other Cain, the murderer, with all his wild talk. No more does the God who later saved him fit in with the God who curses and drinks blood: the change in both pictures is unmistakable. In late Judaism there was a sect of Cainites who thought they could smell powder in the omission of verse 8: powder that backfired and put Abel himself in the wrong. Hence their saying, "In blood lies the pleasure of the Lord of this world."

But already, before then, another, better figure was entering the picture: a God who could decline the sacrifice of Abraham. And, with that we begin to enter the ever-growing area of a conception of God that is incompatible with his eating of men. Though he does fall back into the Moloch-like habit, right from the time of the spirit who waylays Moses and seeks to kill him because the blood of circumcision has not flowed (Ex. 4. 24-26), to the time of the last human sacrifice, which Paul calls Jesus. The refusal of the sacrifice of Isaac, however, already marks a divergence from the blood-series; and it also marks a clearer recantation by God than the recantation implicit in the affair of Cain. It does certainly begin with the despotic, willful trial of God's servant Abraham—the proof of his abysmal, dog-like obedience; of the sacrificial renunciation of his human feelings and not just of his human intelligence (it is, therefore, quite futile for Kierkegaard to praise even this somewhat extended Abraham as an example of the "blissful awareness of always being in the wrong before God"). But when Abraham passes this really steep test on the part of God, the Lord relents, and goes on to take the even less guilty and utterly defenseless ram in Isaac's place. What follows, however, is a sentence which blows up and wakes up the Moloch at one and the same time (Gen. 22. 14): "So Abraham called the name of that place Moriah, the Lord sees."

Quite apart from human sacrifice, however, even the offering of rams, for all its enduring cultic element, was not regarded any more as exactly pleasing to God—at least not in the Prophets, with their very unheathen view of Yahweh. Amos, the oldest of the great prophets, conceives of a Yahweh who rises clean above the incense smoke and above any idea of divine pleasure being taken in it. If the question arises of humoring this new spirit, Abel's firstlings with their blood and fat, the Isaacs of the herd, as it were, are of no more avail: "I hate, I despise your feasts, and I take no delight in your solemn assemblies. Even though you offer me your burnt offerings and cereal offerings, I will not accept them, and the peace offerings of your fatted beasts I will not look upon" (Amos 5. 21-22).

91

How far removed that is from the firstlings and tithes, and indeed slaughtered war-prisoners, which regularly had to be offered to tribal gods, in order to keep these super-human, and frequently inhuman powers in a favorable mood. The changeability exhibited by the divine lord-of-the-manor and exactor of tribute shows that there is in fact a very changeable, movable factor in the concept of Yahweh himself. Right through Greek mythology Zeus just sits there, as stable as a sphere; indeed that was, in a highly secularized fashion, Parmenides' definition of him. But the old Yahweh-figure, full as it is of back-slidings into oriental despotism and of static, vertical pressure from on high, still has room for change, for going along with us, for wandering away from established qualities as no other god can. This comes out most strongly of all (as will be remembered) in the place where Moses asks the fiery vision its name: it comes out there before his very eyes. With the important and noteworthy result that Moses' memory is not linked with a God whose throne is in thick darkness, a God who is nothing but the age-old, tyrannical father-ego of all time, and with that, finis. No, the Yahweh-concept (or representation) of the mountain of Moriah, where the demon of sacrifice finally *sees,* is put now into the future ("*Eh'je ascher eh'je,* I will be what I will be," Ex. 3. 13, and "I will bring you out of the affliction of Egypt"); so it has definitively turned the corner into a dimension of Exodus and expectation.

An image like this one (projected much later *nolens volens* into a real Exodus) causes difficulties even for so complacent a figure as the one-time Lord-of-the-world, and does so with an outbreak of dualism more marked than in the affair of Cain, or even in Abraham's sacrifice. Exodus from every previous conception of Yahweh was now possible, with this *Futurum* as the true mode-of-being of that which is thought of as God; more possible than it had ever been in all the interpolated promises to Abraham. The Bible-of-Exodus became possible: of Exodus away from and against the Pharaoh who, in the person of Yahweh himself, had made only Egypt, not Canaan—not the "new heaven and new earth." —In short: the rebellion, the prophetic witness, the Messianism of a no longer merely underground Bible has, in the Moriah of *Eh'je ascher eh'je,* broken half-way out into the light of freedom.

A great deal of hope must have been there before trust could develop in such a figure, always dashing on ahead. A great deal of seeming deception and betrayal by the Lord must have passed by before the priests could admit that the Redeemer was as exclusively future as that—was to such an extent *Eh'je ascher eh'je,* to such an extent a wandering Where-to, not only in the desert, but in time.

Yahweh was, of course, a new God even to the children of Israel—despite the interpolation in Gen. 4, 26, where his name appears in sudden isolation. The God of the legendary par-triarchs and their Bedouin tribes was called El, or also Shaddai; Genesis actually begins with the not yet henotheistic, let alone monotheistic, plural Elohim. But even where Yahweh has subsequently been set alongside the primitive images of God, the multiplicity of names has testified to the peculiar mutability of the Israelite conception of God. Yahweh, the thoroughly jealous and now thoroughly one God, as yet totally lacking his own style and his future openness, was originally the tribal God of the Kenites, who had their pasture-lands round Sinai. Yahweh ("the blowing one") probably coincided with the storm-and-volcano god of the Sinai of those times. This very suddenness and unforeseeableness, this doubtless awe-inspiring *Tremendum* of thunder and smoke characterizes the Lord whom Moses took over from the Kenites after his flight from Egypt and marriage into their tribe. And the Lord who so much later, in the Temple of Solomon (1 Kings 8. 12), would dwell in "thick darkness," also belongs to the volcano of Sinai. All the more so in Exodus 19. 18: "And Mount Sinai was wrapped in smoke, because the Lord de-scended upon it in fire: and the smoke of it went up like the smoke of a kiln, and the whole mountain quaked greatly." This was still far away from the clear patches of light which were to

93

make God's qualities the model for men. Far too from the Some-day which Moses had before him in *Eh'je ascher eh'je,* as the unfixed *Futurum* of the Ahead-of-itself within the ownmost concept of Yahweh. But it was also entirely free from any naturalistic mountain high up there, and from the astro-mythical constellations of the Above-us, or from a fully formed heaven spread out like a sheet. And, on this border, the local, human border of *Eh'je ascher eh'je,* there lies the decisive feature that Moses invokes this symbol as the *"Signpost out of Bondage,"* as the flag of liberation, and as the horizon of his people's expectations.

This turning of an idol of thunder and oppression into a source of leadership through time, with a still far-distant goal, is historically unparalleled; it is the work of Moses. For despite the gloomy, threatening concept of Yahweh there was still room for the pillar of cloud by day and the pillar of fire by night leading out an *Exodus through the desert to Canaan.* And the regional God, now no longer himself comparable in value, allowed room for the later-interpolated sublimation of the God of pure subjugation into the God of the Book of the Covenant, with its moral code—despite all the cultic apparatus of burnt-offerings and thanksgiving-offerings. The Ten Commandments hypostasize a "doctor of Israel," as the later saying goes; he is no longer the omnipotent autocrat empowered to make the most contradictory demands from his serf-like retinue. Thanks to the element of revolt and to the first incursions of the *Humanum* into the biblical hypostasis of God, there is a different tone here from that of the Greek. Aeschylus could say: "Zeus is there as the punisher of all who bear themselves too loud and noisily, and his judgment is harsh" *(The Persians,* vv. 828 ff.). How strange when compared with this is the idea of a God who is coming: a God who is a sea of righteousness, as Isaiah says in his highly un-Present, Utopian way. And to him alone real praise is now deemed due. The same old courtly service is still there, it is true, along with the old theocracy whose task is to intimidate; majesty is still oppressive—often in the Psalms, and even sometimes in the Prophets. But the

Exodus-light, away from Pharaoh and out of Egypt, his work, could no longer be revoked. The idea of the Creator-of-the-world as well as of its Lord, had to retreat continually before that of the Spirit of the Goal, who has no fixed abode. —All the more so, the more the Promised Land beyond the desert was still conceived of in terms of Egypt. The more the Canaan *here-and-now* was disappointing, in accordance with a God who is himself not yet what he is: who *is* only in the future of his promise-to-be—if he should keep his word—and in no other way.

17. Nazarites and Prophets—Yahweh's Exodus into Universal Moral Providence; Pre-vision

No more tile-carrying for the people now. But no lapping up milk and honey in the Promised Land either, for all the fighting. Hunger did not die out, it grew; and when, after forty years, the Land of Plenty was reached, it had to be conquered, with much difficulty. New enemies continually arose: the house was built only with sword and trowel together. And even when life became more sure, the pressure on the people did not let up. The Egyptian overseers had merely changed their name: they still sat there in the Israelite towns, and on the estates which the people had taken over. The new upper class was a great disappointment; existence became worse than it had been in the nomadic days in the desert and before the time in Egypt. When the Israelite Bedouins moved into the already stratified society of rich and poor in Canaan, they lost the old, simple, partly still primitive-communist life of the tribe. As in all times and places, the riches of the few made the poverty of the many. Communal ownership vanished and private owner-ship took over, bringing with it the well-known distinction between master and serf. Creditors sold their debtors into slavery, and big landowners exported the corn at high prices, causing shortage and crisis at home. The Book of Judges, with its age of heroes, draws a veil over much of this, but the two books of Kings are full of reports of famine and of its converse: "Now the famine was severe in Samaria" (1 Kings 18. 2), but "the king [Solomon] made silver as common in Jerusalem as stone" (1 Kings 10. 27). The patriarchal family did not, it is true, die out completely; nor did a certain limited type of village commune, based on neighbor relationships; but the tribal unit, with its foundation-stone of communal ownership, came to an end. And the concept of Yahweh changed with it.

Against the Baal of the country's previous masters, Yahweh was the bearer of victory, but he had lost the truly Mosaic, Bedouin features of the one who leads out of bondage. Intermarriage and trade with the Canaanites brought the new masters into contact with the native gods, the Baalim. And even more decisive was the fact that these were the gods of fertility, the local deities of meadow and vineyard, whereas Yahweh was a stranger in Canaan, with neither vine nor fig tree, neither homestead nor house. He was a God of the migrant people, a God of the quest for the dream-pastures of Paradise, not a God of landowners—his blessing was invalid for them. Hence the constant "idolatry," conditioned economically—which means magically and religiously too: the blessings of the harvest were from Baal, not from Yahweh. The first-fruits were his from time immemorial; to him the thanksgiving feasts of Canaan were dedicated, and the "horns of the altar," which also adorned the temples of Yahweh (Amos 3. 14). The fact that Yahweh stood firm through all this, that the Baal-sanctuaries of Sichem and Bethel were made over to him, that the earth "yielded produce unto Yahweh," and that the harvest festivals of Baal could be transformed into the Israelite Passover and the feast of Tabernacles and so on—this toughness was due to one thing only: to the memory of the victory they had won with him, the victory which continued to be connected with his name. If he was no God of the ploughlands, he was still the God of lightning, powerfully secure, even in Canaan, in his lofty heaven high above all kings and Baalim. In the very ancient Song of Deborah he appears as the God of sheer raw strength, by whose power the abandoned rule over the mighty: "A new thing God has chosen" (Jgs. 5. 8). Yet despite this he was continually reproached by the people for having deprived them, if not of victory, then certainly of its fruits. Doubts became audible about the God of their fathers—that even he was fickle. And Jeremiah (15. 8) expresses much earlier sentiments when he complains that Yahweh has "become like water that refuses to flow, and like the mirage of a brook in which there is no trust."

Meanwhile, nourished by the traditions of Bedouin days, a semi-nomadic group came forward to oppose the class-structure and the Baal-Yahweh: they were the *Nazirites*. They preached nothing less than a new religious ideal under the mask of the old—return to the *simple communal life,* and Yahweh as the *God of the poor.* The Nazirites were connected with the Kenites and Rechabites, the tribe into which Moses had married, and of which a part had moved into Canaan with the Israelites (Jgs. 4. 11). The Rechabites had remained nomadic, with common ownership, without master and serf. Neither agrarian culture nor the gods of Canaan had seduced them: in their cult they were still faithful to the old Yahweh of Sinai. They disdained wine (an authentic Bedouin attitude preserved and sanctified in Islam), and even in Jeremiah's time their nomadic life, as well as their abstemiousness, was regarded as specially pleasing to Yahweh (Jer. 35. 5-10,18f.). And indeed it was these very same Rechabites (the opponents of the Tel Aviv, and even of the Capua of the day), who served as a seed-bed for the Nazireans or Nazirites (*nazir,* the separated), a sect, not to say institution, whose origins were perhaps justifiably traced back to Moses (Num. 6. 2-5). They practiced abstinence, and allowed no scissors to touch their head, for in their hair lay, as the Samson myth recalls, the magic power no domestication could destroy. Few institutions of the very early days have lasted right down through the Bible—along with their ascetic, "anti-Canaanite," provocative character—as faithfully as that of the Nazirites. Samson, Samuel and Elijah were Nazirites (Jgs. 13. 5; 1 Sam.

97

1. 11; 2 Kings 1. 8), but so was John the Baptist, that unwieldy figure from the desert. He was "clothed with camel's hair, and had a leather girdle around his waist, and ate locusts and wild honey" (Mk. 1. 6); and to his mother it was announced that "he will be great before the Lord, and he shall drink no wine nor strong drink" (Lk. 1. 15). Another theme that runs through the whole Bible is the annunciation of a Nazirite before his birth. It happens in Samson's case, (Jgs. 13. 14) and similarly for Samuel (1 Sam. 1. 11) and for John the Baptist (Lk. 1. 13), and in all these cases no richer man has entered the Kingdom of Heaven. The relationship between the Nazirites and other late Judaic sects of the anti-mammon variety like the Essenes and the Ebionites (*ebionim,* the poor), is not so certain. What is certain, however, is that the early Christian communism of love did not spring from the "Book of *Kings,*" though it could call for support from an Israelite tradition which went straight back to the Kenites, and from the memory preserved by the Nazirites of a nomadic community of goods, indeed even of primitive pre-nomadic communes.

The Nazirite made his appearance as the man of nature, the provo that he was. But he got to his feet when he came into contact with an equally outlandish figure from a different company—the Israelitic dervish, whom the Bible also numbers among the prophets *(nebiim).* There is, it is true, little in common between these prophets and those of later Israel. Amos coolly refuses to be taken for one of them (7. 14). The later prophets thought of themselves as messengers, not just as possessed. But the Nazirites, too, were constitutionally unsympathetic to these foaming shamans of Yahweh whose position was so diametrically opposed to their own, stemming as it did from the orgiastic side of the Baal cult. Like the prophets of Baal (1 Kings 18. 26, 28), whom Elijah mocks so scornfully, these despised figures went in for dislocating their limbs and doing themselves bloodthirsty violence, dazing themselves with orgiastic music and falling herd-like into prophetic frenzy (1 Sam. 10. 5). Naturally a few of them raved for Yahweh instead of for Baal—an example of a Baal-institution which did not, as was the rule, serve the altars of the ruling class, of the Ahabs and Jezabels who had now appeared on the scene. Finally the semi-nomadic Nazirites linked up with a sort of Bohemian Magianism: Samuel is already mentioned as being the prior of a band of prophets (1 Sam. 19. 20), and both Elijah and his disciple Elisha would have presided over such a group.

In the end, then, the pendulum swung back, and an institution characterized by simple archaic frenzy became one of listening, judging and hoping. Naziritism entered the authentic movement of prophetism, bringing about the momentous union of *social preaching* and the *will for a new Yahweh and the coming of his Day*. Samuel, the anointer of kings at the time of the Philistine crisis about the year 1050, did not yet carry his activity into the inner realm of politics, but around 850, Elijah threatened King Ahab and the tyrannical Jezebel, and Elisha destroyed their whole dynasty.

It was, then, the *falling away of Israel from the Yahweh of the desert* that was to throw light on the lesson of her experience—that Canaan was not really Canaan. This desert Yahweh was still the God of the Exodus—even now, when he was in fact drawing them back to the simple community of nomadic times. Even the institution of the Years of Festival and Jubilee (Lev. 25. 5-17, 23-54) bore the mark of Nazirite influence, though the reform here was only partial, not revolutionary. There are pre-agrarian, primitive-communist memories in the demand for the common enjoyment of produce, for a solemn rest for the land, and from labor, and for the re-alignment of private ownership every seven and every fifty years. Yahweh has not at this stage left the old image of a tribal God behind for that of the universal moral Providence, prevision, which he has in the prophets. But he has, in the preaching of the Nazirites, abandoned the class society of Israel. For of all the periods in her history, the tribal period alone has been true to him—the days that passed with no rich, no poor and no revenge. And in this way he seems to have escaped the reproach of not having fulfilled his promise in

Canaan. It was the worshippers of Mammon, the extortioners of the people, who had been unfaithful, not their God.

Doubt, however, still remained—undispelled even by the renewal of the life of their forefathers. Things grew worse and worse. To hunger was added the danger of death from mighty enemies, quite different from the sparrows they had skirmished with during the Conquest or under Saul. What was Goliath compared with the Assyrian chariots, and what the brief glory of Solomon compared with the thousand and more years of fear which followed him?

At this time of wealth the new prophets, from Amos on, fought the involvement of their state in external trade, thinking they could save the land from the great powers of Nile and Euphrates by making it inconspicuous. It was a democratic, pacifist idea in the Nazirite spirit, and partly connected with that movement, inspired by hatred of the lordly ostentation of the Canaanites. It precedes the moral preaching of the prophets and serves as its economic and political foundation. Palestine is to remain a neutral buffer-state between the rival powers of Egypt and Assyria, patient and unobtrusive in the hand of God. Far removed from all association, whether internal or external, with the structure of the great powers and their financial system, their great estates and their luxury. To this movement was now added powerful *socio-moral* preaching which went far beyond just putting a damper on the old ambition for worldly greatness. From Amos to Isaiah, and even further, the moral message was conceived of as Yahweh's primordially human will: "Learn to do good; seek justice, correct oppression; defend the fatherless, plead for the widow" (Is. 1. 7). The exploiters and expropriators are an abomination to him: "And he looked for justice, but behold, bloodshed; for righteousness, but behold, a cry! Woe to those who join house to house, who add field to field, until there is no more room, and who are made to dwell alone in the midst of the land" (Is. 5. 7 f.). All this is the Nazirite heritage, as is the devotion to the times of prophets and the Bedouin days as the childhood, or indeed, in Hosea's image, the courtship of Israel. Private ownership is not opposed now, as it was by the Nazirites: to every man his own vine and fig tree. But only so that none shall be a serf, none choked down any more: "I will punish the world for its evil, and the wicked for their iniquity; I will put an end to the pride of the arrogant, and lay low the haughtiness of the ruthless. I will make men more rare than fine gold, and mankind than the gold of Ophir" (Is. 13. 11 f.). The God who wills that is certainly not the same one whose churches stood, and stand, in the various Fifth Avenues of the world. But, by the solemn affirmation of Thomas Münzer, he is not the opium of the people either. "Surely, thus says the Lord: Even the captives of the mighty shall be taken, and the prey of the tyrant be rescued, for I will contend with those who contend with you, and I will save your children. I will make your oppressors eat their own flesh, and they shall be drunk with their own blood as with wine. Then all flesh shall know that I am the Lord your Savior, and your Redeemer, the mighty one of Jacob" (Is. 49. 25 ff.).

That then is the socio-moral content of the prophetic message; it became thoroughly explosive when the subversive *socio-apocalyptic* preaching began. Outwardly this seemed to make use of the age-old connection between guilt and atonement: bad times are either a punishment or the rod of correction; the just man walks unpunished in the light; all receive their carefully reckoned reward, even in Canaan— especially in Canaan. But this preaching did not rest content with any allegedly infallible justification-automat from one high, though it did undeniably begin with one, and the guilt-atonement account is in fact the last coinage the prophets remember. They remember it for this reason, among others, (and with a temporary suspension of subversive activities here), that it can be seen as a sort of paying-back by proxy from on high. Which, even without bringing in the prophets, relieves Yahweh of responsibility for the misfortunes of Canaan: a mechanical motif employed much later on by the very correct, pastorally concerned friends of Job. Even at the beginning, however, Gideon, on the occasion of a misfortune in war, had put the question that cried out so loudly to the prophets and reached its climax later in Job: "If the Lord is with us, why then has all this befallen us? And where are all his wonderful deeds which our fathers recounted to us, saying, Did not the Lord bring us up from Egypt?" (Jgs. 6. 13). To this question Jeremiah, still keeping to the guilt-atonement parity, gave the orthodox, though insufficient answer: "Thou didst bring thy people Israel out of the land of Egypt with signs and wonders, with a strong hand and outstretched arm, and with great terror; and thou gavest them this land which thou didst swear to their fathers to give them, a land flowing with milk and honey; and they entered and took possession of it. But they did not obey thy voice or walk in thy law; they did nothing of all thou didst command them to do. Therefore thou hast made all this evil come upon them" (Jer. 32. 21-23). That is, of course, no more than sheer Yahweh-apologetics, relieving God of guilt by burdening man—despite his freedom to do evil, it leaves him still a child. In the moral-apocalyptic order this guilt-atonement preaching served only as an initial impulse, but it did so even when it involved the very unprophetic concept of an allegedly inscrutable decision of God to exact atonement where there was no proportional guilt; indeed even when the prophet, introducing his very different notion of the *Deus absconditus*, did not ensure against the dangerous misunderstanding of this in terms of a Lord-God, but actually let Yahweh say: "My thoughts are not your thoughts, neither are your ways my ways" (Is. 55. 8).

The *specific prophetic* contribution to this order, however, lay in the idea of an *unstimulated cooperation of free moral choice in one's fate, right up to the very last.* This cooperation is like a new switching-over of the points, and it marks the difference between the prophet Jonah and the destruction of Nineveh which he averted (without, it is true, comprehending it), and the Greek "prophetess" Cassandra, who could only foresee the curse of the Atrides, without being able, by any appeal for conversion, to forestall it. It is the first preaching and proclamation of the moral trend which goes the *opposite way:* the *Novum* is here, right up to the point of "Repent, for the kingdom of heaven is at hand," and the almost theurgical words "Repent therefore, and turn again, that your sins may be blotted out, that times of refreshing may come from the presence of the Lord" (Acts 3. 19 f.). The prophets taught a mature freedom of choice extending even to fate; they taught the power of human decision. That is why they all speak of the future not as of an immutable category but hypothetically, as a changeable, chooseable one. That too accounts for the leap away from Cassandra (and even from the contemplative seer Teiresias) to Isaiah; and it marks Israel off from the passive type of augury which alone was practiced by other nations. Man can at least now choose his destiny, and the corner-stone of this fact was considered to be a concept of God which, if not hominized, was at all events more broadly humanized to extend its promise to all men of good-will, far beyond the narrow borders of Canaan. *Yahweh became the focus of spiritual unity for the just of all nations.* And the idea that his promise, indeed that he himself, might make another Exodus to fulfillment in a still future dwelling place, that Canaan might be moved into the realm of the eschatological—this idea too is the work of the prophets, beginning with Amos and not ending even with Daniel. The purely apologetic initial intention of thinking of Yahweh and the catastrophe in Canaan together was radically overhauled. The God of liberation was a true God of morality, an ideal God whose qualities could now really be a model for men. The concept of Yahweh begins to draw away even from the allegedly so marvellous Six Days' Work of creation. Significantly, the prophets barely mention what can anyway scarcely be called a success on the part of the Creator-God. Instead: "Behold, I am doing a new thing; now it springs forth, do you perceive it? I will make a way in the wilderness and rivers in the desert" (Is. 43. 19). In Trito-Isaiah this final *Creator spiritus* (still Yahweh?) moves on to what is almost a new, more genuine, seventh day of creation: "For behold, I create new heavens and a new earth; and the former things shall not be remembered or come into mind" (Is. 65. 17). The Exodus from Egypt, the entry into Canaan, are repeated—on a definitive apocalyptic plane, with consolation, but with a palace revolution in the concept of God as well. Morality now gave man a hazardous rule for measuring the ways of the God whom he had been taught to consider a synonym of righteousness itself—*ultima irritatio regis* was no longer enough.

After the God of Exodus, the *second great ideal* of theology is Yahweh as the embodiment of moral reason. Even atheism has not entirely abolished this: it still projects as abruptly as ever out of being, over into the ideal. The future Paradise told of by Isaiah's God—"He shall not judge by what his eyes see, or decide by what his ears hear; but with righteousness he shall judge the poor, and decide with equity for the meek of the earth" (Is. 11. 3-4)—this Paradise treats man as an adult. It is no longer a garden for beasts, a place of hollow innocence and ignorance. Righteousness ceases to come purely from on high as a mechanical accounting-process reckoning out with alleged exactness the atonement due for guilt and the reward for uprightness, as the initial apologetical impulse of prophetic preaching would still have it—evidence, this, of its impermanence. Though it was admittedly impossible for it to stylize fate as the divine tribunal of justice: the real world, so full of unjust suffering, was far too contradictory for that. And if the guilt-atonement relationship was, despite all this, still regarded as one of parity, righteousness turned from being an apologia for Yahweh into being a weapon against him. For this very parity of the fate allotted here to the sinner, there to the self-righteous, was a crying injustice. And a balance day in the next world, terrible for the prosperous evil man but consoling for the poor good one, was not offered in Israel before Daniel. That is why Job, examining his conscience, sets himself energetically against the apparent disparity of the fate sent him by God. Again, however, not without the continuation of the

Exodus, not without a new pre-vision, a new providence having gone on before him in the prophets.

The *verbum mirificum* of the one who founds and saves calls forth in the prophets the very creative essence of a World-creator and infuses it into the promise of a very different Genesis—one which at last is just. Always, however, in such a way that this creative essence, this efficacious word, has its ultimate, formally salvific effect only in the creation of the Messianic nation Israel. Even in their rare outbursts of joyful praise, the other creation, the one around us, never serves the prophets as more than a likeness for a new "Let there be light; and there was light." In itself it is a long way from *Telos* and *Eschaton*. It is, then, the awaited and not in any sense the remembered Genesis that blossoms forth from the words of Trito-Isaiah: "For Sion's sake I will not keep silent, and for Jerusalem's sake I will not rest, until her vindication goes forth as brightness, and her salvation as a burning torch . . . and you shall be called by a new name" (Is. 62. 1 f.). At the same time this *Eschaton* goes far, if not too far, beyond the mere Kingdom of peace on earth, where every man sits undisturbed beneath his fig tree. And this underlines again the antithesis with the first Genesis and its milieu of ease. It underlines it explosively, even though the real, clear *apocalyptic* stress on the *Eschaton* begins only with the last of all the prophets, Daniel. After his time it mounts in ever greater tension from the Syrian apocalypse of Baruch lasting right up to the Revelation of John, with the quite world-exploding signs first hinted at in the writings of the prophets, but not yet detached and isolated there—signs of high eschatological impatience and of closer attention to the end-times, against a gigantic cosmic and anti-cosmic horizon. The prophets preceded the apocalyptic writers in every sense, not least in their Utopian temperament, so radically different from that of late Judaic Wisdom literature—a literature which people tried, so to speak, to hook on to the lightning in the Eschaton. Indeed without the conversion of heaven and earth which the prophets intended, the genre of apocalypse would be unthinkable. It would lack its specifically Hebrew element—Prometheus.

18. The Bounds of Patience

A. JOB GIVES NOTICE

A good man who is honest in his dealings willingly trusts others. But if he is ever badly deceived his eyes suddenly open—very wide. That is Job's position: he doubts, indeed denies, the righteousness of God. While the evil man flourishes the pious can wither away: Job sees it in himself. He suffers indescribably and accuses Yahweh for it. That is, he no longer seeks the fault of his misfortune in his own weakness or guilt—or not there alone. His dreams rise out beyond himself to a different life, a better way than the one he sees; he no longer understands the wretched world. Job's question has never died down: where then is God? Perhaps his suffering did detract from his nobility, but it certainly made him stand up and ask questions.

The lesson of murmuring certainly did not pass him by, nor did his mind stand still. The murmuring of the children of Israel is very familiar in the Bible, sounding ever louder from the priestly text, till it reaches its high-point in this Book of Job. The book itself may be very late in origin, between 500 and 400 B.C., though its framework is much earlier—the folk story of Job, with Satan's temptations and the happy end. The poet has worked his own material into the folk-tale in the same way that Goethe worked his Faust into the puppet play. This folk-story, only retained in the first two chapters and the last, must be very old indeed, for the Chaldeans mentioned in 1. 17 still appear to be Bedouin robbers, and that is something this nation of astrologers could not have been for a long time. Ezekiel also mentions his name some two hundred years before the probable time of composition, in the company of Noah and of an equally archaic Daniel—all are said to be well-known from ancient times (Ezek. 15. 14-20). He was given an interesting treatment by the rabbis too (the Job of the biblical poem this time). Some said that he had lived at the time of Abraham, others took him to be one of Pharaoh's god-fearing servants mentioned in Exodus 9. 20—all with the apparent intention of making this uncomfortable figure a non-Jew, even if a pious one. Despite this, however, the Babylonian Talmud unexpectedly names Moses as the author of the book. Rabbi Jochanaan and Rabbi Elieser came nearer the truth when they explained that Job was one of the Jews who had returned from the Babylonian captivity, and dated the book, therefore, in an outstanding example of early "Bible criticism," after Cyrus.

Despite its alleged Mosaic authorship, the Book of Job was consistently treated by the Judaism of the Law as dangerous and better kept at a distance. It undoubtedly belongs to the late Jewish period of enlightenment; to a milieu which does not spare itself but grapples with the whole man, not just with his skeptical, or even pessimistic mind. The author must have gone to great pains: his language is the richest in the Old Testament, with unusual words of Accadian and Arabic origin, and an unusually broad vision of nature. The dialog-form, too, is an innovation, though one lifted straight from the religious discourse of Jewish life. It does not, as with Plato, progress in a series of objections in the spirit of common enquiry by discussion, but consists rather in attack and defense in an increasingly sharply worded encounter. And it is Yahweh who is on the defensive, thrust back by the most powerful attacks on his righteousness: "Why do the wicked live, reach old age, and grow mighty in power?" (21. 7). And why do the poor go hungry? Not because they are godless, but because the rich squeeze and exploit them while God looks on. "Among the olive rows of the wicked they make oil; they tread the wine presses, but suffer thirst. From out of the city the dying groan, and the soul of the wounded cries for help; yet God pays no attention to their prayer" (24. 11 f.). There was, as it were, anti-capitalist preaching before Job, in the prophets; but the accusation that God does nothing to withstand evil is new. It is here that the fatal need for theodicy begins. The Greek tragedians point to it, but it is really in the Book of Job that the great reversal of values begins—the discovery of Utopian potency within the religious sphere: that a man can be better, and behave better, than his God. Job has not just stepped aside from his cult and his community—his attitude is one of definite, unambiguous attack.

At first the only counter-force was the traditional smoothness which saw itself disturbed by these novelties. The three friends trot out the prescribed, unrealistic clichés, but Job will not be silenced. Neither by the mild gravity of Eliphaz, with his wealth of half-baked preaching, nor by the dull homeliness of Bildad, nor by the coarseness of Zophar. To begin with, the friends just advise and wait; but when Job perseveres in his attack they too become hostile and treat him as a reprobate sinner. For there he sits, breathing enmity at God and uproar at men, preaching an end to patience and criticizing the traditional just God. Job points to his ulcers, his poverty and his abandoned state: "Know then that God has put me in the wrong, and closed his net about me. Behold, I cry out, Violence! but I am not answered; I call aloud, but there is no justice" (19. 6 f.). Even worse, however, he makes no attempt to do conversion-sums with righteousness. Yahweh, like murder, is no respecter of persons: "It is all one . . . he destroys both the blameless and the wicked" (9. 22). The tyrant is irresponsible in, and because of, his almighty power: "If it is a contest of strength, behold him! If it is a matter of justice, who can summon him?" (9. 19). The Magna Charta of common justice is invalid: "For he is not a man, as I am, that I might answer him, that we should come to trial together. There is no umpire between us, who might lay his hand upon us both" (9. 32 f.). The contradiction between the prophetic God of moral providence and the reality of raw chance—or even diabolical chance—was terrible to behold. Canaan had turned into Egypt; only the name was different; Israel was back in her former misery. The guilt-atonement, righteousness-salvation polarity had grown so questionable that even outside the Book of Job it had for a long time now been of no consolation at all. Psalm 88, for instance, is one of the most desperate poems that have ever entered the creed. Not even sin is mentioned there as a possible reason for misery. And, fed up with promises, it gives vent to the truly Job-like question: "Is thy steadfast love declared in the grave, or thy faithfulness in Abaddon? Are thy wonders known in the darkness, or thy saving help in the land of forgetfulness?" (Ps. 88. 11 f.). As for the traditional view of sin, a view that was capable of reading misfortune as punishment or as the rod of discipline, Job counters it with the shattering question: "If I sin, what do I do to thee, thou watcher of men? Why hast thou made me thy mark? Why have I become a burden to thee? Why dost thou not pardon my transgression and take away my iniquity?" (Job 7. 20 f.).

To all this, the three friends, Yahweh's advocates, have nothing to offer except the dogma of atonement for guilt in its most rigid form. Their Yahweh veils himself from sight in this threadbare garment, and the young man Elihu, who appears towards the end, still stresses Yahweh's role as nay-sayer and enemy—in 37. 21 he even speaks as though he were himself come to herald the imminent appearance of the mighty Lord. But all the friends can do is to keep on purveying the dogma of requital from on high, and even then without any of the nuances it had had in the prophets. The weighty influence on the path of fate exercised by subjective factors like morality, the deeply meditated doctrines of choice and decision and of man's co-operation in the world—not a single fragment of these truths, brought home so eloquently from Amos and Isaiah to Malachi, remains present in the bigoted babble of these four religious hypocrites. Job's moral conscience, on the other hand, provides a firm stay against the highly questionable judgments of Yahweh and of the friends, his fellow magistrates. And even if it should waver there is still this truth, that a God worthy of the name should save, not punish; that he should, at the very least, right the wrongs which occur secretly and unprovoked.

A man has overtaken, has enlightened his own God. That, despite the apparent submission at the end, is the abiding lesson of the Book of Job. The elemental category of Exodus is operative, in a most powerful transformation. After the Exodus of Israel from Egypt and of Yahweh from Israel, Job makes his exodus from Yahweh. And we may well ask: where to?

The tormented man naturally wants to get away from his tormentor. He attacks because he wants to be left in peace. He is afraid and does not heed. "Commit your work to the Lord, and your plans will be established" (Prov. 16. 3)—that sort of thing is just no longer credible.

Job challenges his mighty enemy to give an account of himself: "Here is my signature (on the indictment)! let the almighty answer me!" (Job 31. 35). And Yahweh replies from out of the storm. He replies in a very strange way—with more questions and still more questions, interspersed with wild descriptions, of the peacock, the horse and the eagle, the storm, the Pleiades, the untamed birth of the ocean, the clouds, Behemoth and Leviathan. Implicit in Job's critique of the actual world is the presentiment of a better one. But Yahweh's answer is to propose one riddle after another, taken abruptly from the wonder and might of nature: a sector on which neither Job's questions nor his accusation touched, despite his leprosy.

"Who is this that darkens counsel by words without knowledge?" —Yahweh's opening question (38. 2) is that of an intimidating schoolmaster. His second, "Where were you when I laid the foundation of the earth?" (38. 4), is the snub of injured majesty. It is followed by a psalm in praise of himself: "When the morning stars sang to me together, and all the sons

110

of God shouted for joy . . ." Yahweh's questions have been called sarcastic, but it was Job's sarcasm that drew first blood when he cried, "What is man, that thou dost make so much of him, and that thou dost set thy mind upon him?" (7. 17). The sarcasm is really very fine, for the skeptic, writhing with pain, is scornfully quoting a passage from the Psalms which, in its original setting (Ps. 8. 5), expresses the worship and thanksgiving of the creature towards his creator. It is the sort of sarcasm a God would use to a worm. There is a remarkable rhetorical parallel, too, between Job's account of his works in chapter 31 and Yahweh's in chapter 38 onwards—except that Job's list, apart from coming first, puts morality where Yahweh puts nature. Nor do Yahweh's questions, even from the viewpoint of nature-study, possess the stamp of eternity which marks out other writings as worthy of the word of God.

Only a few centuries later, with Pliny and Plutarch, some of the natural wonders he relates were not really considered wonderful at all. And besides, they just do not correspond with Job's concerns: the connection is unfair. Yahweh is replying to moral questions with physical ones, beating down the blinkered insight of an underling with blows of wisdom formed in the impenetrable darkness of his cosmos. The nature-pictures are undoubtedly powerful, but there is also a strange, unmistakable whiff of almost demonic pantheism (prefigured in, or contemporary with, Psalms 65 and 74). Nature is no longer the mere arena or show-place of human action, as it is in Genesis 1; it is the clothing, or at least the cipher concealing the majesty of God. Yahweh's works have ceased to be anthropocentric; human teleology breaks down; firmament and colossus tower over it. The stars, in contrast with Genesis 1. 10 and 14, now precede the creation of the earth (Job 38. 7), and there is no sign in God's words of a teleology of man—of a promise of salvation for him lying hidden in the downfall of nature, as it does in the prophetic apocalypses. To prove his majesty, Yahweh chooses senseless, monstrous, even crude and bloody examples from the world of beasts; and here too there is no rational design. The peacock "pays no heed that her work is in vain, because God has made her forget wisdom" (39. 13 f.); the eagle's young ones "suck up blood; and where the slain are, there is he" (39. 20); Behemoth, the hippopotamus, makes one think he "wants to swallow up the Jordan with his mouth" (40. 23); and not of man but of Leviathan, a sort of sea-dragon, is it said that "upon earth there is not his like, a creature without fear" (41. 33). The Behemoth and Leviathan hymns are probably later additions, but they represent clearly and pictorially the unhuman spirit at work here. And it is with a stroke of consummate evil that this Yahweh brings down everything the prophets had said about his rational moral providence, centered on the land of milk and honey. For he makes the overweening, heteronomous boast that he can "bring rain on a land where no man is, on the desert in which there is no man" (38. 26).

The whole theophany is so alien to the Bible that it is almost as if another God were there: one who has nothing in common even with the perilous Yahweh of the volcano, but is reminiscent, rather, of some demonic Isis or of a simple nature-Baal—or even, disconcertingly enough, *mutatis mutandis,* of another God some two thousand years later: Spinoza's. As if one could hear Yahweh's irrational, senseless speech echoed in Spinoza's assertion that God guides nature by the light of his own universal laws, not by the particular laws and purposes of men *("adeoque Deus non solius humani generis, sed totius naturae rationem habet").* Of course the ratio, and the autarchy of ratio, which Spinoza referred to, are totally absent from the Yahweh of Job, but, for all that, the anti-teleological bias is a remarkable point of contact between them. One of the earliest sources for Spinoza's religion could in fact be these last chapters of the Book of Job, though as far as Spinoza is concerned there is nothing demonic in his Pan.

But why, then, does Job make out that he has been converted, or even convinced? Why does he say: "I lay my hand on my mouth" (40. 4)? In his book *The Idea of the Holy,* Rudolf Otto has sought a solution in the wasteland of Beyond-good-and-evil, for that is the Beyond this Yahweh manifests. The picture Yahweh paints is quite atrociously disedifying, calling to mind as it does the eleventh song of the *Bhagavad-Gita,* where Krishna reveals himself to Arjuna as a repulsive maelstrom of death and monstrous birth. But none of that would have done anything to convert, let alone convince Job. It would simply have thrust him down again, thrust him spiritually back, by *metabasis eis allo genos,* into the depths of pre-prophetic, pre-Canaanite demonism. There is this point, too, that the author of Job may have found Yahweh's straight-forward, declared demonism (especially in its elevated cosmic instrumentation) more consoling than its alternative: the injustice of the God of righteousness. In any case this poet is no forerunner of Rudolf Otto, and even less so of those indiscriminate modern devotees of the night of blood who shelter under the mask of mysticism. His despairing hero was still cast in a rebel mold; he was still, unmistakably, a biblical Prometheus who could never in fact have spoken the words: "I lay my hand on my mouth" (40. 4).

The final conversion scene stands from ancient times in close proximity to the traditional ending of the popular story, in which Job is healed and reconciled to God; it is in fact the bridge-passage to this conclusion. It may have been added by the author so that he could safely give vent to his heresy—which he succeeds in doing. Or it may be that the storm and nature scenes were interpolated later—which, in view of their poetic power and linguistic unity with what came before, is unlikely. Or, finally, it may be that the author of Job had two disparate strands of thought, the rebellious human one and a heteronomous, extra-human, cosmic one (a dichotomy at the heart of his theme which would be almost without parallel in great writers). There is, then, little choice but to interpret the problematical storm-scene in the first sense: as a cover for the heresy Job so fearlessly wanted to proclaim. The praise of God's greatness in nature (already given powerful expression in the Psalms) was interwoven with the old mantle narrative of the popular story—and the mantle was embellished with stars.

The decisive point in all this, however, is often overlooked:

that the author had already, a long way back, proposed *another solution—one which sprang straight from his rebellious depths:* A solution only deprived of its unequivocal clarity, only deprived of the salt of its meaning, by the hopeless corruption of the text, and by the harmonizing indulged in by the Christian churchmen who translated it. In the Vulgate, as in Luther's Bible, Job says: "For I know that my Redeemer liveth, and at the last day I shall rise up from the earth; and once again I shall be clad in my own skin; then in my flesh shall I see God: whom I shall see for myself, and mine eyes shall behold, and not another" (19. 25-27 [translated from Vulgate, following Authorized Version where possible]). Since then a host of Protestant theologians and Old Testament philologists have made conjectures about the corrupt text of this passage: Duhm, for example, in his *Kommentar zu Hiob* (1897), and Bertholet after him. But even the Hebrew word *goēl,* transmitted unexceptionably in the text, cannot possibly be translated as "Redeemer," at least not in view of the mild sense this word has assumed in Christianity. Nor does it mean Yahweh as Redeemer, as the orthodox Jewish interpretation would have it, for the sense of *goēl* is a man's closest relative and heir, who has the duty of avenging a murder—in ancient times it was the *goēl had-dām,* the Avenger of blood mentioned in Numbers 35. 19. The extant text, corrupt and incoherent, reads verbally thus: "And I know that my avenger lives, and at last [as the last] he will stand up [stand by, stand firm, stand his ground] upon the dust. And after this my skin are destroyed, and from the flesh I shall see God. When [whom] I see for myself, and my eyes beheld, and no stranger." Bertholet arranges this chaotic text, tentatively and conjecturally, in the following way: "But I know that the avenger of my blood is alive, and at long last he will raise himself above the dust. The witness of my innocence will be with me, and I shall see for myself the deliverer of my guilt; with my own eyes I shall see it, and not as a stranger" (cf. *Biblische Theologie des Alten Testaments,* II, 1911, p. 113). In later Hebrew, it is true (and that means in the Book of Job, too, presuming that a solemn passage like this does not in fact invoke archaic usage), the word *goēl* more generally may also be taken to mean advocate; but this weaker sense in no way fits Job's bitterness and his outright warfare against Yahweh. It does not fit in with the crime he feels has been committed against him, the crime he has just denounced so strongly: "O earth, cover not my blood, and let my cry find no resting place. Even now, behold, my witness is in heaven, and he that vouches for me is on high" (16. 18 f.). All interpretations point, then, to the figure of an Avenger, the avenger of the downtrodden Job whose blood is crying out to heaven, the unnamed, unknown one who pursues with justice and redresses the murder of the innocent. There is, of course, no "prophecy" of Christ here if one reads "Avenger of blood" instead of "Redeemer"; but it does avoid taking the enemy for the advocate. *The friend Job seeks, the relative, the Avenger, cannot possibly be that same Yahweh against whom he invokes the Avenger*—that Yahweh whom he again attacks straight after, and before whom, in chapter 31, he unfolds the testimony of a righteous man. The traditional exegesis of 19. 25-27 has always conveyed the accents, or at least the mood, of Job's three traditionalist friends; even when, philologically at any rate, the reading "Avenger of blood" could no longer be suppressed. Harmonization to preserve a staid theocratic tone has always won over the—other Bible, however much that other Bible has stood out incorrupt against a sea of corruption. Job and his unequivocal message continue to be turned upside down, so necessary is it, even after the horrors of Auschwitz, to misconstrue this message if men are still to abandon themselves to God. Even now, thousands of years later, the three friends still have their followers; but that is *ad minorem gloriam* so far as the innovator Job is concerned.

The thesis that the world can get on quite well without man, that it is not centered on man, is very far removed from the Messianic teaching he had hoped for. The Avenger-figure is in fact closer to the Yahweh of the Exodus, the Yahweh of "Israel's courtship"—a spirit who has nothing at all in common with the present state of creation and world order. The sharp

115

edge of Messianism is here in fact made manifest, in all the strength of its antithesis to the given world. The answer to Job's questioning, to his despair and hope for change, is given *in terms of an Avenger, terms connected intimately with his own clear conscience*, and in no other way. That is the solution proposed by the author of Job; it makes mincement of the Yahweh-scene with its dead end in a view of nature that has no place for man—or none yet. "My eye pours out tears to God, that he would maintain the right of a man with God, like that of a man with his neighbor" (16. 21). This most ardently longed-for Thou certainly does not lie in the Tohuwabohu of fate, but it does not lie either in the mere *Tremendum* of nature.

B. PATIENT SUFFERER, OR HEBREW PROMETHEUS?

As is well known, the most bitter of men has been made out to be the most patient—has really been put on display as such: Job was to bring the doubter back into the fold. The popular story has beaten the poet: the rebel has been received into the Church as the epitome of long-suffering. The words from the opening, "The Lord gave and the Lord has taken away," have, together with those from the ending, "The Lord blessed the latter days of Job more than his beginning," succeeded in extinguishing the whole fiery center of the book. In the Orient, in fact, Job has become proverbial for his opposite—to such an extent that among the many nicknames of the camel there is: abu Eyyub, father Job. The Koran praises a Job cut down to size as a patient sufferer, a model of resignation outstanding even in Islam. The ninth Sure speaks quietistically of his deepest struggles: "There is no flight from God except to him." In orthodox Judaism, it is true, he has always been a stumbling-block; but the Church has made him the prince of all submitters. The general verdict of the Talmud is *ba'at*, he was indignant. Admittedly, in one place Moses is credited with the authorship of Job, but it could only be the Moses of the Waters of Contention, or of the rebellion against Yahweh's angel of death. The Church in her turn confuses Job all too frequently with his three friends: with the conventional platitudes ever-ready as a muzzle in the hands of the clerical party. She reduces him to the banal level of Eliphaz, or at least to that of the victor over temptations, the hero of the popular story. He becomes in fact the model of patience under trial—and that is meant to be the same man who called Yahweh a murderer: "It is all one . . . he destroys both the blameless and the wicked" (9. 22)! That is the Titan who challenges God, and who needs no demi-god to be his champion (after the model of the Greek tragedy against Zeus), but who places himself fair and square in the fight and takes his stand as a man against an enemy he believes to be almighty.

Job stands in a world where terrible experience has proved the requital-dogma empty. It is not alone that he suffers: he protests as a representative. Even the teaching of the prophets, about fate being conditioned by moral decision, had long ago been lost in the simple requital-dogma of the three friends, with its mechanism of reward and punishment. But reality knew nothing of this; knew nothing, either, of a benevolent providence. The Yahweh of the storm, who dashed mankind to pieces, reducing him to a fraction of the world, certainly showed no trace of that. Indeed this Yahweh himself, in the final scene, revises the ideal of providence Job's friends had made of him. It is with deep irony that he addresses Eliphaz: "My wrath is kindled against you and against your two friends; for you have not spoken of me what is right, as my servant Job has" (42. 7). The resignation, however, that Job was meant to draw from this sort of divine instruction had nothing to do with a message of joy. It was a question of pure surrender, devoid of consolation; even the future is blocked. The Yahweh of the finale, as one would expect of a nature-demon, speaks no single Messianic word. He makes no murmur of response to the hope which Job, in 19. 25, is supposed to have placed in him; on the contrary, the foundation of all hope is and remains Job's own good conscience, with its rebellious quest for an avenger. In fact, Yahweh's appearance and his words do everything to confirm Job's lack of faith in divine justice; far from being the theophany of the righteous God, they are like a divine atheism in regard to (or rather paying no regard to) the moral order. There is almost a hint there of that most paradoxical of all visions—the one Jean Paul entitled "Words of the dead Christ down from the edifice of the world: that there is no God."

So much the less chance, then, of resignation; and all the more certain that the would-be theodicy will turn out to be its opposite: the exodus of man from Yahweh, with the vision of a world that will rise above the dust. Not that this world is, in Job, any sort of after-life where just recompense is made for everything. The Judaism of his day knew nothing of that. Man's body just went down into the earth, into the land of the shades. Job meant, then, a world he himself would see, perhaps after some renewal; a world ushered in by the avenging libertator, who would take the principle of unrighteousness to trial. He meant a path forged by man and his morality, cutting a way through both nature and God. Theodicy is now inevitable; and all the excuses of theology fail it—all the apologies and alibis made necessary by the ever-widening circle of Job-like experience and thought. The doctrine of the Fall breaks down, with the elaborate way it uses Adam's sin and the idea of demonic intervention to whitewash an evil creation. So too does the developed idea of Satan, the most monstrous of all Yahweh's scapegoats, the one on whose head the whole havoc of existence can be heaped. In the popular story he is no more than an accusing angel, or at the most an envious sceptic, and in the body of the poem he is not even mentioned. In former times he was perhaps taken to be an evil seducer ("Satan stood up against Israel, and incited David to number Israel"—1 Chron. 21. 1), but in no sense was he the author of evil. The motif of the fall of Lucifer, found in the First Isaiah ("How you are fallen from heaven, O Day Star, son of Dawn!"—Is. 14. 12), was only later applied to satanology; the quotation actually refers only to the king of Babylon.

To all these white washing theodicies Job would have replied: Yahweh cannot be both almighty and good if he gives Satan free rein. He can only be almighty and evil, or good and weak: the union of the Almighty and the Good leaves as little room for the devil as it previously did for evil unpersonified, evil without a dummy or facade.

There is, however, another sort of dualism, often scarcely noticed, to be found in the prophets and in the interpolations they inspired in the Pentateuch. This dualism is less susceptible to Job's objections, because, among other things, the dichotomy here is not between good and evil, Ormuz and Ahriman, but between indifference, so to speak, and love. The prophets, still persevering in the topos of Yahweh, generally treated misfortune as being the discipline and trial imposed by a righteous father; but sometimes they saw it as something that simply happened on its own account, when Yahweh turned his back on men. Yahweh himself expresses it towards the end of Deuteronomy: "I will forsake them and hide my face from them, and they will be devoured; and many evils and troubles will come upon them, so that they will say in that day, Have not these evils come upon us because our God is not among us?" (Deut. 31. 17). Here evil and trouble seem to be not realities willed by Yahweh or by a God opposed to him, but realities in their own right, which exist and flourish in and through the distance kept by God. They are fate, let loose in complete indifference, and indifferently frustrating man's concerns—like the cosmic nature-demon at the end of the Book of Job. God's almighty power and goodness diminish in unison; in his absence Egypt or Assyria can descend on Israel as evil fate, just as a self-induced whirlwind can. In the prophets this doctrine was an attempt at a theodicy without the Fall or Satan; and it conjures up an echo as late as Augustine who, for all his widespread use of Satan, could still remark: evil comes from the deprivation of God—God is not its *causa efficiens,* but its *causa deficiens.* Job's indignation, however, would find no solace in this theodicy either; all the less so since he considers Yahweh to be just such a disparate nature-demon himself. An

119

alibi is no excuse, given the wretched state of the world; it is no substitute for true responsibility: real goodness and almighty power would never grow so tired and indifferent. Not even to the sinner, let alone, as Job in his realism so constantly pointed out, to the just.

Measured against the rigor of his questions, no theodicy can still stand up as honest. The Book of Job has set to work the advocates of almighty power and goodness, but it has also, *a limine,* put a stop to all their harmonizations. Men who have stepped so radically beyond the concept of a Creator-God or a God of righteousness that they can deny his existence, do not have any more problems about justifying him; or if they do they are purely historical ones. According to the French Enlightenment, the simplest solution to theodicy is: *que Dieu n'existe pas.* But this just turns into moral atheism; which, ontologically structured, is what the whole concluding theophany of the Book of Job can be seen to be. And then the whole problem of theodicy turns into an apologetics without a cause. But, what *is* important, Job's whole rebellion, all his questions and accusations, seem, when God is dethroned, to go up into thin air.

Can that really be so? Does the Book of Job, with all its bitter questioning, possess no more truth for easy-going atheists than the historical or the psychological or, of course, the poetic variety? Is there not a great deal there apart from this? The unfeeling cruelty of nature, even without Yahweh, its unconcern for man? And then: disease, disorder, alienation, the cold shoulder of existence? And that strange Something in existence (whether concretized, whether hypostasized transcendentally or not) of which Job says that it "destroys both the blameless and the wicked" (9. 22)? Is there not also death, about which Job says the terrible, timeless words: "If I look for Sheol as my house, if I spread my couch in darkness, if I say to the pit, You are my father, and to the worm, My mother, or My sister, where then is my hope? Who will see my hope? Will it go down to the bars of Sheol? Shall we descend together into the dust?" (17. 13-16)?

An unfeeling universe remains; one still so badly adjusted to human finality. And if we can no longer react to this with accusation, we can and do react with searching questions, and with massive negative amazement. So far as those questions deal with what used to be called theodicy (now reduced to a *problem:* that of immanent sense—all superstitious, whitewashing apologias for some supreme, transcendent authority having been cast aside), we are led to ask if all the idealistic dreaming that is now in such sore straits does not in fact need some consolation, some hope that despite everything it may yet reach its goal. Man's works against inhumanity, his attempts to achieve Utopia, his plans for what is-not-yet—do they not call for some corresponding factor at the heart of the world? Can there be no understanding of the harsh clash of misery and the drive to overcome it, no insight into exploitation and its progressive dialectics? And does not dialectical materialism itself need some justification for invoking such a dreary and repulsive process? Where does this realm of necessity come from, with all its long oppression? Why is the realm of freedom not suddenly there? Why must it work its way with so much bloodshed through necessity? Why the long delay? All these questions remain there for atheism to answer—that is, if atheism is not just the unhistorical, unrealistic folly of optimism, or of equally unhistorical nihilism, with man as a laughable begetter of illusions (despite the fact that he is himself part of the world), and with the alien specter of death all around us, and that gorgon of cosmic inhumanity which can never contain any shred of concern for man.

Job's questions are not entirely answered by his exodus from the Yahweh of apparent righteousness. They remain, transferred now and transformed, to address the paralyzing storm and the silence of the world where no Yahweh dwells. The simplest solution for theodicy is not just *que Dieu n'existe pas,* for the questions then rise up again to confront the dark, unfeeling way of the world itself, and the intractable matter which moves there. The simplest way is this: that there is always an exodus in the world, an exodus from the particular

121

status quo. And there is always a hope, which is connected with rebellion—a hope founded in the concrete given possibilities for new being. As a handhold in the future, a process which, though by no means achieved, is yet by no means in vain, thanks to the never-abating pregnancy of its solution, our solution. The exodus begun by Job from the Caesar-like concept of God, when he placed mankind above all forms of tyranny—above the very questionable tyranny of righteousness from on-high and the neo-mythical tyranny of majestic nature—*this exodus is not one away from Exodus itself.* Far from it: it is precisely the rebel who has trust in God, without believing in him. That is: he has trust in the specific Yahweh of the *Exodus from Egypt,* even when he has seen through every concretization of myth, and when every subservient reflex to a master on high has died away at its source. The God who appears in Job, ruling and oppressing with so much power and greatness, but known by his fruits, is a mere Pharaoh from heaven. Job is pious precisely because he does *not* believe. Except in Exodus, and in the fact that the last human word has not yet been said—the word that will come from the Avenger of blood who puts an end to blood, the word that will come from the Son of Man himself, and not from any mighty Lord. The word, finally, that will allow of no more exodus but will move in, utterly fearless, to take the place of a now-revoked On-high.

AUT CAESAR
AUT CHRISTUS?

19. How Restless Men Are

We in our turn have never emerged from ourselves, and we are where we are. But we are still dark in ourselves; and not only because of the nearness, the immediacy of the Here-and-now in which we, as all things, have our being. No—it is because we tear at each other, as no beasts do: secretly we are dangerous. And because in so many other ways we are hidden: unrealized, unachieved as no other living being, still open to what lies ahead. With a finger even in the Yet-to-come, which is coming, far ahead.

And at the same time we start, over and over again, at the beginning, ever restless. But with a sign that our plan is good; a sign called Jesus: one that is not yet rid of restlessness and journeying; but one that is bound in unique intimacy to man, and stays by him. As the mildest of signs, it is true; but precisely for that reason as the most fiery, the most disturbing, the most uprooting. If it had not been so, if the hypocrisy had continued, no shoot would ever have blossomed, there would have been no "I am he," but just more soothing words. Something else is afoot here, though; for this Jesus calls us by our name, and stands by it. The awakening can be a quiet one and yet still be unsettling. It is a renewal.

20. Mildness and "The Light of His Fury" (William Blake)

Some men are born lambs; they duck and dodge with ease and alacrity. It is in their nature. To them Jesus did not preach with the power the Scripture speaks of. And least of all is he himself the mild figure some meek spirits make out. The figure the wolves have dressed for the sheep, so that their wolfishness may become twofold. The pseudo-shepherd is portrayed as so quiet, so infinitely patient, that one might think he really was like that. The founder figure *must* have been free from passions . . . Yet Jesus had one of the strongest passions there are: anger. He overthrew the tables of the money-changers in the Temple, and did not forget to use a whip. He is only patient in the affairs of his own quiet circle; he shows no love at all for its enemies. So far as the Sermon on the Mount is concerned it does not, it is true, speak of one man being set against another for the love of Christ, as do some other zealous words (Matt. 10. 35 f.); but then it is not a sermon about the days of battle at all. With its blessing on the meek and the peacemakers, it is concerned with the last days: with the End, which Jesus (according to the Mandaean John) thought close at hand. Hence its *immediate,* chiliastic references to the Kingdom of Heaven (Matt. 5. 3). There is quite a different message for the battle, for the achievement of the Kingdom: "I have not come to bring peace, but a sword" (Matt. 10. 34); or, in more outward-looking, outward-burning terms: "I came to cast fire upon the earth; and would that it were already kindled!" (Lk. 12. 49). Which is exactly what William Blake meant by his corollary in verse, applicable to 1789, "The spirit of turmoil shot down from the Saviour/ And in the vineyards of red France appear'd the light of his fury."

124

The sword in Jesus, preaching, and the fire which purifies as well as destroys, are certainly directed at more than mere palaces: they apply to the whole of the old aeon, which must pass away. But at the head of the list stand the enemies of those who labor and are heavy laden: the rich, for whom it is more difficult to enter the Kingdom of Heaven than it is (with all the irony of the impossible) for a camel to pass through the eye of a needle. The Church has widened that aperture considerably since then, and her Jesus has of course now left the focal point of mutiny. Mildness—to the unjust, that is—has come up trumps, not Jesus' anger. And yet even Kautsky, who only saw in it a "minor religious mantle," had to admit in his *Foundations of Christianity* that "The class hatred of the modern proletariat has scarcely ever reached such fanatical forms as that of the Christian proletariat." Jesus would spew the lukewarm out of his mouth; no single word of his can fit ideologically into any of the social structures we have so far known—least of all the words of Sermon on the Mount. Everything he said is full of expectation, and preparation for the End. His moral teaching is incomprehensible without its apocalyptic counterpart—even prescinding from the (very late) Revelation of John, which, though not confined to Jesus' doctrine, was continually hinted at in his preaching.
"He who endures to the end will be saved" (Mk. 13. 13): a strict complement indeed to the demands of the Sermon on the Mount. "And what I say to you I say to all: Watch" (Mk. 13. 37). There is no quietism there; rather, in the words of William Blake, these sayings relate to the light of that undeniable fury.

21. Jesus' Exodus into Yahweh

BAPTIST FOR THE ONE-TO-COME

Suffering alone does not bring a man to his feet. Unless he fights the pressure that is beating down on more than just his soul. Seeming to hear words which turn his life around; seeing a door. . . . Doing so above all when the times themselves spell

125

change: change that jerks one forward, and does so suddenly. It was like that in the days of John the Baptist: time seemed complete; the measure of the past was full. Penance must be done, for the Kingdom of Heaven was at hand, and it was worthwhile to cleanse oneself for it—by baptism in the Jordan. For it was the age-old function of that water to purify more than just the skin.

But a new figure was now there: one who baptized in a special way, fulfilling baptism; one who went beyond the common ritual washings to a purification which made ready, once for all, for someone yet to come. John's claim to be the messenger sent on ahead was endowed with a quality of immediacy that no one in the Scriptures had yet possessed, not even Elijah—a quality that made him more than a messenger. This herald did not himself know the Mightier-one who was coming after him, whose baptism would not be with the traditional water, but with a new spirit and with fire. Hence, the offensive, baffled question, "Are you he who is to come, or shall we look for another?" (Matt. 11. 3), and Jesus' reply, directed to one he had not counted among his own: "Blessed is he who takes no offense at me" (Matt. 11. 6). But, for all this—and that shows how little the youthful Jesus saw himself as the One-to-come—at the beginning of his mission Jesus went of his own accord to be baptized by John. For his part, John may well have incorporated Mandaean, Persian influences into his character of Nazirite from the desert. But in any case he went further than anyone had gone before, in calling for a more than merely national stand and witness. His God "is able from these stones to raise up children to Abraham" (Matt. 3. 9). Another covenant is waiting in the wings; but not yet a covenant of joy.

GOOD NEWS AS THE OPPOSITE OF FEAR
OF THE LORD: JESUS' EXODUS INTO YAHWEH

One was coming, who would make the crooked straight at last. First of all he was to come from on high; then, when nothing happened, he was expected from below: a hero from among the Jews. An envoy, but one who carried out his mission better than the figure who made the mission necessary. For if the world were not in such sore straits, no Messiah would be needed.

Jesus hesitated a long time before he appeared in this guise; at first he considered himself a disciple of the Baptist; he felt unclean and was baptized. The story of the temptations (Matt. 4. 3-6) shows his conviction that it was for the devil to call himself the Son of God. That is why Peter is rebuffed so harshly when he first gives Christ the name (Mk. 8. 33). Only the "Transfiguration" six days later, with the outwardly audible voice from the cloud (Mk. 9. 1-7), seems to have brought him to the definitive awareness of his mission. This much is clear by then, that however mild this mission was, it was by no means a purely interior one, as was claimed later on when it had failed. Jesus accepted the Hosannas when he entered Jerusalem: and *Hosanna!* was the ancient acclamation of the kings. Politically it was unequivocal: it was directed against Rome—"Blessed is the kingdom of our father David" (Mk. 11. 10), "Hosanna! Blessed is he who comes in the name of the Lord, even the King of Israel!" (Jn. 12. 13). Standing before the High Priest Jesus confesses himself to be the Messiah, with all the signs of power which, since Daniel, formed part of the traditional expectation—not, therefore, in any merely interior or abstract way (Mk. 14. 62). And before Pilate he takes on the title of King of the Jews: the title under which he was crucified (that was the Roman punishment for rebellion). If Jesus was not in fact the Messiah of Jewish expectation, one is left with the puzzle as to how he came to have scruples about declaring himself to be so, and why he overcame them. He would have called himself a good man, a pastor of souls, and at the most a successor of the prophets of old. No heavenly hallucination would have been called for to venture the words *Tu es Christus.* The task of separating Jesus from the Messianic dream of the Jews, and therefore from an eschatology which was also political, was begun by the Enlightenment, and continued, somewhat less innocently, by the anti-Semitic liberal theologians of the nineteenth century. Renan was the unfortunate instigator of it all, with his *Life of Jesus*. The scientific preparation was done by Holtzmann, Wellhausen and Harnack, and the conclusion was a Christ of pure and quite unparalleled interiority. Again it was Wellhausen who reached the lowest depths when he said of this King of the Jews that "the kingdom he had in mind was not the one the Jews had hoped for. He fulfilled their hope and longing by directing it to a different ideal, a higher order. Only in this sense can he have called himself the Messiah" (*Israelitische und jüdische Geschichte*, 1895, p. 349). So eschatology was thrown out of the gospels, although philologically its credentials were excellent; and Jesus became the prophet of a purely ethical Kingdom of God: one that lay right outside the apocalyptic dream which had, since Daniel, characterized the whole of Jewish piety.

Thanks are due to Albert Schweitzer (*Das Messianitäts-und Leidensgeheimnis*, 1901; English translation, New York, 1914) for seeing things in proper proportion again, even within the bounds of liberal theology: Jesus put ethics (seen as penance, preparation for the Kingdom) in the context of eschatology, not *vice versa*. But even in Schweitzer, eschatology is not thought of in an earthly-political-materialistic way; it is exclusively supernatural: far too supernatural—far too far removed from both the new heaven *and new earth*. But, for all that, the coming Kingdom is the primary thing in Jesus' mind, not love. His concern for love only comes from his concern for the Kingdom, which is no psychological event, but a catastrophic, cosmic one, directed towards the new Jerusalem. Jesus had no time for the defeatism of pure interiority; he lived entirely in the order defined by the public prophecy of John: "Repent, for the kingdom of heaven is at hand." He sent his disciples out in pairs into the Jewish towns (Matt. 10) to spread the gospel; and he prepared them for the Messianic affliction which was soon to come: days of harsh persecution for them as for all the elect, though some of them would perhaps find the right tone for these hard times. He did not even expect the survivors of this mission to return to him as they went, so near did he deem the end of this world, and the coming of the new one: "You will not have gone through all the towns of Israel, before the Son of man comes" (Matt. 10. 23). Even the Our Father contains the same sort of immediate reference to the tribulations of the imminent *Eschaton;* only false translation can give it a tone of complete interiority. "And lead us not into temptation, but deliver us from evil." Temptation (*peirasmos*) does not mean here the temptation of the individual to sin; it means tribulation, eschatological affliction, persecution by the Antichrist at the end of days. The prayer is that this chalice of persecution should pass away, and the new aeon be born, without a long delay which would give time for counter-revolution. Jesus believed so firmly that he was to bring in the new Sion, that this faith only left him on the Cross—in the most terrible Moment any man had lived, a moment stronger even than the death-agony which came with it. In that most concrete of all cries of despair: "My God, why hast thou forsaken me?" Only a man who has seen the concrete feasibility of his work completely disappear could say that; not any mere leader of souls; not any Heavenly King of purely spiritual realms. Even the message to the laborers and heavy-laden is shot through with the social impulse of the Nazirite and prophetic movements, not with any death-wish or lofty consolation. "For he taught them as one who had authority, and not as their scribes" (Matt. 7. 29): least of all as some sort of sublimated Christ with a message only for the soul, and a mind and spirituality focused only on eternity. The saying of Matthew 11. 25-30 is a politico-religious cry of jubilee; it signifies quite unequivocally the Messiah-King's entry into power, and its last words are a reprieve: "My yoke is easy, and my burden is light." Which certainly does not refer to the yoke of the Cross. For that is of all burdens the least mild and light, and one that could certainly not have yielded any tidings of joy.

Subjectively, then, Jesus considered himself the Messiah in the thoroughly traditional sense; objectively he is anything but an artful dodger into invisible inwardness, or a sort of quartermaster for a totally transcendent heavenly Kingdom. On the contrary, salvation is identified with Canaan, as the fulfillment of the promise to the fathers, with no escape-clause, no hair-splitting and no omissions—a Canaan which is in fact essentially surpassed: "There is no man who has left house, or wife or brothers or parents or children, for the sake of the kingdom of God, who will not receive manifold more in this time, and in the age to come eternal life" (Lk. 18. 29 f.). There was already quite enough interiority in the mere expectation of the Messiah, and more than enough heaven in belief in the Up-there: it was the earth that needed the Savior and the gospel.

If any doubt should remain that Jesus—before the Cross-catastrophe—intended to appear as an earthly Saviour, it is dispelled by the word "gospel" itself. Jesus did not disdain to play the part of a medical wonder-worker, and he uses the word gospel in the sense of a wondrous healing of all the earth, brought in by the Kingdom of God (Mk. 1. 15). He sent this highly un-interior definition to the Nazirite John in prision: "The blind receive their sight and the lame walk, lepers are cleansed and the deaf hear, and the dead are raised up, and the poor have good news preached to them" (Matt. 11. 15). Even if there are some places where Jesus speaks of the gospel as one would of a legacy (Mk. 13. 10; 14. 9)—places which may well have been neatly interpolated later on—the word itself is certainly not a late one; it is certainly not what Johannes Weiss called it. "simply an expression from the language of mission": post crucem, then and spiritual. Quite the opposite, in fact. Precisely at the time of Jesus, it conveyed the unmistakable politico-religious meaning of a salvation which lay concretely in the end of misery and the beginning of good fortune. Nor was it only the subjugated Jews who at that time cherished hopes or feelings of a very tangible advent: all the peoples of the Orient did so. Indeed, even their oppressors, the well-fed Romans, used the word "gospel" as a word of peace, a Sibylline sort of term connected openly with good fortune (against the background of bleak insecurity provided by the last century of the Republic). Virgil's prophecy of a divine and royal child in the Fourth Eclogue was widely known, and applied to Augustus: the golden-age of Saturn, the Saturnalia, are coming back—and it is this that is here called gospel. In this sense, too, an altar-stone at Priene in Asia Minor honors the birth of Augustus quite literally as the beginning of *"evangelia"* for the world. In this way the word penetrated into Palestine, a world which more than ever now had room for good news; it drove home the meaning of final and irrevocable, socio-political good fortune, and joined forces smoothly with the *Olam-ha-Shalom,* the Kingdom of Peace, of traditional prophetic Messianism. It would never have done this with pure inwardness or Other-worldery. The general shift of meaning brought in by the language of mission was necessary before that could happen; and that is something Jesus never undertook. The Christians of the catacombs, too—no peaceable dualistic, transcendent, escapists, these—made no peace with Nero and his kingdom; otherwise they would not have been thrown to his wild beasts. And, not least of all, this same highly virile Christian impulse inspired the Peasant War, which, not without reason, was an exercise in practical chiliasm. In its true, original sense the gospel was identical with its down-to-earth revolutionary realism: "The time is fulfilled, and the kingdom of God is at hand" (Mk. 1. 15). *In summa,* Messiah and gospel mean just this, that Jesus never conceived his mission in watered-down, unworldly terms.

This is not contradicted in the slightest by the two ostensibly spiritual sayings of Christ which, for the last two thousand years, have been used to prove, and even to lay claim to, the harmlessness of Christianity: the sayings about the interior *kingdom,* and about the *kingship that is not of this world.*

Jesus never said, "The kingdom of God is in you." Properly translated, the phrase (Lk. 17.21) read, "The kingdom of God is in the midst of you" (ἐντὸς ὑμῶν); and he said that not to his disciples but to the Pharisees, indicating his disciples as he

131

spoke. His words were an answer to their catch-question as to when the Kingdom of God was coming; what he said was that the Kingdom is close at hand, even spatially: it is here in the community of his followers. He did not say what Luther translated, "The kingdom of God is in you": that would, *e contrario,* have been to emphasize the unworldliness of a realm of pure spirit. And Luther renders the previous phrase: "The kingdom does not come with outward gestures"; but, translated literally, what Jesus really said was " The kingdom is not coming with observable signs" *(meta paratērēseōs).* And, in the language of Hellenic culture which Luke, the doctor, here makes Jesus speak, observability, *paratērēsis,* was a medical and astrological term relating solely to symptoms and previous signs, and having nothing to do with interiority. What Jesus meant, then, was that there will be no time for tranquil observation: the Kingdom will break through *suddenly,* in a single all-transforming bound. He speaks about this breakthrough in the community of his followers: the only ones who will survive the abrupt dawning of the Kingdom, with its very un-interior apocalyptic traits, are not those who hold their finger gently up to the wind and observe the long-range signs and cycles of astrology, but those members of the new community who are armed and sealed in constant readiness for it.

And now the saying: "My kingship is not of this world." These words of Jesus before Pilate are quite clear grammatically, at least as to their ordinary sense, but they appear only in the largely unhistorical Gospel of John (18. 36) with its already Pauline slant, and they serve a reconizable purpose in the posthumous community. They are placed there so that the Christian who is brought before a pagan court can call on his Master's words to testify that Christ and the Christians have nothing to do with treason. That is why John leaves so many more gaps in the scene before the High Priest than the other evangelists do, drawing out the scene in the Roman court to make up for it. And that is why he portrays Pilate so much more favorably than he does the Jews: the high-ranking

Roman officer is to be a precedent in his threefold assertion that he could find no fault in Jesus, and his three attempts to set him free. John uses the judgment-scene above all to make Jesus say words which, in the matter concerned, were quite harmless—and in Jesus' own case almost saved him. But they were not words taken from the tradition of Jesus' sayings; they originated rather in the needs of the community and the desire to alleviate them. Their motive is not primarily Christological but forensic and apologetical (cf. here J. Baur, *Kommentar zum Johannesevangelium*, 1925). It is incompatible with the courage and dignity of Jesus that he should use such defeatist words in front of Pilate, presenting himself to his Roman judge as an outlandish enthusiast, and, by Roman standards, an almost comically un-dangerous one. But it was not at all incompatible with the dignity of the Christian community for its members to appeal to these words before the court (at least not until the time when the martyrdom cult broke out). Hence the stress on the ill-will of the Jews and the noblesse of Pilate, and the clear *captatio benevolentiae* in this post-Jesus world. One may well doubt whether this passage in John saved any Christians from Nero; but later on it would have helped all the more towards the abandonment of the earthly claims of Christianity, once the Pilates and Neros had themselves turned Christian. Then the phrase was no longer interpreted as an apologia for the victims of the world, but became one for the lords of the world—which certainly was not John's intention.

Jesus could still not have spoken these words, however, even in this wider sense. Nowhere did he set up a dualism between this world and the other, in such a way that this world remained unassailed, and could survive alongside the next by a sort of non-intervention pact. This world must pass away before the next: it will be judged by it in the terms the Baptist used when he announced Christ: "His winnowing fork is in his hand, to clear his threshing floor, and to gather the wheat into his granary, but the chaff he will burn with unquenchable fire" (Lk. 3. 17). Whenever the words "this world" and "the other world" appear, except in this interpolation in the court-scene, they are entirely free from any undertone of alibi. "This world" means the same as "the present aeon"; "the other world" means the same as "the better aeon that is to come," the *mellon aion,* the coming world-period which stands in opposition to the present world. Hence Matthew 12. 32; 24. 3. What is meant is eschatological tension, not some sort of geographical separation from a fixed This-world here and a fixed Beyond there. The only real thing now about this world is its submergence in the next, when the better aeon finally breaks in on it at the last day. But there is no point in preaching that Kingdom to the dead; it is for the living to hear of it—the ones who are gathered here already. No death is necessary, no post-mortal Beyond (Matt. 16. 28; Lk. 21. 32). Not even the words of the dispute about the coin of tribute, "Render therefore to Caesar the things that are Caesar's, and to God the things that are God's" (Matt. 22. 21)—not even these words support Jesus' defeatism before Pilate, however much they were flogged to death by Paul, not to mention the later Christians of compromise. On the contrary, the disinterested-ness of the dispute about the coin of tribute is itself truly eschatological: Caesar does not matter precisely because the Kingdom is close at hand. The disinterestedness before Pilate, however, takes no account at all of eschatology—of this most firmly-established of all the elements in Jesus' preaching. It was an absolute disinterestedness, not the conditioned, ironi-cal, scornfully dangerous type which stamps all the rest of Jesus' sayings about the present world. "Now is the judgment of this world, now shall the ruler of this world be cast out" (Jn. 12. 31). Room is made for the new aeon of heaven and earth: for the most actual then, of all Here-and-nows.

However much Paul and then Marcion stressed the trans-cendence of Christ, this transcendence is by no means a simple removal from, and beyond, the world. It is, rather, a new world, coming with power to establish itself in the ruins of the old. The Son of Man does not stay in the realm of the Utterly-other; even after the catastrophe of the Cross, and after the resurrection, he still comes down to earth; and not in any disinterested mood, but "with power and great glory" (Lk. 21. 27)—a true ascension to the new earth, just like the dawning of the heavenly Jerusalem, adorned as a bride, in all the might of the apocalyptic End. The old earth, too old now, has reached the *kairos* of this urgency; indeed it sometimes seems that the kingdom, which is anyway so near at hand, has *no need of power any more.* And that is where the Jesus of the Sermon on the Mount fits in—the Jesus who, after every benediction bestowed on powerlessness, immediately affirms the proximity of the Kingdom (Matt. 5. 3-10). And not, or not only, as a merely popular reward: the essential "for" which precedes "theirs is the kingdom of heaven" means rather that all use of force, all driving of the money-changers from a Temple that in any case is passing away, is herewith proclaimed superfluous, in a time whose time has come. The power-revolution that is to raise the lowly and humble the great is brought to its climax and conclusion by the *apocalyptic* Jesus in the realm of *nature* with all the mighty power of a cosmic catastrophe, and as a substitute, as it were, for a revolt among mankind. That certainly does not imply any ultimate love of one's enemies; it is, rather, a sort of automatic faith in the *Kairos* (the measure is full, the time complete), but not a peace-treaty with Belial and his realms. And the spirit of patient non-combatance which precedes the catastrophe relates always to the injustice inflicted on *one's own self,* and to that alone: it is not a toleration of the injustice done to *others*—to the *weak* and the lowly. The Kingdom of Heaven is the last thing that can be called on to sanction that widespread and comfortable attitude. The relevant words there are those about the lukewarm, whom Jesus will spew out of his mouth. The fact remains, however, that at the center of Jesus' preaching stands love, *Agapē*—and that is the hardest thing about it; that is its enduring moral paradox. An all-embracing human love, of course, implying the so far unheard-of reversal of all aggression, only has a place in Jesus' message (and in the social set-up still prevailing at his time) in the light of an imminent Exodus and Advent. For the contents of that Ad-

135

vent, its very *raison d'être*, must be *Agapē:* the love of God's children now that they have attained the Kingdom of Peace, where no other deeds exist but those of Christian discipleship. Where the background is not so much that of the realized Kingdom as that of the division and decisions of the last days of turmoil and crisis, Jesus' preaching is far tougher than that of all his prophetic predecessors, with their *Olam-ha-shalom.* There is not much talk then of loving one's enemies; the scene is rather one of unexpected spiritual warfare. Nor is this a later interpolation—"I have not come to bring peace, but a sword" (Matt. 10. 34); "He who rejects me and does not receive my sayings has a judge; the word that I have spoken will be his judge on the last day" (Jn. 12. 48). Over and over again, when he is not dealing with the time of Advent, Jesus, the arch-heretic and rebel, proclaims warfare between this present world and the one that is coming to take its place—the one whose first faint stirrings can already be detected, and which will bring with it a time of persecution and great endurance for the elect (Mk. 13. 8 f.). *This aeon and the coming aeon intersect upon earth in a sudden dawn of change.*

That is why the Romans convicted Jesus as a revolutionary; that is why the High Priests and the Pharisees quite justifiably feared the man upon whose words the people hung (Lk. 19. 48): the man who condemned to destruction the entire priestly theocracy and the religion of Law, which had reigned undisturbed from the days of Ezra and Nehemiah. This Jesus was dangerous; it was not entirely due to misunderstanding that a community of interests grew up between the Jewish upper class and the Roman oppressors against him and his eschatological radicalism. It was, in the eyes of this world, no harmless enthusiast whom they nailed to the Cross, but a man whose Advent was to turn their values upside down: the supreme model of another world in which there was no oppression and no lordly God. It was only as a facade that the priests appealed to the fact that Jesus had declared himself the Son of God (that is, the Messiah), and that he therefore had to die "according to the law" of blasphemy (Lev. 24. 16; Jn. 19. 7). For in the century before his birth, since the end of the Hasmonean dynasty, there had been other enthusiasts who announced themselves to be the Messiah, and, as enthusiasts, no harm had come to them. In the same way, too, Bar Kochbah (son of the stars), the hero of the uprising against Hadrian after Jesus' time, was declared Messiah by no less an authority than Rabbi Akibah himself. But Bar Kochbah fought for the Judea of the here-and-now, with rich and poor and priests together. He fought on the verge of despair in rebellion against Rome, but he upheld the values of the traditional Jewish world with its priestly theocracy. So he could be blessed by the priests and given the title Messiah: that mighty, once-for-all-time name was not deemed blasphemy here. It is not of course that Jesus was too peace-loving to be considered the Messiah, but rather that his Kingdom of the Son of Man was too remote from the *lordly* Yahweh, the Yahweh who had not led the people out of Egypt, the Yahweh who was now the normative figure. This Son-of-Man Messiah did not claim to be a fighting preservationist, or a romantic restorer of some Davidic kingdom with its lordly God. No; he proclaimed himself as the new eschatological Exodus, overthrowing all things from their beginning to their end: the *Exodus into God as man.*

MORAL AND ESCHATOLOGICAL LIGHT IN THE GOSPELS

Even the best things cannot be done at once. Especially when it seems that to do one thing is to detract from another. Or when, at the very least, the situation calls on all the forces of the will to achieve at one blow what, by slower methods, would take an age—if it ever got done at all.

This sort of antithesis reaches its peak in the contrast between the moral and the soteriological preaching of Jesus. Is there really time for moral change? Is there any breathing-space for it in the short period before the Kingdom comes? The Ten Commandments were designed for long life on earth—though not for a comfortable one: stealing, perjury and murder make things much easier. And even the commandment "Thou shalt love thy neighbor as thyself" has a long-term situation in view—it was promulgated in Leviticus 19. 18, and Jesus confirmed it, not as being his personal doctrine, but as the corner-stone of the Law and the Prophets (Matt. 22. 40). It establishes egotism as the norm, and then curtails it by including one's neighbor in one's own self-love. What time, however, what space, what social (or even non-social) dimension can exist for the commandments of the Sermon on the Mount? "Do good to those who hate you, and to him who strikes you on the cheek, offer the other also; from him who takes away your cloak do not withold your coat as well, and of him who takes away your goods do not ask them again." Is that meant to be advice for this present world? Anyone who follows it is *ipso facto* guilty, for he must tolerate not only the injustice done to himself, but also that done to his brethren: unless non-resistance to evil and rejection of the sword are meant to refer solely to the events which lead directly (and intentionally) to a sacrificial death—which is surely not the case.

Another factor that has often been remarked on is the economic naïveté of Jesus' preaching: he treats work and nourishment in terms of the lilies of the field and the birds of the air (Matt. 6. 25-28). Which resulted in the rapid impoverishment of the Jerusalem community and the consequent need for Paul to beg on its behalf in Corinth and Rome. The words of a rabbi of the early Christian period proved true: that man is easier to save than feed. How often, too, the parable of the unjust steward was told—a strange and, from the standpoint of business ethics, quite shocking one, with its counsel to resort to embezzlement and to make friends with the mammon of iniquity (Lk. 16. 1-9).

Both these strands in Jesus' preaching—the exhortation not to care, and the exclusion of all moral differences in the world of mammon—only make sense, in fact, if the world is, in its essence, soon to pass away. For then eschatology draws all

138

else to itself, in accordance with the words of Jesus' masterful début: "The time is fulfilled, and the kingdom of God is at hand; repent and believe in the gospel" (Mk. 1. 15)—the world has really become a matter for indifference. The unheard-of prescriptions of the Sermon on the Mount relate in this context not to any lengthy scheme of things, nor to one that is of great importance for this earth. And the same holds for the saying, "Render to Caesar the things that are Caesar's, and to God the things that are God's." Though pregnant with later consequences (through Paul and Luther), it has, on the lips of the Founder, not yet acquired a dualistic sense—not even that of keeping twin accounts. For all its outward pomp, the Roman Empire is as irrelevant and unessential as an overnight stay in an inn which one is going to leave at daybreak. Far more decisive in Jesus' mind is the truly chiliastic admonition to give all one has to the poor, and so to withdraw as subject (as well as object) from Caesar's sphere of interest—that petty circle with its already numbered days.

Seen from this angle the Gospel is *not a social thing,* not even *primarily a moral thing.* Its concern is eschatological redemption: "I must preach the good news of the kingdom of God; for I was sent for this purpose" (Lk. 4. 43). From the earliest days in Galilee, Jesus' preaching is founded on eschatological hope. This is no addition made by the evangelists (like the notions of sacrificial death and of resurrection); on the contrary, it is philologically one of the best attested strands in the whole New Testament. But it is, for all that, only one side (albeit the stronger one) of Christ's message. With it, within it, and at times even above it, there appears the doctrine of a love attainable on earth, a love for the sake of love, which is there already in the counsel to give all one's goods to the poor.

The complex relationship of these converging strands of thought gives rise to the problem of a twofold intention and light in Jesus' preaching—in the tension between the mutually illuminating aspects of Now and Hereafter, of Here and There. The Dutch Masters grappled with the problem of double lighting in their pictures inasmuch as they would paint an object illuminated by the light of the moon and by the light of a candle as well. And men have wanted to see a similar double lighting in the gospels: that of the social and that of the eschatological gospel—two sources, this time, which resist all harmony. Albert Schweitzer went into this question most thoroughly of all *(Das Messianitäts- und Leidengeheimnis*, 1901). For him, Jesus preached a constant "interim ethics," while the Kingdom itself lay in a "supramoral" realm beyond good and evil. The fact of the matter is that the eschatological light in all its force falls on the prescriptions of the Sermon on the Mount, which are incapable of fulfillment over any long period in this world; and it falls in particular on some of the counsels rooted in economic indifference, such as the parable of the lilies of the field. Contrary, however, to Schweitzer's total relativization of the moral source of light, it does not fall on Jesus' teaching about love, the ethics of which, in Schweitzer's theory, is seen as making man ready and worthy for the Kingdom and, at its deepest level, as already sharing in the Kingdom's eschatological content. From time to time Jesus even gives directives for this world that are stricter than any Mosaic or Talmudic ones—for example the prohibition of divorce (Mk. 10. 2-12); a strictness which stands out as all the more isolated and this-worldly in that he paid no attention to the family ties of his followers (Matt. 10. 35-37), and taught that in the Kingdom there is no distinction of sexes, and therefore no marriage (Mk. 12. 19-25).

The only *purely socio-moral* element in Jesus' preaching is that which is concerned with brotherliness for its own sake; and into this category falls the teaching about love. The teaching which culminates in the profoundly immanent, yet vivid and practical words "As you did it to one of the least of these my brethren, you did it to me" (Matt. 25. 40). Simple love of God is here converted into love for those who labor and are heavy-laden, and it is of the essence of this doctrine (as opposed to the Sermon on the Mount) that it is not entirely unfeasible, even over a long period. The dream of fraternal kindness could be fulfilled in the tiny infant community with its communism of love centered on the giving of gifts. And that key-point in Christ's morality, the warm breath of mercy, could find fulfillment there in a manly way, in and above the community. Detachment from creatures had not yet reduced them to short-lived, pathetic monstrosities, nor had detachment from the world uttered its smooth dismissal of economic discrepancies. Wealth was an enemy, the gospel was concerned only with the laborers and the heavy-laden, and the rich young man was told to sell his goods and share the proceeds among the community (Mk. 10. 21)—not as a purely formal directive either, a sort of *medicina mentis* to detach him from creatures, but as an instruction of clear and substantial moral content, rooted in the ethic of non-ownership. Again, there is the plain and factual statement of the Acts of the Apostles which has served for centuries to propagate the communism of love, despite the non-arrival of the Kingdom: "Now the company of those who believed were of one heart and soul, and no one said that any of the things which he possessed was his own, but they had everything in common" (Acts 4. 32). Ordinary poverty, too, was held in high esteem, and considered *in its own right to bear a special functional relationship* to the Kingdom. To be more precise, this communism of love, this city of Philadelphia, was the basic condition for the advent of the Kingdom: so it also became its *wordly norm*. That is the gist of many parables: that the giving away of one's goods is a treasure laid up for one in heaven, where no moth destroys (Lk. 12. 33); but also that brotherliness makes this treasure present here and now. The Kingdom is present in this world only as a tiny seed, but this seed is already a crystallization of the next world: an element of that final state of things has been set into the midst of our existence, without calling for any vast, unthinkable self-destruction in love (as does the Sermon on the Mount), or for social disinterestedness. However, precisely because Philadelphia was founded as the place of preparation for the Kingdom, the place of advent, it too only enjoyed in the end a short-term validity. Its community of brotherly love began to revolve around itself as though in an already abandoned realm. From the Utopian point of view, it certainly belonged to the Kingdom: it crystallized it. But its relationship

141

to the Kingdom was really that of the seed to the tree; and in this case the tree manifested not only greater love, but love of an entirely different sort. The same sort of thing can be seen from the passage: "Sell your possessions, and give alms; provide yourselves with purses that do not grow old, with a treasure in the heavens that does not fail, where no thief approaches and no moth destroys . . . Let your loins be girded and your lamps burning, and be like men who are waiting for their master to come home from the marriage feast, so that they may open to him at once when he comes and knocks" (Lk. 12. 33-36).

The constancy of these two elements, the moral and the eschatological, could not, in fact, be clearer. And, "taking this to its extreme, it is true of Jesus himself, inasmuch as he is himself the eschatological Event" (Käsemann, *Exegetische Versuche und Besinnungen* 1/2, Göttingen, 1964; English translation, London, 1967, pp. 199, 200). This does not mean simply abandoning life-orientated morality; but it does mean that even for the historian of Jesus' life it is quite essential to relate this morality to his life and preaching in an apocalyptic way; and this apocalyptic awareness is all the more essential when it comes to exegesis of the unwieldy relationship between morality and the Kingdom. As it is, too, for any *historically* accurate exegesis of Jesus' preaching in the context of the original community: "the apocalyptic world is the spiritual world in which the men of the New Testament were at home" (Stauffer, *Theologie des Neuen Testaments,* 1948, p. 6; English translation, London, 1963). And in which they continued to be at home even when the moral beatitudes of the Sermon on the Mount led not to the Kingdom of Heaven but to the disappointment of yet another dispensation of providence. For the former times, so long established, cast their pall right over and beyond even the last day.

The disciples hungered and thirsted for brotherliness, but things went on as before. Love did not come down on men, except within the confines of small groups, which was not new. Apart from the veil of the Temple, nothing split in two; the Kingdom was not close at hand. Its supposed imminence had made men indifferent to the things of the world, where it had not subjected them to unimaginable demands. And as the days went by, life became rather less well defined from the economic and social, but also from the moral point of view. The counsel to render to Caesar the things that were Caesar's, uttered in a mood of indifference verging on scorn, now began to jeopardize love for the laborers and heavy-laden. For indifference to the world leads to things being left as they are; and, where Paul is concerned, it leads to the old order being granted implicit recognition. What extraordinary equanimity he showed in the face of slavery (which had already roused the protests of the Stoics); he even tried to convince the slaves that they ought to obey their masters. Inward-looking spirituality and concentration on the other-world began to take the place of the Kingdom coming down from heaven. The rich were pardoned and almost assured of their place in heaven if they gave alms, "for God loves a cheerful giver" (2 Cor. 9. 7). What a difference from the words about the camel and the eye of a needle. There is no sign, either, of tension with the state, whether national-revolutionary or even purely moral: Paul was a *civis Romanus.* In his eyes, no Christian who does God's will can come into conflict with the state; and this is also a reflection of the fact that for him morality, too, is thrust into the background. Here in fact lie the roots of Luther's *sola fides,* the doctrine Thomas Münzer later called "Chalking up the bill to Christ." The world is looked on as perishable and yet at the same time unchangeable: perishable according to the promise of Christ, unchangeable (so long as it endures) as the realm of Satan. The persecutions still lay round the corner, so Paul could look calmly on the dualism between Caesar and God. Far more calmly than Augustine who, later on, could see nothing but enmity between the *civitas terrena* and the *civitas Dei.* Far more calmly, too, than those Fathers of the Church like Chrysostom who, after the time of Constantine, sang the

143

praises of love-centered communism—of communism already in a social form.

The converse of this is the eschatological slant of Paul's preaching, the stress laid on the Kingdom—now, of course, a Kingdom *after death*. And the dualism between the world and God penetrates even the person of Jesus, for as well as the Jesus who lived on earth and practiced love for men, there is the other, risen Jesus. That is the point of the strange antithesis which runs, "If for this life only we have hoped in Christ, we are of all men most to be pitied. But in fact Christ has been raised from the dead, the first fruits of those who have fallen asleep" (1 Cor. 15. 19 f.). The present Christian life is one led "in faith and not in vision"; or only in indirect vision "in a mirror, dimly" (1 Cor. 13. 12): its essence lies in waiting for the revelation of Christ, a waiting which eventually came to take the place of expectation, bringing with it the psychology of patience, and the justification of the Cross by the notion of sacrificial death. This sacrificial-death theology is not, of course, the only thing that came from Paul; he also developed to the full the idea of hope in the resurrection, and with it the idea of the destruction of those powers which hold sway over the present age, and the idea of the dawning of a new creation. This was a different eschatology from the one which Jesus preached. There was no imminent Kingdom here, but just hope, and the feeling that kept hope alive. Pauline eschatology did, however, preserve something of the social threat of Jesus' teaching in its stimulation of the will through hope: its strengthening of the desire for Exodus and for a break-through into the Kingdom—sentiments which have inspired men from the Montanists right through to the Anabaptists and even further, summoning up a faith that was by no means passive or ineffective in good works. Paul's conservatism, though, succeeded in strangling his own eschatology at birth, by making salvation already present and anticipated in the Christian community (later on Agustine, motivated by similar considerations, was to redirect the dream of Christ's thousand-year reign onto the Church on earth. The upshot of this was that not only the moral gospel, with its communism of love, took a step backwards; that very eschatological system centered on the resurrection of Christ, for which Paul had given the go-ahead, did so too. And this culminated in those supremely interpolated last words of Jesus on the Cross, "It is finished": words which barred the door once for all to any real eschatological future.

Crux locuta est, resurrectio finita est; history will from now on run its course in the vale of tears, which is all that is left for us. The world of apo-calypse has been cut off by being taken literally as the mere unveiling of what has already been achieved, and not as the revelation of what is, for all its radiant clarity, still quintessentially unachieved: still *per definitionem et per effectum* really lacking that presence which is thought of as its Messiah. Despite all this, however, the active fragment of the original gospel retains its openess and unity: morally it is full of love for the laborers and heavy-laden, eschatologically it is full of hope in the revelation of what is called our "unveiled countenance."

22. Christ's Secret Name Is Son of Man, Not Son of God; The "Mystery of the Kingdom"

It is easy enough to say that man has not got very far. It sounds like the voice of experience—even of deep thought. Especially when the voice speaks not so much in tones of self-hatred as in tones of self-righteous hatred of mankind, decked out in Christian garb. The will to work for the improvement of life seems an empty thing then, or an arrogant thing; useless in any case. When man is measured by so small a scale, the picture he makes can best be held in focus when there is nothing in it but evil: when he is incapable of anything else. Then he waits for help from on high, often as an excuse for leaving everything in a mess here below—a very comfortable mess for those who live from it. Adam fell, so the story goes, and, from then on, nothing more than patchwork has been possible.

But what, in fact, if man has got on? If in the Bible he has got further than ever before? For the Bible contains that strange expression "Son of Man"—that expression which, on Jesus' lips, is the most intimate title of the Messiah, and which shows that the Messiah is no mere ambassador from on high. "Son of Man" only appears modest or powerless when set alongside "Son of God." But in fact it is the highest title of all, and it means that man has got a very long way indeed: he has become a figure of final, all-conquering strength.

The words "Son of Man" have sometimes been taken as a literal (and meaningless) rendering of the Semitic expressions *bar enâsch* (in the Aramaic) and *ben adam* (in the Hebrew), which meant simply "someone," or "a man." Wellhausen, again with his anti-Semitic slant, subscribed to the opinion that υἱὸς ἀνθρώπου was a sort of Jewish Greek, and to translate it as "Son of Man" was just bombastic. Which is why Paul avoided the expression as a barbarism incomprehensible to the non-Semite. But in the New Testament these words are used almost exclusively by Jesus when he is describing himself as suffering and dying and, above all, as victoriously returning (Mk. 8. 38). The authenticity of these passages has indeed been doubted (without any unpleasant remarks) by Bultmann and, on other grounds, by Käsemann; they considered them to be additions made under the apocalyptic influence of the Post-resurrection community. But the expression "Son of Man" can be found as early as Daniel, although it does not have its full Messianic dimension there; and the peculiarly human quality of its apocalyptic tone would undoubtedly have appealed to the living, pre-resurrection Jesus. In truth, then, as it is used in the Bible from Daniel 7. 13 on, the title means, even in its Semitic form, something both unusual and very powerful. The Son of Man, *ben adam,* is in fact the son of the *Heavenly Man,* of the divine Adam. Not as being the offspring, but rather as being the form or configuration of the essence which appears within him. Paul could refrain from using the term "Son of Man" because the incarnation veiled the glory of the figure to whom it referred; but he by no means refrained from using the specific element involved: that of the Heavenly Man. Jesus did not, simply speaking, become man in the incarnation; he is Adam in his very essence, the second, spiritual Adam, who is in fact the first: ". . . the second man is from heaven" (1 Cor. 15. 47).

The idea of a pre-existing archetypal man was already present in the Old Testament: in the Book of Job, Eliphaz asks: "Are you the first man that was born? Or were you brought forth before the hills?" (Job 15. 7); he supposes, then, a figure created before the world, and mockingly infers that Job falls rather short of this. The same figure is hinted at as early as Ezekiel, where Yahweh, ostensibly referring to the king of Tyre but with the heavenly Adam unmistakeably in the background, cries out: "Son of man, you are a pure seal, full of wisdom and perfect in beauty. On the day that you were created your drums and pipes were prepared for you. You are like a cherub who spreads his wings wide to cover himself. I have placed you on the holy mountain of God, and you walk in the midst of the stones of fire" (Ezek. 28. 12-14; [translation taken from the German]). The cherub is one of the highest angels, possessed of perfect knowledge, radiant in gold and glory; so this Adam is very different from that other dour figure molded out of clay. As we have already remarked, the term first took on its eschatological connotation in the Book of Daniel: "And behold, with the clouds of heaven there came one like a son of man, and he came to the Ancient of Days and was presented before him. And to him was given dominion and glory and kingdom, that all peoples, nations and languages should serve him" (Dan. 7. 13 f.). This Man-figure, this Son of Man cannot be the people of Israel, as is the Suffering Servant of Isaiah 53, for he comes on the clouds of heaven. He is, rather, the eschatological expression of the Heavenly Man; he is a mystic Adam who has taken on, now, the form of a redeemer.

To this context belong those singular personifications of "wisdom" in which it comes forth from God *ab initio* as a being in its own right, without any dualism, and yet as autonomous and personal, dwelling not with God, but among men: "On the eights beside the way, in the paths she takes her stand" (Prov. 8. 2). And this "wisdom" goes on to say: "The Lord created me at the beginning of his work, the first of his acts of old. Ages ago I was set up, at the first, before the beginning of the earth. When there were no depths I was brought forth, when there were no springs abounding with water" (8. 22 f.). This personified "wisdom" is quite clearly related to the "heavenly man," and to the logos of Philo and the Gospel of John; but clearest of all is the fact that here, too, just as with the category of Son of Man, we have a *topos* that is both pre-existent and almost entirely emancipated from God.

It is of course true that while none of this evidence is post-resurrection, none of it is very old—none can claim to be unequivocally *pre-exilic*. Ezekiel, around 570 B.C. is exilic; Job and Proverbs, both about 400, are post-exilic; and Daniel, about 160, is from the very last period of Old Testament writing. It is possible, too. that Ezekiel 28. 12-14 is a later interpolation; that would perhaps account for the strangely composite picture formed from the king of Tyre and the cherub-Adam. This absence of the Heavenly Man and of the Son of Man from the ancient sources of Judaism has led some scholars to wonder whether his first God-man was perhaps of non-Jewish origin. According to Reitzenstein the Heavenly Man is a figure from ancient Iranian mythology: one that first became known among certain Jewish sects at the time of Christ. Judaism before the Exile, indeed before the time of Jesus, knew nothing of a pre-existent Adam; he was imported straight from Iran (*Das Iranische Erlösungsmysterium*, 1921, p. 117; and cf. Kraeling, *Anthropos and Son of Man*, New York, 1927).

None of this, however, can detract from the fact that just as the reception of Jesus as Davidic Messiah led the way to his reception as Son of Man, so the doctrine of the Messiah was, in the later books of the Bible, first widened and then surpassed by the doctrine of the Heavenly Man. Not that the Messiah was put harmlessly away into some spatially transcendent other-world; on the contrary, the expansion of Messianic doctrine was into a macrocosmic, metacosmic dimension. Apocalyptic literature changed the well-worn stage-set of Davidic glory into one of new heaven and new earth, where the ancient stock of David was no longer sufficient on its own, but had to widen itself into that pre-existent being in the form of a Man which corresponded geometrically, so to speak, with the new environment. Which corresponded with it above all from the point of view of *content,* for this Heavenly Man was a member of that ancient line which runs from the *serpent,* through Cain, to the Avenger of Job: a member of the *underground opposition movement* to Yahweh.

Once this new dimension had been reached, the two accounts of Adam's origin in the Book of Genesis suddenly took on fresh importance; they could not just be explained in terms of the late redaction of the book. The *priestly code* runs: "So God created man in his own image, in the image of God he created him; male and female he created them" (Gen. 1. 27); but the Adam of the *Jahvist* document (which begins at Gen. 2. 4) is by no means created in the image and likeness of God: "Then the Lord God formed man of dust from the ground, and breathed into his nostrils the breath of life; and man became a living being" (Gen. 2. 7). This Jahvist document is far older than the priestly code, but the sources of the priestly code are quite as old as those of the Jahvist—only the redaction is post-exilic, is the work of Ezekiel, Ezra and Nehemiah. It is admittedly impossible to say in detail how much new material was added to the ancient saga during its redaction; the picture of Adam as a figure of brilliance, made in the likeness of God could be a post-exilic interpolation from Iran. But that is highly improbable, for the priestly code would not have added anything that could detract from the unity and sublimity of Yahweh. The most probable solution, then, is that there is an ancient, subversive saga at work here; it may well be of Iranian origin, but even then it is by no means "a complete novelty, utterly foreign to the conceptual world of Israel" as Bousset liked to think (*Die Religion des Judentums im neutestament-*

lichen Zeitalter, 1903, p. 251). The question is not in fact whether the priestly code interpolated the "image and likeness of God," but why it did nothing to remove or nullify this image—like the *Eritis sicut Deus* of the serpent. In the final analysis, then, the doctrine of the Heavenly Adam as the prototype of man belongs in its turn to the biblical Azores: to the remaining mountain-peak of a submerged, subversive, anti-theocratic tradition.

The twofold story of the creation of Adam was given considerable attention in the late Judaic period, sometimes even being related to current ideas about the Messianic Son of Man; and, after the *breakthrough made by Jesus,* these ideas now took the form of the equation *Messiah-Son of Man.* Philo, in his *magnum opus (Legum allegoriae,* I, 12), tackles the question speculatively, for the tools of Bible-criticism had not yet been developed. He saw in the contradictory texts of Genesis a profound, almost Christological mystery, concerning Adam. The first-born of creation, formed in the image of God, contained within himself the mystery of the Heavenly Adam, of the archetypal Man himself. He did not go so far as to identify this Heavenly Man with the Messiah, but the decisive Messianic attributes of heavenly birth and likeness to God were certainly there. And Philo's Logos-Messiah, without which the Logos-Christ of John and Paul would be unthinkable, was the "image of the divine essence," the "first-born son," the "high priest uniting man with God," the "visible God in whom the invisible dwells."

All this helped prepare for the *specifically Christian* attributes of the Son of Man, and formed a link between them and the heavenly Adam; a link that was sealed by the decisive text of John 3. 13: "No one has ascended into heaven but he who descended from heaven, the Son of Man who is in heaven"; and, above all by the text of John 17. 5: "And now, Father, glorify thou me in thy own presence with the glory which I had with thee before the world was made." As has been remarked, Paul did not himself use the expression "Son of Man," but he was certainly well aware of what it meant and what lay behind it. In Colossians 1. 15 he speaks of the Jesus-Adam figure: "He is the image of the invisible God, the first-born of all creatures"; and in 1 Corinthians 15. 47, 49, he says: "The first man was from the earth, a man of dust; the second man is from heaven. Just as we have born the image of the man of dust, we shall also bear the image of the man of heaven." This "first man" is not the same as Philo's: he is the old, weak Adam, the Adam who "became a living being"—as opposed to Christ, who is the "last Adam," who "became a life-giving spirit" (1 Cor. 15. 45). Christ, then, is not the *Protos* here, but the *Eschatos;* except that that this *Eschatos* is in fact the *Protos* of Philo, the "image of the heavenly man," for he repairs the sins of Adam and restores his weakness to its primal glory. He restores the image and likeness of God, liberating Adam from the clay: "For as in Adam all die, so also in Christ shall all be made alive" (1 Cor. 15. 22). The same parallelism with the work of creation appears in Romans 5. 11-21, where Christ stands for righteousness as against sin, for life as against death, and for grace as against law: the orders of the earthly and the heavenly Adam are opposed. The corner-stone of apocalyptic thought is presupposed here: that the last days are a repetition of the first days in reverse. They are *apokatastasis,* restitution. But (and this is, for Messianism, decisive), they are imbued with the pathos of the new and the unknown. They are a restitution of something quite novel: the forest has at last been cleared, and the image of God has come. Similarly, in 1 Peter 1. 20, Jesus takes on the form of the returning archetypal Man who "was destined before the foundation of the world, but was made manifest at the end of times for your sake." And, as this Man-made-flesh, co-ordinating God, Jesus is the pretender to the Kingdom of God. Just as in his human substance he precedes the world, so in this same substance he outlives it, and with his disciples inherits the Kingdom, and makes it one for men. So it is that the *macrocosmos-metacosmos,* the apocalyptic setting for the Son of David, becomes in the end the *makanthropos,* the Great Man: "Until we all attain to the unity of the faith and of the knowledge of the Son of God and become the perfect man, in the measure of the stature of the fullness of Christ" (Eph. 4. 13). But that measure is one for a new world, not for the old—not for a Yahweh set apart from man and incomprehensible to him, a God of whom one of Job's friends could say: "He is higher than heaven—what can you do? Deeper than Sheol—what can you know?" (Job 11. 8). The answer to this supercilious agnostic lies in the Letter to the Ephesians, and it is based on the *makanthropos*—the new, adequate measure of man in and through Christ: "that you may have power to comprehend with all saints what is the breadth and length and height and depth" (Eph. 3. 18). So highly does the writer of this letter think of man—or rather of his mystery. *Looking backwards as well as forwards, man had come a very long way indeed.*

It was not easy to swallow the idea that man was made from clay. The solution was to see Jesus as the returning Adam: then the first Adam, too, was the image of God. There is in fact a *second strand* to the archetypal notion *Son of Man,* a second lineage which by-passes Jesus and comes to rest in another *Christos-figure:* that of Moses.

It is a strange, instructive, Utopian doctrine. In the Haggadah, the Great Prophet was, simply speaking, pre-existent: the angels in Jacob's vision of the ladder (Gen. 28. 12) were Moses and Aaron. The climax is reached in the *Ascension of Moses,* an apocryphal text of the first century A.D. (*Die Apokryphen und Pseudoepigraphen des A.T.,* ed. von Kautzsch, 1900, II, pp. 311 ff.), in which Moses is placed on a footing of complete equality with the Heavenly Adam. Moses here speaks to Joshua: "God did indeed make the world for the sake of his law [var.: people], but he did not reveal this first-born of his creatures from the very beginning of the world. . . . That is why he chose me out and found me, for I was ready from the beginning of the world to mediate this covenant" (1. 12). The same majestic tone appeared in Joshua's last words to him: "All who die receive on earth a grave which accords with their greatness, but your grave reaches from sunrise to sunset and from the south to the outposts of the north: the whole world is your grave" (11. 8). Moses is now one and the same person as the archetypal Man, enshrined and immanent in the world. But in another, earlier document he is even more: in the *Book of Enoch,* preserved in Ethiopian from the second century B.C., this figure of Man pre-exists with the Ancient of Days in heaven, as an essence without any *physis* or any form of incarnation at all. A hundred years later, in the "Images" of the Ethiopian Enoch, he has taken over the role of Messiah: the Heavenly Adam has become the bearer, and indeed the content, of the new age—an age in harmony with the aims and objectives of man, which the first era had left undone.

The expression "Son of Man" is also now a constant feature of Jewish apocalyptic writing; it can be found in the Book of Enoch, the Fourth Book of Ezra and the apocalypse of Baruch. In Rabbinical circles, too, and all the more so in the occult literature of later Judaism, the Heavenly Man is given great importance. Man is a figure of radiant glory, at the end of time as at the beginning; and mankind's self-worship in the form of the Adam-Messiah becomes an almost independent factor alongside or within his absolute worship of Yahweh. This is a totemism of man greater, almost, than the Christian one. In the Talmud the first Adam is a giant, filling heaven and earth with his great stature. And in the Cabbala "Adam Kadmon" is the mystery of the world itself, and at the same time the key to this mystery: "Man's form," says the Sohar, "is the primordial image of all things in heaven above and earth beneath; for that reason the holy Ancient One [God] chose it to be his own form." Adam Kadmon is, then, at the same time macrocosm and model of God. The ten *sephirot* (the attributes emanating from God) are applied in a thoroughly anatomical fashion to his figure, making the macrocosm a *makanthropos:* the sephirot "crown" and "understanding" are applied to his head and neck, "beauty" lies in his breast, "love" in his right arm and "righteousness" in his left; in his genitals lies the

153

"work of creation," in his left thigh is "strength" and in his right thigh "glory"; the "kingdom" resides in his feet. The Cabbala also indulges in some adventurous philology in order to have its Adam Kadmon at the very beginning of biblical creation instead of, as in Genesis 1. 27, at the end of the sixth day. The Bible begins with the words *"bereschith bara elohim"*: "in the beginning God created." But a different, "esoteric" word-division with correspondingly different vowels, gives the reading *"bara schith bara elohim"*: "he created the ram, he created elohim (divine powers)" The "he" is then the *"Ainsoph,"* the primordial Nothing which emanates creatively into Something; and *"schith,"* the *ram,* is *Adam Kadmon.* The *"elohim"* are the categories on Adam Kadmon's body, which is the world. All of this is, of course, pure fantasy; but it is a kick against the Adam of clay and of nullity—against the orthodox view of Yahweh with his worm-man far below. Only the *Ainsoph* remains on the non-human plane—an unfathomable figure in the background, the sacred and primordial Nothingness, into whose lonely darkness the head of Adam Kadmon fades away.

There is much here that is borrowed, and much that derives from contact with Neo-Platonic emanation-systems and from Genesis (which is at the root of the Cabbala). But, more importantly, there is close affinity with the anthropos-logos doctrine of the radical Ophites, those fellow-travellers of the serpent, of Adam's enlightener, who now reappear on the scene. Even they had got as far as portraying their Serpent-spirit as the great World-man—or rather as the Great Man of the frustrated, hidden Paradise that is the world. He was for them the *Okeanos* of Paradise, the river Jordan, of which it is written: "A river flowed out of Eden to water the garden, and there it divided and became four rivers" (Gen. 2. 10). Or, in another place, Eden, which is the source of this river, is the brain of the Great Man, and is enclosed in the heavenly spheres as in a garment or a skin. Here too high fantasy is at work, but it is a very human fantasy. It takes the land of heavenly Paradise and bliss away from the paternal throne of

God, and makes it the realm of the archetypal Man. Adam Kadmon is, it is true, the cosmos reposing in God; but in the final analysis he is first and foremost *all that remains of this cosmos after the consummation of the present age.* This present world fills a space in which it does not really belong: its form is that of the *makanthropos.* This massive yet thoroughly man-centered hope runs through the Cabbala with a new tone of triumph, which though not post-vital, is post-mundane. It can be linked through the apocalypses with the Gnostic idea of resurrection—this is evident in the teaching of Valentine, the most important of the Gnostics, who, according to Clement of Alexandria (*Stromata,* IV, 13. 89), said: "From the very beginning you are immortal; you are the children of everlasting life. You share out death among yourselves in order to exhaust it and abolish it—in order that through you and in you death may die. *You do away with the cosmos, but you yourselves remain* to rule over the whole of perishable creation." And not only the present world, but also the very principle of creation and conservation that was substituted for it is finally dissolved in the new heaven and new earth proper to the Man-hypostasis. The old father-image is, in the light of this man-centered mysticism, one of long-forgotten aloofness.

To this mysticism belongs the most beautiful and most permanently valid of all forms of prayer, a godless prayer which stands above all simple a-theism and sees the *unio mystica* in its most human form as *unio* with the Son of Man. It is found in an apocryphal Gospel of Eve: "I am you, and you are me; and wherever you are, there am I. My seed is sown in all that lives; you may gather me wherever you will, but when you gather me you gather yourself" (cf. Wendland, *Die hellenistisch-römische Kultur,* 1912, II, p. 298). These supreme words of confidence need no Our Father to give them life. They are in complete harmony with the *Anthropos agnostos:* the one being that will be left when all has been gathered in from the diaspora. The yearning for identity that appears in this religious movement works to make the *makanthropos*

155

present, but as a figure of the Kingdom now, rather than of the world.

23. The Diminishing Greatness of the Son of Man— The "Smallness" of the Kingdom

The question now was whether so colossal a being could be related to actual present life. In reality the *makanthropos* began to turn into its opposite extreme, taking on the aspect of a new sort of astral myth. Nor was the process confined to superstitious circles. It underlies the well-known macrocosm-microcosm equation proposed by the Stoics—an idea rooted ultimately in that of the Great Man. Man is a miniature of the world, and the world is man writ large. In this analogy, however, man is foreshortened and the cosmos magnified. For Paracelsus, man is the "quintessence" of cosmic power, containing a supreme concentration of the essence of all things. He is the homogeneous Lord of the World—but by that very fact he is also little more than its mirror. Significantly, this microcosm idea (the secularization of the makanthropos idea) came to the fore in cosmocentric rather than man-centered periods: in the Stoa and the Renaissance—both very world-conscious times—in the writings of Paracelsus and Leonardo. Under the influence of this equation the microcosm once again took on gigantic proportions and macrocosmic range; it too became a colossus and a monster.

In the context of systematic superstition—especially in the work of Swedenborg—the *makanthropos* idea also fell into a strange sort of decadence, without reaching quite the same depths of cosmomorphism. Kant, in his *Dreams of a Ghost-seer*, poured biting scorn on the views and visions of this magus. It is interesting to see how, in him, the human, and indeed mystical, instinct for moderation (as well as sheer cool-headedness) reacted in satirical protest against the Swe-denborgian *makanthropos*-in-space as against a *World-colossus* of interiority. He mocks at the monstrous notion of a cosmic *makanthropos* as at a mere childish fancy. But, as well as being childish, it was also astromythological; it turned the dream of "Man and nought but man in all the world" back into a cosmic Leviathan again, and delivered the *Humanum* up into the hands of the universal giant. In the end, of course, Swedenborg did not say that his Great Man was a figure in space, or that it filled the universe. It was composed, rather, of the relationship between souls or spirits; and in this respect Swedenborg himself left the scene of cosmically extended Man behind and, with the idea of a *purely social Adam Kadmon,* entered upon a trail that was reminiscent of the *other, post-mundane makanthropos idea: that of the Mystical Body and the Kingdom.* Kant's mockery was not aimed at this; indeed the concept of society in the form of a Great Man—of the greatest of men in the final analysis—is the mystical background to his own ethics. Society is, for Kant, a community of intelligible worlds, of which man, because of his moral character, is a fellow citizen. And, being the ethico-religious ambience of the human race, society possesses man's intelligible form.

This latter-day, Utopian context is, in fact, the only one in which the *makanthropos* can be taken seriously again, after the flood of idle, vulgar enthusiasm and empty analogy. For now the *makanthropos* is a goal: Adam Kadmon was the Alpha and Omega, and that alone—and only the Alpha so that the Omega should be the goal of the *whole* creative work. *Makanthropos* is the Great Man at the world's end, the form and figure of the future Kingdom: a profoundly humanistic vision, carried over with justification into the tradition of Christian speculation, where it continued to live in what was now no longer a cosmocentric system, but one which believed in man. It is not, then, that the Son of Man grew to be as great as the world: he grew to be as great as the "quintessence" of the world—as great as the one thing necessary.

So a new, more silent grandeur dawned. Jesus did not take up much room as a child, though he surpassed his believers in everything. Despite the closeness of the Son of Man there is no thunder, no alienation in the experience. The unfathomed depths of space are not unfathomable; the Kingdom houses neither Behemoth nor Leviathan. The rule of the Son of Man, the realm of the *makanthropos* at the end of time, did nothing in men's minds to diminish the importance of the present world and its expansion. However totally he was conceived, he did not recede into the immeasurable background—though of course for this very reason he did not fit entirely into the measure of man given in and by this present world either.

That is where the New Testament God-man leaves the apparent anthropomorphism of the Greeks behind, for all they did was take the naturalistic figure of man-as-given and make this the framework for the incarnate *numen*. They even ignored the drive to transcend, present in man-as-given: what they took to be God was a sort of resplendent animal-man, beautiful, ultimate, and crystal-clear. Their "naturalism" destroyed even the element of mystery preserved by the animal image in religion. (The only Greek God with any *numen* is Medusa.)

Those early images of Jesus—the Orphean Good Shepherd, and the bearded Christ based probably on a youthful version of the Zeus of Phidias—are also naturalistic rather than humanistic in the sense in which the idea of the Mystical Body is humanistic. The mystical archetypal Man was not thought of as human in this way, any more (and even, perhaps, less) than he was thought of as the macrocosmic colossus. What all classic and classicistic religious anthropomorphism lacks is the element of the unknown, the feeling of being at the brink of the unknown, it lacks the *openness* of the *Anthropos agnostos*.

And, for the same reason, every attempt to take the precise measurements of the Son of Man and his earthly realm must in the end fall outside that realm. An example is Hegel's concept of the Son of Man; or, above all, of the human order he sees as Christianity, the product of the long divinizing process. "In the course of this history, consciousness came to men; and the truth they lit upon was this: that, for them, the idea of God had certainty, that man is himself God as immediate and present"

158

(Hegel, *Werke, XII,* 1832, p. 253). But the subject who takes the idea of God into his self-consciousness like this is a different figure from the Son of Man. For Hegel's religious man does not touch the brink of the human mystery at all; he remains complacently within the limits of man, the community and the world, as present and given: the limits of a pre-ordained, paternalistic faith. The ego, existing for its own sake, which Hegel retrieved from alienation, was itself something fixed and objectified, with its own history and its own remoteness. And his *Humanum* ("the kingdom of the substantial will") was lost in the state, unredeemed and indeed un-recognized by religion.

It is, then, to be expected, that even in the religious sphere, classicistic humanism should fall back behind Job, behind the idea of the Son of Man, behind the realization that a man can be better, and more important, than his God. In fact a religion of pure beauty and clarity *vis-à-vis* the Son of Man reduces, as in Hegel, to "an awareness of the reconciliation of man with God." As opposed to the religion of the coming Kingdom, which does not shackle the godly within the well-known dimensions of man, in order to achieve the equilibrium of atonement, but preaches a Son of Man whose dimension is human in a *non-given* way. This figure and this dimension bear about as much resemblance to the available subject as they do to the gigantic proportions of the available cosmos; and to the crude unfathomability of the Yahweh-idea the *Anthropos agnostos* bears no resemblance at all.

No, a more silent, more secret grandeur is dawning; for the *makanthropos* of mysticism is small—such is the paradox—and his very smallness makes him the *makanthropos*. It is a smallness unopposed to greatness, a smallness of proximity and compenetration, the quintessence of the one thing necessary. It is the smallness of the *Moment of Fulfillment,* fore-shadowed in the religious sphere by the moment of *unio mystica.* This Moment is in fact an Always and Everywhere, containing all that is human; it is reality uncovered in the here and now; and in Christian terms its religious dimension is the

159

Kingdom and that alone. This is the land that lies behind the Avenger of Job, the wondrous land of Deutero-Isaiah: "And the ransomed of the Lord shall return, and come to Sion with singing; everlasting joy shall be upon their heads" (Is. 51. 11). Everlasting joy, just that. That is the point where all Christian ideals and mysteries meet; they are not concerned any longer with external, unthinkable objectivity, treating it as alien to man. Yahweh's despotic grandeur is eradicated, and that being who was the God of the Exodus is now made godless, and put forward as the Son of Man. This, however, is by no means the final solution.

24. The Title "Son of Man" Is Eschatological, The Later Title "Kyrios-Christos" Wholly Cultic

According to Wellhausen, the expression "Son of Man" meant in Aramaic usage simply man as an individual, as opposed to the genus "man." It was far too ordinary an expression to be taken as a title. The trouble arose from the false Greek translation νἱὸς τοῦ ἀνθρώπου, which made the Son of Man uncomfortably independent, removing him from the sphere where the titles "Son of God" and "Lord" would be competitive; and these titles were so much easier to manage and manipulate—down from on high.

But it has been shown that the term "Son of Man" was by no means common in Aramaic; it is, in fact, an ancient poetic expression which could, for that very reason, bear a quite unaccustomed meaning. It could bear the meaning of Daniel 7. 13 with its speculative, and by no means purely grammatical, problems about who this figure was. So important and so mysterious a being connected with the very deepest layers of the problem of Jesus, and expressing the depths of his pride, cannot possibly be dealt with in terms of a sort of scribal error. Son of Man is not a title given by the disciples, it is Jesus' name for himself: none is more frequent on his lips. And the decisive point is this: the key-word *Man* in Son of Man, along with the intentional element of *novelty* and *mystery,* defines the expression as belonging to a line of tradition, to a Christ-*topos* that is different from the so to speak legitimate, dynastic title, *Son of God,* which has been far more common. This latter title has a history stretching from the countless morganatic offspring of Zeus to the neo-Egyptian Son of God, Alexander, and even further. *Son of Man,* on the other hand, belongs exclusively to the infant community in Palestine. He belongs there, and there alone, despite the foreign, and again genealogical tradition flowing in from Philo, with his concept of the Logos-mediator, and above all of the "first Adam," the "heavenly man," first-born of Yahweh's creatures—a tradition which influenced Paul in 1 Corinthians 15. 47, and, in a very different way, left its mark on apocalyptic thought.

Even here, however, the accent is far more on the "pre-existence" of the Proto-man than on his having been created, like the second Adam, by God. Indeed Philo even adds the legend of Melchizedek, the "first high priest" (cf. Gen. 14. 18 f.), to his picture of Adam—all for the sake of that other line of tradition; for this legend is singularly lacking in references to Yahweh. It appears again in the letter to the Hebrews, where Melchizedek is made the predecessor, if not the double, of Jesus, precisely on the basis of his being his own forefather—which is going one better than the first Adam, or even the autochthony of Jesus. The passage runs: "He is without father or mother or genealogy, and has neither beginning of days nor end of life, but resembling the Son of God he continues a priest for ever" (Heb. 7. 3)—though the resemblance to the Son of God is such that this Son of Man has, and needs, no created sonship, no origin that is unoriginal or dependent. But to get back to Philo: he is not concerned with any difference, any otherness in relation to the Father-God which might bring the figure of Melchizedek or, later, that of Jesus to mind. But he is concerned to divide up the creative, "speaking," logos-element in Yahweh, which is akin to this—and that all goes to help the birth of the later Pauline concept of the Heavenly Man, existing before the creation of the world.

According to this division, the creative Logos is indeed on the one hand the divine Wisdom, which remains strictly within itself; but at the same time this Logos is the independent image of the godhead, the first-born, and yet unborn, Son—the "Logos which steps outside the godhead" (λόγος προφορικός). He is a "mediator" of a sort that belongs not less but all the more (that is, without transcendence) to the category of Proto-man, to that which is really human in the world. He belongs to it and cares for it, and does so notwithstanding the fact that Philo himself does not call him Son of Man, any more than Jesus' disciples use this, his *own most personal title,* of their master—that only happened later, under the influence of apocalyptic thought. Which leads us to the conclusion that this forward-stepping Son of Man can—on the model of the not so much pre-cosmic as out-and-out eschatological prophecy of Daniel—become completely active and visible only in the apocalyptic context of the returning Christ. Outside this context it cannot involve more than a description used by Jesus of himself in his effort to get to know himself. It is, admittedly, so strong a description, and it recurs so frequently, that all others pale into insignificance beside it; but this is precisely because it is the most eschatological description of all. This is so much the case that in apocalyptic literature (for instance, the Ethiopian Book of Enoch) the Son of Man, for all his pre-existence, and as opposed to the teaching of Philo, does not play any part in the creation of the world, precisely because he is to be the active principle at the end of time—active in the creation of a new heaven and a new earth—and not before. The *lordly, majestic* element of apocalyptic thought does, as we shall see, lead away from the innate humanness of the archetypal Son of Man; but there is still a long way to go to the later Hellenistic picture of the Kyrios-Christos who does not dwell among us, but descends upon us from on high.

The category Son of Man resonates, in fact, on two planes: that of present-day life between man and man, and the total plane of future life. For the coming Son of Man must first of all pour himself out in the life of the gospel, but the equation Jesus = Son of Man only reaches its climax within the framework of eschatology. That, finally, is where the mystery lies—the perpetual mystery no philology will solve, for it is in the end nothing less than the secret of *homo absconditus* himself.

We are its starting point, yet it remained among us as if in darkness. The title Lord *Jesus* did not yet exist: Jesus was not yet elevated and publicly proclaimed, like other princes. At the summit of the primitive community there stood the Son of Man and him alone—not the Kyrios-Christos with his utter otherness and opposition to men. Bousset, in his great work *Kyrios Christos* (5th. ed., 1965), opens up new ground in distinguishing the primitive Palestinian picture of Jesus from the cultic image of Hellenistic Christianity, and doing so on these very grounds of the difference between the titles *Lord* and *Son of Man.* Even in the relatively late Johannine writings (the Fourth Gospel and the Letters) the title *Kyrios* is lacking—perhaps it is intentionally avoided. Instead the Son of Man speaks always in the Philadelphic terms commensurate with his *topos*—even when he is already touched by the halo of future glory; and his *topos* is not theodynastic, and therefore not theocratic either. He speaks to men as the vine speaks to its branches: "You are my friends . . . No longer do I call you servants, for the servant does not know what his master is doing" (Jn. 15. 14). These writings, in fact, place the disciples, with all their piety, so close to Jesus "that they solemnly reject the expression Servants of Christ, and, obviously for the same reason—perhaps concealed opposition to Paul—avoid the title *Kyrios"* (Bousset, *loc. cit.,* p. 155).

It cannot, of course, be denied that the Son of Man, raised upon high, and unveiled apocalyptically, is thought of in the gospels as a judge, coming in the glory of the Father, surrounded by angelic hosts (Matt. 16. 27; 25. 31 f.): an awesome vision, not of the Hellenic or Byzantine Church, but of the primitive community. But the important thing to remember in the face of this already enthroned majesty is that the real Son

163

of Man is not lost here, even in his elevation; he is not subsumed into some *Dominus maximus triumphans,* but thought of still in the image of the shepherd, separating the sheep from the goats (Matt. 25. 31), or, above all, in the image of the lamb—the lamb which, in the full blossoming of apocalyptic thought, is the lamp which alone illuminates a heavenly Jerusalem (Rev. 21. 23). So, even in the incipient Church of a cultic God, of an hypostasized Kyrios, where the figure of the Lord Jesus is unmistakable, his *a priori* antecedent, the Son of Man, is still retained, and retained recognizably as the *a priori* of what alone can call itself the *mystical Humanum.* For those were the terms of his début, the terms by which he said not only "I and the Father are one," but also "If you did it to the least of my brethren, you did it to me."

Only in later Hellenistic Christianity was divine cultic status granted to the imperial figure of Kyrio-Christos, which appeared alongside the apocalyptic Son of Man, and then began to take its place. When that happened, the Son of Man passed over to the poor: to those who inwardly, and above all outwardly, kicked against the realm of the On-high, where there was no room for man. It passed to the heretical Brethren—of the Common Life, of Good Will, of the Freedom and the Fullness of the Spirit. And it passed to Thomas Münzer with his Allstedt sermon on the vision of the Son of Man in Daniel, and on Jesus the true corner-stone, whom the builders rejected. Meanwhile the Kyrios-Christos God admirably suited the purposes of those who would reduce the Christian community to a sort of military service of their cultic hero, with the inevitable consequences in terms of allegiance to worldly rulers whose authority, according to Paul and others, is likewise "from God."

It may have seemed that the future belonged entirely to this Kyrios; but the only future to do so was that which lay under the hand of Church and state authorities. The other future, the dawning of the "better age," belonged to the early community and to its Son of Man. This future has, to put it mildly, been a constant stone of contradiction to Christianity with its Lord

Jesus—a stone which Christian hypocrisy has always tried to hide. For even if the Lord-Jesus figure did set himself up as the official Son of God in the place left by the Son of Man, he did so, despite everything, despite the official myth of sonship, not as Kyrios, but once again as Son of Man. *Deus homo factus est*—this final twist to the biblical Exodus, making it an exodus from Yahweh, too, transformed his triumphant Day at the end of days into the unveiling of quite a different face: the face of man, and of the Son of Man. And this was true even for Paul (2 Cor. 3. 18).

Or again, if earlier eschatology had foretold the coming of God, Christian eschatology foretold the Parousia of Christ. That is the Bible's last and greatest word on the *topos* Son of Man—a *topos* which is not even anti-theocratic any more, but just untheocratic. And one whose inner depths remain in profound disharmony with the haze of titles cast over Jesus by the court theologians—notably the pagan, cultic title *Kyrios,* and its ultimate development, the Byzantine Pantocrator.

25. The Total Christocentricity of John 17, the "Key to the Gospel"

The poor were not put out when they were spoken to by one as poor as themselves. Poverty made him one of them—not a lord for them to mistrust. On the other hand, however, they could never expect much from a Son of Man who had nowhere even to lay his head. And that is another reason why Jesus was constantly elevated in the popular mind to the rank and cult of Lord, and surrounded with an aura of glory in whose reflected lordliness we men can share.

This happened above all in the fourth and most recent of the gospels, the one farthest removed form the primitive community—a gospel that was certainly not the work of the apostle John, but rather of a group of writers dependent on a Pauline tradition about Jesus. The chief characteristic of this already speculative work is the frequent occurrence in it of the

165

pre-Gnostic *excursus*—for instance the almost naïve miracle-stories of chapter two onward. These additions, however, do not (yet) constitute a second conformist "priestly code": that is the difference here between Old Testament criticism and gospel criticism. The priestly Church had not yet been established in the milieu from which this gospel came, although the transition to a cultic community had begun, and the radical idea of Christian break-through had been tempered by Paul to a state of relative peace with the world. Another, surprising characteristic of the Fourth Gospel is, as we have already remarked, the absence of the Kyrios-title of Hellenistic Christianity, and what is tied up with this, the solemn rejection of the description "servants of Christ" (cf. Jn. 15. 14). Even the "Lordship" of Christ, which is essentially the theme of John 17, does not thrust on men the indigestible deoctrine of the Kyrios-on-high as the dynastic Son of God. Indeed this gospel, for all its lateness, has not only preserved the expression "Son of Man," but has made it an integral link with the Christ of sacramental life: it is no cult-God, but the Son of Man, who *expressis verbis* gives himself as food and drink to his disciples (6. 53). And even the title "Son of God," with its mild pathos of Yahweh as father-figure, and its possible undertones of Kyrios and of paradoxical conformism in the absence of the Son of Man—even this title does not touch the peculiarly Christocentric, non-theocratic kernel of this gospel. Least of all in John 17, that late blossoming of the Founder's farewell speech—a chapter that has justifiably been called the "key to the gospel." And one whose Hermetic doctrine has been handed down powerfully by the founder of the Christian idea.

It is no death-bed speech, but a farewell discourse, and one without much mention of the Cross. The legacy Jesus leaves is not, as such "incomprehensible," despite the fact that it is given as a "secret instruction to the disciples" (Käsemann, *Jesu letzter Wille,* 1966, p. 17; English translation, London, 1968). Jesus speaks once more as the uncreated proto-Man.

When he speaks of the Father, therefore, it is not as of one who had begotten him: "And now, Father, glorify thou me in thy own presence with the glory which I had with thee before the world was made" (Jn. 17. 5). He has *ipso facto* placed himself, as uncreated, within the ambit of the Lord of Creation; the passive formula of "being sent" does not detract from this, for it is not specific to Jesus.

There is, too, the straightforward Christocentric statement, "I and the Father are one": a statement which goes to the heart of this most esoteric of the gospels, and has its counterpart in the words "All that the Father has is mine" (16. 15). These words are homoousian to the utmost degree; their message is one of *equality*, and if it is not equality with the Father, the World-creator, to whom does it refer? *What is the Johannine idea of God?* Jesus undoubtedly means by *Father* the traditional Creator of the world. Indeed in the course of this gospel the Father is made the dispenser of all the gifts which the Christ had claimed as his own: light, truth, life, and the bread and water which come down from heaven; the only thing Yahweh does not do is rise again—but then he is eternal anyway. And yet all this is really no more than window-dressing, for Jesus, from the very word go, says that he is himself the light and life of the world. When the eschatological light of this gospel seems to give way to the protological (the light that was "in the beginning": cf. the prologue), this is only in order that the Logos of the prologue ("In the beginning was the Word, and the Word was with God, and the Word was God") should appear unmistakably as the Alpha of another world—one to which, at the end of time, he and the Christ will accede. The reference to the proto-Logos of the first Genesis is merely polemical; it in no way relaxes the eschatological tension or allows it to revert towards some primordial Creator-figure (or some Gnostic principle of emanation) of the present world. On the contrary, the true Proton of primeval light, which "the darkness has not overcome," is precisely the Eschaton, of a *second* Genesis: a Genesis through the Logos who is Christ. He will be the true Creator of a new creature; he

167

will form men in his own image, and they will be hated by the
"ruler of this world" (16. 11) because "they are not of the
world, even as I am not of the world" (17. 14). The Logos/Son
of Man is, with his *Veni creator spiritus*, set clearly apart from
the *Deus creator*, and the dualism of the two of them begins. It
only just begins, for in this farewell speech the purely transcendent, acosmic, nirvana-like motif of eremitical flight does
not as yet appear, despite, or rather because of the "departure" of the disciples from their allegiance to the so-called
"ruler of this world." Not that the world is in itself finished and
done with, for the disciples are sent into it as into the arena of
history; and the paraclete, too, will eventually appear in this
arena—though not in the aeon of this world.

For all this, however, there is still a peculiar dualism in
Christ's farewell discourse: a dualism in the *idea of God*—in
that very figure of the "Father" through which the *homoousios*
is so strongly asserted. This, at last, is the decisive point which
makes the Fourth Gospel a key to the gospels; this is the
focal-point of *opposition to the idea of God as Lord*. The
following passages speak for themselves. They refer in the end
to that other theophany, in the person of the Son of Man, and
to a God who is by no means unknown to the heathens alone:
"They do not know him who sent me" (15. 21); "And they will
do this because they have not known the Father, nor me" (16.
3); "Father . . . thou hast given me thy love . . . before the
foundation of the world. O righteous Father, the world has not
known thee, but I have known thee; and these know that thou
hast sent me. I made known to them thy name, and I will make
it known, that the love with which thou hast loved me may be
in them, and I in them" (17. 24-26). These passages are
concerned with the naming of a name which belongs to the
category of Exodus, a name as yet unknown even to the Jews:
one that is indeed not opposed to the ideas of the prophets, or
of Job, or even of *Eh 'je ascher eh 'je* (as the Manichean Marcion
later thought), but which, for all that, deals a blow to every sort
of lordly picture of God, striking at the very heart of its Kyrie.
The reality of the ancient hypostasis of lordship was not totally

denied in the presence of the disciples—that is true; but the opposite of this hypostasis, the new Exodus-figure, could not have been made clearer, or brought closer, to the laborers and heavy-laden, the degraded and the despised. It was as in the Our Father, where the name which is hallowed, the name of him who is "in heaven," is very different from the one that is usually the object of such lofty praise. The power of real hallowing and the standard of real godliness is sought elsewhere: not in theocratic terms, but in the terms of Christ-like goodness among men. "Forgive us our trespasses *as we forgive them that trespass against us*": that is the model for the age-old jealous God. The name here hallowed is, then, the name of one like Christ in the *homoousios*-sense; in the sense, too, of the Paraclete who, in Christ's last testament, is designated the helper against the "ruler of this world." Until the Parousia comes, the "Spirit of truth" will be there to testify to Christ—not to the old religion with its "fear of the Lord." And his words will have come from Christ, not from any theocracy, nor from the heavenly Father's cherished "throne of grace." "I have yet many things to say, but you cannot bear them now. When the Spirit of truth comes, he will guide you into all the truth; for he will not speak on his own authority, but whatever he hears he will speak, and he will declare to you the things that are to come. He will glorify me, for he will take what is mine and declare it to you. All that the Father has is mine; therefore I said that *he will take what is mine* and declare it to you" (Jn. 16. 12-15).

These are indeed "words of the dead Christ down from the edifice of the world: that there is no God"—none, that is, apart from "what is mine." There may well be Persian, and even pre-Manichean influences (the Spirit of truth, *Vohu mano*) at work in these key-passages of the Fourth Gospel, but that was the privilege of this latter-day Zoroaster. For the Spirit of truth, from whom the Paraclete will take his words, is not a falsifying, but a *deeply-penetrating* interpolation, reaching to the heart (the Son of Man element) of the hallowing of God's former name. Which is why, later on, from the time of Origen

169

to that of Joachim of Floris, this Spirit could inspire the heretical mysticism of a "third gospel," an "age of the Holy Spirit," lying pregnant in the world after the age of the Father and that of the Son. Such was the scope and power of Christ's entry into the formerly theocratic realm of the On-high, where no man trod, least of all one who was man "in truth"—or, in the words of another biblical formula emphasizing the specifically christological element of radiant recognizability, one who was man "with unveiled face." In this way, then, the enigmatic expression Son of Man brought home to their resting-place in an equally hermetic *Humanum* the treasures once squandered on an hypostasized, paternal Heaven. For the words "with unveiled face" refer not only eschatologically, but also apocalyptically to our real identity as men: they un-cover what was always pointed at, and reveal it as the *universal Kingdom* of the Son of Man. The Fourth Gospel joins the old theme of the "Day of Yahweh" at the end of time to a Parousia of Christ, the Son of Man—a figure who stands alone, without Yahweh, a-*Kyrios* and a-*theos,* at once in the true sense of *Cur deus homo.*

Jesus gave his last discourse as a secret instruction to the disciples. There is perhaps one sentence—a sentence of Augustine's—which heard these words truly as inner sentiments coming at last into the outer world, and as outer sentiments able to reflect the inner man. It runs: *Dies septimus nos ipsi erimus.* This is, of course, no more than an ideal horizon to the constant interchange, and constant support, of our tasks both *proximate* and *ultimate,* saving the former from blindness, the latter from emptiness. But Christianity, the heir to the longed-for Exodus, has, with these words, staked the best claim to be man's home. Often, alas, merely to be a haven of consolation for those who take flight from the real issues. But even then, when things are seen in perspective, how much better orientated a haven than others which are easier to gain—including that of the outsider. Christianity does not conceal its punch in the folds of inwardness, or pass clean over this life in other-worldery—which is only apparently the opposite. No, the real gospel took place right *in* the world, and *for it* in its sorry plight.

26. *Paul's So-Called Patience of the Cross. His Appeal to Resurrection and Life*

There were no disciples any more at the end. It was not even as if the death on the Cross had been anything particular or outstanding. Common criminals died like that every day, and slaves, who did not count as men, hung by thousands from the cruel wood. That, we can be sure, is not what the disciple, or the legendary shepherds out in the fields, understood as good news.

Nor had the historical Jesus expected a death like this, despite the bleak vigil in Gethsemane: in his very dying moment he felt himself abandoned. When he assured the disciples that some of them would live to see the Kingdom, which was close at hand, he by no means excluded himself. The new Moses did not envisage death on the threshold of Canaan, least of all death as the Messiah, with the good news in his hand. To the disciples nothing could have been clearer than that the king had been defeated by the gallows, the life-bearer by death. Even his miraculous cures—indeed these more than anything else—pressed home the question as to why this healer of the blind and raiser of the dead could not bring himself down from the Cross. But illusionary wish-fulfillment, and paradox, did more there than move mountains: more than merely transform a mean and cruel death into a mighty victory. The living and undefeated Jesus was three times denied by Peter—by the same Peter who had in Caesarea been the first to say "Thou art the Christ"—only to withdraw now in cowardly disillusionment. But later, after the catastrophe, when Jesus was no longer present in the flesh, Peter was to die the proud death of a martyr; and countless others followed him. There were, it is true, stories about an empty grave, and about a youth in white garments standing nearby (in Luke and John

171

there are two); and there were the very life-like appearances to various disciples at Emmaus and at the Sea of Tiberias. But in this age when belief in ghosts was general and almost taken for granted, were these apparitions really something special, something reserved to the Lord? Could they, when compared with other apparitions (however realistically these might have been believed), actually turn back the hand of death? Above all, were they confined to this unique case of the resurrection, once for all time, of the One who had been nailed to the Cross? In other words, did a man have to be God's Son in order to go around after his death? Was that the proof of Messianic grace? And the doctrine of the resurrection, which came a bit later, was also alien to more people than Doubting Thomas; or at the very least it did not provide any eye-witness account of any really extraordinary event which could overshadow the catastrophe for good and all. Even Paul's doctrine of sacrificial death, quite apart from its complexity, only came some decades after Peter. The driving-force, therefore, in the minds of the early disciples, was simply their disinclination to accept Jesus' death as true, which, coupled with the *growing strength of his memory,* germinated the active pathos *that his soul cannot perish, and in its hope we cannot come to nothing.* And this, in turn, allowed his end to appear as a beginning, as a wide-open door—which could never have happened with the downfall of a simple hero.

This could not, however, last for long; it could not suffice for those who had not known the living Jesus, nor for so religious a race as the first disciples. A proper *theology* was necessary, and a theology was produced: that of sacrificial death and the apparition of spirits, and of Easter as the end result won dialectically by the repayment of our debts in a death of torture. To this, Paul, who already stood outside the original Christian circle, added the powerful paradox, necessitated by the extension of the mission to the heathens, that Jesus was not the Messiah in spite of the Cross, but because of it. Earlier ages had read that "a hanged man is accursed by God" (Deut. 21. 23), but Paul, with unparalleled dexterity, twisted this round to say that "Christ redeemed us from the curse of the law, having become a curse for us" (Gal. 3. 13); for "God has made him both Lord and Christ, this Jesus whom you crucified" (Acts 2. 36). Again, the Messiah did not appear in the man who lived and taught and moved around (as the disciples thought), nor in the entry of the Son of Man into the realm of Yahweh (as priestly orthodoxy thought), but on Golgotha, through Golgotha, and there alone. There was even a passage in Deutero-Isaiah, and a very detailed passage, too, which seemed to reach forward from within the very bounds of Judaism to the birth of the Messiah on the place of the skull: "Surely he has born our griefs and carried our sorrows. . . . Therefore I will divide him a portion with the great, and he shall divide the spoil with the strong; because he poured out his soul to death, and was numbered with the transgressors; yet he bore the sin of many, and made intercession for the transgressors" (Is. 53. 2-12). The text admittedly refers not to the Messiah but to *Israel,* whose very existence was so deeply threatened—Israel, specially chosen now, in suffering, for a distant reward. It was, however, possible to link it with the later idea of a suffering Messiah, Son of Joseph (the Joseph who had been thrown into the pit): a figure not to be confused with the victorious Messianic Son of David.

The decisive element in Paul's doctrine of sacrificial death (called by Harnack a gospel *about* Christ rather than the gospel *of* Christ) came, however, from extra-Judaic sources, though very disparate ones. These sources were motivated largely by the desire to free from the reproach of treason, or of full-blooded Satanism, the figure of a Father-God who so utterly and entirely abandoned his innocent son—where he did not, as the Marcionites later taught, murder him himself. For the unfathomable decree of God's holy will, which Job's friends had used to white-wash Yahweh, was, in later Judaism, and above all in Christian-paganism, no longer enough. In order to reach terms of intimacy, if not of complacency, with Golgotha, there grew up instead the idea of a fault solely on the part of man, and the far more refined idea of the equation of moral

173

fault and guilty culprit, which was, in fact, an appeal to the Roman law of rights and duties in the Father's defense. Hard justice now, not grace, reckoned up the debts which called for payment, and Christ, in this theory, paid them with his innocent blood, whose superabundant merits went so far as to heap up a treasury of grace for the Church to dispense. But there was another, quite different, source which had even wider implications for Paul's apologia of the Cross. Mythological this time, rather than logical and juridical, it lay especially close to the heart of the pagan world of Oriental Hellenism in which the Apostle worked. It was the idea well-known in cultic circles, of the death of a god. With it a different note was struck from that of the law of rights and duties, for in the background here was the age-old, thoroughly pagan archetype of a god who died and rose again each year. Even gods of vegetation like Attis-Adonis, the Babylonian Tammuz, died (though not in vicarious satisfaction), and came back to life each spring. They even had their vicarious Good Friday liturgy to counter the fear that the god might remain under the earth, in Hades; and they had their acclamation "Attis-has-risen": a real Easter resurrection *sui generis.* The echoes of this are still with us in a more than merely secular *Ver sacrum,* along with the theological construction put upon it that "Nature celebrates the Christian mysteries unawares." A further cultic settlement brought in the Dionysian mysteries (by no means "pan-Babylonian" this time) with their God who was destroyed and then came back to life and victory over the powers of winter. All of this foreshadows, in a pagan, mythical way, the Pauline dialectics of death and resurrection, the dark night of negation and the break-through into the chaos of light: otherwise there would have been no mythically inspired reverence for the Cross to save the day when the *experience* of the charisma of Jesus as "light and life" had passed away.

The idea of a sacrificial death taken by God the Father as a *conditio sine qua non* payment, with the slaughtered Lamb of God wiping out the debt, was not, of course, part of this mythology of an annual calendar-God, but was Paul's own contribution. Here too, however, the roots stretched back further than Roman law, further even than the vegetation and calendar-god myths which Paul had taken over. Their ultimate source was very bloody, and very primitive: it was the ancient idea, so long shunned, of *human sacrifice*—and this, in the final analysis, was made to *Moloch*. Which was, of course, simply anti-Christian. But that was the price Paul paid for his new mission-text: that Jesus was not the Messiah in spite, but because of the fact that he ended up on the Cross.

The gentle Lamb was very roughly slaughtered in this doctrine. As though the God who stood over him was a God of simple fear, only to be appeased with bowls of blood. The regression to barbaric times and usages is gross indeed, and even more astonishing is the regression from "hallowed be thy name" to this barbaric conception of God. It cannot be explained by any infectious memory of remote national customs either. The king of the Canaanites had indeed sacrificed his son in times of national peril; so had the Phoenician king. But their Moloch would have been thought of now as a very strange being indeed—Jesus certainly did not invoke him. Even the remaining animal sacrifices had been attacked with unforgettable vigor by Amos, the oldest of the prophets, some seven hundred years before Jesus (Amos 5. 22), and by Hosea after him: "For I desire steadfast love and not sacrifice, the knowledge of God rather than burnt offerings" (Hos. 6. 6)—a text which Matthew 9. 12 explicitly repeats. And, so far as human sacrifice was concerned, it could no longer appear with a clean conscience in a liturgy which hallowed the name of God; for the sacrifice of Isaac had been refused—however much that incident may have been interpolated. "Abraham called the name of that place The Lord will see; as it is said to this day, On the mount where the Lord sees" (Gen. 22. 14): but Paul, with his Golgotha of sacrificial death, revoked this mountain and rewrote the Prophets. The story of Jepthah's daughter and her fate—in Judges 11.30–40—shows that human sacrifice did reach into historical times—but not liturgically. The demon who took his tithe in human blood had

175

been thrown off, and the Cannibal in heaven long forgotten—or at least no longer honored as God. It was all the more extraordinary, then, that he should reappear behind the Pauline theology of rights and duties, accepting the satisfaction made by Jesus' self-sacrifice (a sacrifice, so to speak, without alternative, thanks to all the ordinations of an inescapable providence). Marcion, who generally admired Paul, reduced this doctrine not without justification, to an upside-down belief in Yahweh: Jesus did indeed die as a victim, but as the victim of what was a "murder from the very first"—the work of the evil that is in the world. And Origen, that heretic among the ranks of the Fathers, could find it comprehensible, to say the least, that Satan, rather than Yahweh, should be thought of as the one who received the ransom money of Golgotha. How different from all that is the love of the Son of Man when he gives his flesh and blood to his brethren at the Last Supper, after "the Lord's will must be done"; how different this is from the will of a remorseless creditor arranging the payment of his debts and collecting the money of the Lamb whom he sends to the slaughter-house.

It goes without saying that this merciless doctrine, thought up as the justification of the Cross, does not touch the actual resurrection myth at all; for this myth, with its wish-*mysterium*, could live happily without any need for torture or execution. The lonely death with its unbearable negation was sufficient to nourish the longing for an Easter faith: just as while Jesus walked on earth this faith found nourishment in his light and life: in the sign formed by the Christ himself. The motive and the effect of the doctrine of sacrificial death was, in fact—so far as an overlord exacting payment in bodies, lives and blood was concerned—something far more earthly than any consoling thoughts for death, or any resurrection. And it is this that explains the regression to the Molochism of former ages—or rather this that saw political and ideological reasons for allowing such a regression to take place—a regression from a concept of Yahweh which had long ago been humanized. This facet of Paul's thought stretched far beyond Luther to complete its destructive work; for its aim was to break the subversive element in the Bible once and for all, with the myth of the victim Lamb. It was to be a sanction for the so-called *patience of the Cross*—so praiseworthy an attitude in the oppressed, so comfortable for the oppressors; a sanction, too, for unconditional and absolute *obedience to authority*, as coming from God. Every theology of hope which might have placed itself in the front rank of change opted instead for conformity when it accepted these ideas—an acceptance whose convenient passivity broke the fine edge of Jesus' own hope, which had led all through his life, right up to the Cross.—All this with reference to those Pauline passages about the Cross which do not belong to the *Quod ego*, and belong even less to the rebellion against dialectics than to that against apologetics. "Suffering and the Cross, suffering and the Cross is the Christian lot"—that was Luther's gloss on the subject (directed to the sweating peasants, not to their masters). In short, Paul's political commandments from the Cross would, even in the political sense, be groundless, without his regressive doctrine of sacrificial death, and the corresponding regression in his concept of Yahweh. This regression pervades even the pathos of his doctrine about *change, salvation and newness of life*, and his mighty antitheses about "the law." He says in this context: "Let every person be subject to the governing authorities . . . he who resists the authorities resists what God has appointed" (Rom. 13. 1 ff.); and later he adds a quite intolerable parallel between slave-owners and the Lord Jesus Christ: "Slaves, obey in everything those who are your earthly masters . . . Whatever your task, work heartily, as serving the Lord and not men" (Col. 3. 22 ff.)—the patience of the Cross could not have been more expedient, especially now, in the continued delay of Christ's return.

And yet there was another side to the Man of Sorrows, the victim sacrificed to Moloch: there was the massive, and equally Pauline, stress on the manifestation of an image of incorruptibility in a radiant earthly Jesus. The Apostle of the Gentiles, fresh from his paymaster-tricks—and despite his adoption of vegetation-god mythology, could propose to his followers the idea of baptism in the death of Christ: a death

177

which was more-than-death. Speaking always in terms of *Phōs kai zoē*—the light and life of the anointed Jesus—he prepared their minds to receive a highly unempirical and speculative wish-*mysterium*, a joy-*mysterium* such as had never before been known: "If for this life only we have hoped in Christ, we are of all men most to be pitied. But in fact Christ is risen from the dead, the first fruits of those who have fallen asleep . . . For as in Adam all die, so also in Christ shall all be made alive" (1 Cor. 15. 19-22). This was not, it is true, of much help to the laborers and heavy-laden in their life of misery, and above all in their struggle against those who were responsible for that misery in a more real way than Adam. But it did try to conjure up an element in man which had so far not been grasped—an element which lay, as it were, beyond the reach of the jaws of death—inasmuch as man himself is extra-territorial to that realm. Paul's doctrine about Christ, based on an anti-death mystique whose roots lay further back than any mere highlighting of the harrowing nature of death on the Cross, was in this way an effective force against the phobia of *nihilism*, which had just then begun to show itself in late antiquity. It was a Tribune of humanity, sent out against the hardest of all forms of anti-Utopianism that we encounter in our present supremely heteronomous world: sent out in the face of death.

27. Resurrection, Ascension, and Parousia: Wish-Mysterium in Spite of Sacrificial Death

Goodness lived on—perhaps it was unforgettable. But behind all this (and not only in the Sermon on the Mount) there was the saying that the Kingdom was close at hand. So when it did not come and did not come, its place was filled by three aspects of that invisible realm into which Jesus was presumed to have departed. The first of these earthly, supra-earthly mysteries was the resurrection, the second was the ascension, and the third the Parousia.

The *resurrection* men talked about did nothing to help Jesus down from the Cross, but it was calculated to help him up out of the grave which awaits us all. And that was interpreted as a different, more introspective, occurrence than the common and merely external ascension of some vegetation-god, which was the source of Easter. For the Jesus who was given such prominence as the first fruits of those who have fallen asleep and who now reawaken, was not a god at all, but one of us: even at the Last Supper he was dispensing to us for the first time the *pharmakon* of our own immortality.

But now the second mystery, the *ascension,* tore Jesus away from man's estate again. A sort of ennoblement from on high removed him far from the world of men, as a veiled *Kyrios/ Son of God,* a super-Hercules in a super-firmament. The gospels themselves made light of this ascension: Mark 16. 19 and Luke 24. 51 give very brief reports, when compared with the good news of the resurrection. The first real report is that of Acts 1. 9-11, where the ascension takes place, like the Second Coming, on a cloud, bringing to an end the forty-day-long intercourse of the risen Jesus with the disciples, who had believed him to be among them in a bodily way. Apart from reminding one of Hercules, the story also has biblical over-tones, recalling the ascension of Elijah, with horses and chariot of fire (2 Kings 2. 11), which was equally abrupt in its separation from Elisha. But this story, too, is of the dynastic-solar variety, with the chariot of a sun-god and the general style assumed by ascending heroes when they quit the earth.

The ascension phenomenon also fitted in well with the very lightly drawn figure of Christ (after the manner of high feudalism), which now came on the scene in the form of Docetism—the doctrine that Christ's body was only an ap-pearance, which he had already shed before the crucifixion, and his death only a mask; his pure and immaculate pneuma, clad in white, had already stepped aside to a place where it could even look on now in contempt. The doctrine made use of a curious little passage in the Gospel of Mark on the subject of Jesus' arrest: "And a young man followed him, with nothing

179

but a linen cloth about his body; and they seized him, but he left the linen cloth and ran away naked" (Mk. 14. 51 f.). According to the Docetists, this youth was the real Christ, who did not, therefore, go to the judgment-house at all, nor to death on the Cross. It was all the easier to bring out the same non-human pneumatism in the ascension, and to make sense of the way it revoked the notion that Christ had come among us in the flesh, and the whole notion of the Son of Man.

In the final analysis, though, the ascension was not, in the minds of the faithful, the *disappearance* of one who was not, for them, a Lord at all. This whole build-up of a purely spiritual higher being, with its peculiar pathos of a *spatial On-high,* was in the end no more than a façade for something which, far from being noble, actually *broke in on* the On-high. Jesus' words, "the Father and I are one," took on in this context their true sense of simple *usurpation.* The Son of Man not only broke through the myth of the Son of God, but also through that of the throne "at the right hand of the Father": now a Tribune of the people sits upon that throne, and so revokes it. For all his celestial dignity after the ascension, Christ is still, even for Paul, the man Adam—indeed Paul is explicit: "The first man was from the earth, a man of dust; the second man is from heaven" (1 Cor. 15. 47). And his human character stays with him there: that of a *Tribunus plebis* from first to last. The enduringly anthropological nature of the New Testament picture of Christ is made clear in the very book which deals most speculatively of all with the ascension-myth: the Letter to the Hebrews. If the gospels had neglected the ascension, this letter puts it in the central place: "For Christ has entered, not into a sanctuary made with hands . . . but into heaven itself, now to appear in the presence of God on our behalf" (Heb. 9. 24)—the former "sanctuary" of God has passed over into the "heavenly Jerusalem," even if this is still a place where "innumerable angels" gather (12. 22). The model of ascension here, even if it is still the ascension of Christ that is in question, is no longer the departure of a mighty lord for high places, but is, instead, one of the most striking of all images of hope—that of the archetypal anchor pulling us home. "We have this as a sure and steadfast anchor of the soul, a hope that enters into the inner shrine behind the curtain, where Jesus has gone as a forerunner on our behalf" (6. 19 ff.). So much for the other side of the second of the wish-*mysteria*, the side of the Tribune, and intended liberator of the people. Or, as another (equally questionable) letter of Paul would have it, quoting the Psalms on the subject of this ostensible ennoblement: "He ascended on high and led captivity captive" (Eph. 4. 8).

Christ's office was all the more clearly that of Tribune, for here Paul ascribes to him what Psalm 68. 18 ascribed to the chariot of Yahweh. Christ was to take over what had come to be seen more and more as the function of Yahweh, who, because of the sheer loftiness of his throne, could no longer fulfill it himself. This function had, for a long time now, been thought of in the sublime but euphemistic terms of the heavenly Czar as the "healer" of Israel (Ex. 15. 26): "for I am the Lord your Saviour and your Redeemer" (Is. 49. 26). Yet, despite the unique symbolic force of the Exodus, that image of Yahweh could make no headway against the hypostasis of unapproachable majesty. The Exodus and the conquest certainly lay behind the idea of "taking captivity captive," for this was the annexation of the highest of all regions by the head of mankind; but in the fairy-tale land of religion one had to turn a blind eye to the essential difference that the ascension-myth with all its implications was a simple personification of man's hope, whereas the conquest had been as real as Canaan. On the other hand, while unrealistic, this myth of usurpation did aim to put the Son of Man in the place filled by an hypostasized On-high; that was, in fact, its whole point, for it drove the consequences of "I and the Father are one" right into the realms of a long-credited transcendence.

The third wish-mysterium, the *Parousia*, also flowed from belief in the On-high; but here, too, in the Eschaton, Christ was no longer a mere being from up there. The Lord who rejected

181

lordship was not only gazed after as he went; he was also expected to come back. Nor had the human element dropped out of his Second Coming; otherwise it would not have been a return of man's Jesus to mankind. He appears now, however, more as the Avenger of Job than as the preacher of the Sermon on the Mount. Only for the laborers and heavy-laden, the degraded and despised, will the Second Coming be a mild one: only for those who are more than prepared for it. To them the Lord will come as a bridegroom to wise virgins, but the lukewarm—not to mention the real oppressors—he will spew out of his mouth. The Parousia is, admittedly, in one way just a reversal of the old power-structure rather than something really new; for the lowly will be exalted and the mighty brought low, and, above all, Christ will return as another archangel Michael sent down from the heavenly throne. That is how the faithful sometimes see it—as though the breaking into the On-high had really done nothing to transfigure the Lord of hosts at all: "For the Lord himself will descend from heaven with a cry of command, with the archangel's call, and with the sound of the trumpet of God. And the dead in Christ will rise first; then we who are alive, who are left, shall be caught up together with them in the clouds to meet the Lord in the air; and so we shall always be with the Lord" (1 Thess. 4. 16 ff.). But in the end it is again the figure of the Son of Man that strikes the loudest note: "Behold, I stand at the door and knock; if any one hears my voice and opens the door, I will come in to him and eat with him, and he with me" (Rev. 3. 20). There seems to be quite as much love here for the oppressed as there is justice for the evil-doers and salvation for those who have been freed. Or, as the highly Christocentric interpretation of Jacob Böhme would have it, the same apocalyptic light which shines with anger on the wicked also lights the way to the wedding feast of the elect.

Finally, the Second Coming revealed both the real point of the ascension-myth and the full force of the reaction to it. The point of the myth was the transformation of heaven as the preserve of God into heaven as the city of man, the new

Jerusalem. And the point of the reaction was that this heavenly city was to come down to man "prepared as a bride adorned for her husband" (Rev. 21. 2): the new heaven and the new earth were fully anthropocentric. The *homoousios* of Jesus has completely taken over the old paternal picture of God with its subordinate worlds of sun and moon: "And the city has no need of sun or moon to shine upon it, for the glory of God is its light, and its lamp is the Lamb" (Rev. 21. 23)—the Lamb whose radiance thereby equals the glory of God. For this Christ was far more than any non-Messianic founder-figure: far more then Moses, or even Mohammed. He was not just similar to God *(homoiousios)*, but equal *(homoousios)* to the very last degree. The Arians held to the thesis of mere similarity, but that would have ruled out any real entry of the Son of Man into the domain of the Father—any real equation of the radiance of the Lamb with the divine glory. So they were condemned, and the council of Nicea canonized the orthodox doctrine of Athanasius that Christ was *homoousios* with the Father: the doctrine which bestowed on him the most revolutionary *topos* any founder-figure or any Parousia had ever had. That is the light which dawns, and dawns inevitably, when the category Son of Man enters the mythical, but also mystical, wish-*mysterium,* making the Christ-impulse live even when God is dead.

28. Second Thoughts about the Serpent: The Ophites

The moment has come to recall a very bold stroke indeed: one that belongs closely to our own self-proclamation, but does so in a very strange guise: that of the serpent who, coming from the Garden of Eden, was also the first seducer of youth, the first gatherer of disciples. These associations were not forgotten, though they were continually distorted. They were taken up again after the time of Christ by the Ophites (*ophis:* snake), a Gnostic-Christian sect active in the third century.

We know the teachings of this sect almost solely from the writings of their opponents. The age-old cult of Ophis came down from matriarchal times or even earlier. It can be found in a positive or, later, mostly negative sense in many religions, though not with the edge it has in the Bible. The serpent was the double-dealing beast from the earth's secret depths, from whence came noxious gases and healing springs, dreams, prophecies, volcanoes and treasure. He was, from the very first, a complex being, the source of poison, but also of healing (the Aesculapian rod), the god of volcanic eruption and also of eternal rejuvenation and renewal. On the one hand, as Hydra, Python, Typhon, he was a creature of the abyss, subjugated by the gods of heaven; for Hercules defeated the Hydra and Apollo the Python, erecting Delphi over its cave, and both Siegfried and Michael overpowered the "dragon of the pit." But at the same time he was the snake of lightning, the fire in the heavens. Uraeus, the regal sun-serpent of Egyptian diadems, belonged to these same upper regions.

The Ophites, however, enthusiastically recalling other traditions in the Bible, clad their serpent-idol in quite a different skin. In an astonishing way they related to religious rebellion what was in itself simply a primitive cultic nature-myth. This they did by invoking the serpent of Paradise. The text runs: "This serpent is the strength which stood by Moses, and the staff which turned into a snake . . . This all-comprehending serpent is the wise logos of Eve. That is the mystery of Eden, the sign set over Cain, that no one who found him might kill him. The serpent is Cain, whose sacrifice was not accepted by the God of this world: he accepted the bloody sacrifice of Abel instead, for the Lord of this world is well pleased with blood. And it is the serpent that in latter days, at the time of Herod, appeared in the form of a man . . . So none can be saved and rise again without the Son, who is the serpent . . . His image was the bronze serpent set up by Moses in the desert. That is the meaning of the words (Jn. 3. 14): 'And as Moses lifted up the serpent in the wilderness, so must the Son of Man be lifted up, that whoever believes in him may have eternal life'"

184

(Hippolytus, *Elenchus*, V; cf. Leisegang, *Die Gnosis*, 1941, pp. 147 ff.). They interpreted the serpent of Genesis, therefore, not only as the principle of life, but also as world-shattering reason itself. For, hanging from the Tree of Knowledge as the "larva of the goddess Reason," he had taught the first man to eat of its fruit. *Eritis sicut deus scientes bonum et malum*—out through the gates of the garden of beasts where the real original sin would have been not to have wanted to be like God at all.

But instead, what came on men was the wrath of their petty demiurge, even though, according to the Ophites, the Tree of Knowledge had bestowed on them the first-fruits of emancipation. And however much the light-bearing serpent was served up by redactors as the dark satanic grandparent of evil, he was still, according to the text quoted above, indefatigably present at all the Bible's subversive breaking-points, from the bronze serpent raised by Moses to save the children of Israel in the wilderness (Num. 21. 8-9), right up to Jesus—nor was he present as a symbol that would crawl all its life along the ground. His seed was the desire to be like God; but this Promethean urge had more than a purely personal dimension. It appeared equally well in the desire to create as God created, as the myth of the Tower of Babel shows—a myth which likewise received the worst possible clerical press. And one that was answered with another expulsion, this time from the unity of language and country to dispersal over all the earth; for Yahweh could tolerate no point where man reached up to heaven.

But to get back to the visible symbol, the serpent of salvation, the Savior-serpent raised up by Moses in the desert. Its image stood, unforgotten, on the high places right up to the time of King Hezekiah: "He broke in pieces the bronze serpent that Moses had made, for until those days the people of Israel had burned incense to it; it was called Nehushtan" (2 Kings 18. 4), which means "the thing of bronze." That took place about the turn of the seventh century B.C., and still 700 years later the Gospel of John could put on Jesus' lips the parallel so stressed by the Ophites: "And as Moses lifted up

185

the serpent in the wilderness, so must the Son of man be lifted up" (Jn. 3. 14). Ophitism moved on from this point to draw the most astounding picture of the similarity between Christ's death on the Cross and the curse that fell on the serpent of Paradise because he had "opened the eyes" of men. Both of them suffered the wrath of the Demiurge, and the Saviour-serpent was nailed to another tree: that of the Cross.

But Christ was to return. Here the Persian myth of a third, definitive appearance of Zoroaster had some influence, for the new Parousia, when it comes, will be in the form of a snake of lightning. "The Lord will break in at midnight" and will throw down the whole vile world of the Demiurge in ruins. Here, only too clearly, is a rebellion myth second to none; the surprising, and unfortunate thing is that it appears to have lasted only in a purely spiritual form. The high defiance, the unique reappraisal of the serpent's words, the hard bite of *Eritis sicut deus* made themselves felt only at the level of theoretical exegesis. It is, in fact, almost beyond belief that the momentous equation of Christ with the serpent, the sole ancestor of Mephistopheles, could be reduced to complete zero, to utter silence, not only on the political plane but on the purely spiritual plane as well—along with the Ophites' abrupt realignment of the Cross's function with the devil of this world, rather than with the goodly Father who yielded up his Son. This devil now stamped out the guiding light of freedom for the second time, and more radically than ever before.

So the strange doctrine of the Ophites did not, in fact, fare well. More than any other heresy it was consigned to the realm of the merely curious. The teaching it has handed down is not only full of gaps—it has also been polluted with a fog of Gnosticism which covers up its dangerous, well-knit essential content. The momentous Christ-serpent equation must, *ab ovo,* have seemed a monstrous blasphemy. That is why the Fathers of the Church, and her history, have played the Ophites down, not even accepting them for the wicked heretics they were, but simply brushing them aside with repulsion as fools who are best forgotten. And doing so all the more readily

for the fact that the real impetus behind them, the disproportion between the eating of the apple from the Tree of Knowledge and its penal consequences, continued to give trouble. Its
disturbing influence was felt, understandably enough, in non-
Christian, rabbinical theology, too, although in these circles
Christ's role as serpent might have seemed very apt.

The *thorny problem* of the so-called Fall, however, did not
depend on the Christ-serpent equation. It was a problem
primarily of the Old Testament, passed down to scholasticism
by rabbinical theology, above all by Maimonides. He was a
real thinker, and no parrot, but he posed the question in
exactly the same way as the long-forgotten Ophites, although
at the back of his mind there was still the conventionally
correct but profoundly inadequate solution. He begins (*Führer
der Verirrten,* I, Meiner, pp. 30 ff.): "Years ago a learned man
asked me the following grave question, which calls for serious
attention ... The questioner said: It appears from the
straightforward words of Scripture that the Creator's original
intention was for man to be like all other living beings, without
reason and the power of thought, and unable to distinguish
between good and evil. But when he disobeyed, his very
disobedience brought him the reward of perfect fulfillment, a
fulfillment peculiar to himself ... But this is as much as to say
that because a man has sinned and committed a particularly
grave crime he will be made a better creature, and set as a star
in the heavens." The question passes over the punishment for
the sake of the reward—that is only too clear; but it does see
the resultant state as the otherwise unobtainable reward of
"disobedience." For, as the "questioner" goes on to say
Adam and Eve were made as beasts, and only through their
"sin" did they become men. Maimonides' reply—he may
himself have set the question, too—was, of course, an apologia
for the Creator, starting from the point that he had in the first
place given Adam the power of reason, but not the dim and
turgid reason which makes value judgments: the power he
gave him was non-sensual, non-affective reason, and this
power fallen man had lost. His conclusion is thoroughly

187

tortuous: "That is why it is said, You will be like God, knowing good and evil. It is not said, Because you know or grasp true and false. For with unconditioned being [viz., the object of knowledge rather than of mere opinion] there is no question of good and evil, but only of true and false."

Ophitism lived on, therefore, in the problem still posed, and posed perhaps ever more intensely, by Maimonides and by Aquinas after him—at least in so far as it gave the spur to a long overdue apologia for the God who outlawed knowledge. It was, of course, the question that lasted, rather than the futile, tortuous reply; the serpent himself could have given an answer more in keeping with the simple directness of the questioner. The Ophite doctrine also lasted in itself until the sixth century, and it was evidently still regarded as worthy of persecution, for Justinian issued a law against it in 530. The serpent of Paradise was, according to Bishop Theodoretus (c. 450), also worshipped for a long time by the Marcionites, as opposed to the Creator of the world (though Marcion himself, the evangelist of the God-against-the-Demiurge may not have been a party to this); indeed the Marcionites are even said to have used the symbol of a bronze snake at their mysteries (cf. Harnack, *Marcion,* 1924, p. 169). This bronze snake lasted, in fact, right into the late Middle Ages in the eucharistic cup, and in the mystic-Oriental decoration found on Templar churches. Hammer-Purgstall, the great Orientalist, who was in general anti-Templar, even claimed to have discovered the "Ophitic diagram," described by Origen, on some reliquaries of this strange order. It consisted in a line of contrast between the world of Yahweh-minus-Exodus and the serpent-spirit of the better world. Similar illustrations can even be found in a few sectarian Baroque Bibles: the bronze serpent pictured as the crucified Christ, for instance, standing in the forecourt of the Temple, with the Cross of Golgotha as the Tree of Knowledge, and the serpent nailed upon it.

So, although we have to rely almost entirely on cagey references (especially those of Irenaeus) for our knowledge of the Ophites, the so-called Fall would not allow them and their arch-heretical emphasis to be forgotten. It is a long way from an animal cult to the siren of the Tree of Knowledge, to a Christ-Lucifer, to the third serpent, the apocalyptic, and finally successful, snake of lightning. And the pre-Gnostic fantasy at work there is also very great. But even greater is the will for light: the struggle for a light that will burst out across all deserts. We can in the end repeat words which have a place in more than just the history of myth, words which have set their seal, in place of the Ophitic "diagram," on all that we have been saying here: the serpent of Paradise is the larva of the goddess Reason. Fortunately, there *is* an element of reason present in the history of revolution: the seal of the serpent can still be seen. And not now as something strange; rather as something taken for granted.

29. Second Thoughts about the Exodus-Light: Marcion's Gospel of an Alien God Without This World

And now the moment has come to recall another bold stroke—a doctrine not from the mainstream of the serpent tradition, but one, if possible, even more seductive.

Marcion lived about the year 150 in Rome, an embittered Christian, sharply opposed to the "law" of this world and of its Creator. The key-word to his work is "antithesis": *"Antitheseis"* was even the name of his book, which, though itself lost, has been half-preserved in quotations by his adversaries. It is directed towards everything connected with the life of this world in its burgeoning and in its decay—against the well-being of the flesh, and against the death which goes with it. All is deformed, rotten from its so-called maker on down, our own "Father" who, in his justice without grace, is a figure of unquestionable cruelty. In the long gallery of the Vatican Museum, leading to the library and the collection of sculpture, there is, among hundreds of inscriptions largely taken from the catacombs, one in the spirit of Marcion (which in this case is

189

not far from the spirit of Job). A relief shows the raised forearm and hand of a girl pointing upwards, but in an attitude far from prayer. Under it, in three stiff but pointed lines, are the words: "O Procopus, I raise my hand against the God who tore me away, an innocent girl who lived to be twenty; *pos. Proclus.*" Though the stone evidently comes from the Christian milieu of the catacombs, the hand on it is raised like a Marcionite's *against* the Lord of life and death. The inscription does not invoke any pagan planetary gods who might rule over a predominantly evil fate (the impersonal *"Heimarmenē"*): *contra deum* is singular, and refers to the familiar God of monotheism. For that is the mood and ethos of Marcionism: *contra deum* = *contra Yahweh* as maker and Lord of the world.

Marcion gave the word for a thoroughly Christ-conscious antithesis. He tried to break a way for Jesus out of the Judaeo-biblical framework of God. Not, it must be said, from any feelings of tension or enmity vis-à-vis the Jews (he honored the Jew Paul as his master), but because Jesus should have nothing at all in common with the Bible of Yahweh—inasmuch as it is this. Christ's message was, for him, not only opposed to the Old Testament, but entirely different from it; the break from the old follows from the incomparable leap of the gospel into the new. In fact the very concept of the New Testament as a separate entity comes from Marcion, although he himself, put off on every hand by the scent of old wineskins, only admitted into his canon ten of Paul's letters, and Luke, who was Paul's friend—only these were the new wine. He also removed all references to the Yahweh of the Old Testament, who was fully re-demonized; and he threw out all the disturbing allusions to the prophets, and the baptism of John, the "returned Elijah." At the same time he aligned himself more and more explicitly with the Paul who was so emphatically antithetical in his approach, and consequently so opposed to the former law—Paul who had, in fact, spoken against Yahweh, if not as Creator, then certainly as Ruler of the world, and, to be even more precise, as Law-giver. For Paul had, as an apostle, established the hiatus between "law" and "gospel," between the "commandments" and "freedom," and between "justice" and "grace"; and this should have removed all possible confusion about where Jesus stood.

But, not wanting to fail in his duty to the evil Creator of the world (as opposed to its Ruler), Marcion also went beyond Paul to the primitive *dualism,* revived in his day, of ancient Persian religion. He seized with enthusiasm on Ahriman and Ormuz, the evil principle and the good, who were also interpreted as the Creator and the Redeemer of the world. That made room for the mythology of an evil Creator as well as an evil Ruler, as can be seen a little later in the work of Mani and the Manichees, and even in the struggle between the *"civitas Dei"* and the *"civitas terrena"* in Augustine. In Marcion himself this Persian dualism intensified the radical nature of the *Novum* that was his gospel; and it also intensified the Pauline antithesis between law and gospel to the point of irreconcilability, for Ahriman, the simple principle of evil, was the only alternative to the good. Paul had certainly gone far beyond the Old Testament Law, but he still acclaimed it as the *paidagogos,* the "guardian" leading to Christ (Gal. 3. 24). And, above all, he seldom or never so much as touched upon the question of the identity of the Demiurge with the great God—despite 2 Corinthians 4. 4 about the "unbelievers" whose minds have been blinded by the *god of this world,* "to keep them from seeing the light of the gospel of the glory of Christ, who [alone] is the likeness of [the true] God."

As opposed to this, however, Marcion, like Paul, differentiated to a considerable extent between the various Persian and Gnostic dualisms he took over, above all in the matter of the reduction of the Yahweh-principle to that of evil. Marcion's non-gospel God is not just the evil god: this latter is, for him, subservient to the *cruel, merciless God of justice.* And Christ has as little in common with all of these as has the God whom he revealed: the God who is *utterly alien to this world and not guilty of it,* the *Deus contra deum huius mundi* (cf. Harnack, *loc. cit.,* pp. 106 ff.).

191

Marcion's scheme of things goes further, therefore, than the related idea of a *Theos agnostos* which grows to maturity in his work—that is, the idea of the simply unknown God about whom Paul preached in Athens (Acts 17.23), and to whom the Athenians had built an altar. For however much this God might imply the other so far utterly alien one, he did not, in Marcion's thought, deliver man from the flesh and from power, from the world and the stars and the God beyond the stars in the same way as did his own God of simple abduction.

About one point, though, no doubt was left, and this was that Marcion's gospel, this final Exodus, bearing man off in jubilation to his heavenly home, was straightforwardly antagonistic to this world: empirically it was a thing of gloom. For not only did it bring release from bondage—in which it was like the great archetypal Old Testament Exodus which Marcion excluded—but it also freed man from the flesh and from all that was of this world, while providing nothing better. This purely spiritual, purely logos-inspired wave of farewell to the world has no land on its ascetic horizon where, even comparatively speaking, milk and honey flow; and least of all does it have room in its pure Docetism for a Christ who has risen in the flesh. Indeed, according to them, Christ was not even born in the flesh—a gospel so burdened could not have given the pure impulse provided by the gospel of the entirely new and utterly alien God.

But even here, even in this ethos of abstract and often banal asceticism, and of a God whose other face is one of utter strangeness—even here there is no revulsion from *man:* indeed the idea was to focus on him more closely than ever. To focus on his ownmost transcending, on the point where he really transcends into the foreign territory of a home that is once and for all identical with himself. No simple maiden from a foreign land will show the local people how to bind their flowers into better garlands than before, and no strange traveler will tell romantic and disturbing tales of a blue flower far away, or with trembling hands demonstrate new ways of doing things. But rather something never heard nor seen before, yet something very familiar, was coming; something that has never been here before—something that for that very reason is Home. That is why Marcion's Christ, for all the empirical gloom of asceticism, will come to the strains of a music which is quite manifestly that of abduction. Or, as Tertullian himself put it, Christ was to rob from their false paternal home those who were longing to escape: those who were creatures of the good God. As in all mysticism, too, even when it has no statutory *askesis*, Christ was to bear away his bride not to a place of less light and life than here below, but of more. That is the point of Marcion's appeal to the Pauline text (quoted with minimal ideas about the way to publicize joy): "What no eye has seen, nor ear heard, nor the heart of man conceived, what God [the object of unconditioned expectation] has prepared for those who love him" (1 Cor. 2. 9). This *alien yet welcoming distance*, never before heard of and only conceivable through Christ, provides the required sense of "freedom," "grace," and "homecoming" for Marcion's anti-"law" and anti-"justice" figure, who is also anti-"creator and ruler of the world." And this in turn is above all calculated to proclaim, through the Exodus, and by the power of the good news now reached at last, the world-creation and the *"Deus"* creator: *ultima Antithesis est creatoris finis.*

The most surprising thing about all this is the Surprise in person. The Surprise which comes like lightning, as an absolute break with all that has gone before and is now due only for destruction. That which lies in wickedness can only bring forth wickedness—in Marcion's eyes that goes for the whole of history up to Jesus: history in no way leads to him. It is with real meaning that his birth is put down as the year naught, the beginning of a new time-series which in itself has no *real* place, but only an apparent one, in history. The Marcionite year naught is a different matter from the beginning of those calendars which are set in history and issue from it, like the Roman calendar *ab urbe condita.* Paradoxically enough, the only real parallel lies in the Jacobin calendar, whose year naught was "also" intended as a totally new beginning, with its break from the entire "old testament" of history as a sheer trick on the part of the princes and priests. Marcion's *topos* defied comparison with this, however: his concerns were religious, and here he rejected all historical mediation of his *Novum*—not only that of works and deeds, but that of premonition and promise, too. Not even the prophets, not even the Ophitic serpent of Paradise could have held the unforeseeable gospel of Christ in their hands. The historical dimension is simply of no value in the abrupt light of a revealed salvation, with its *gratia* which, even historically, is *gratis data*.

Marcion, then, gave birth to that "break" mentality which was always to militate against any idea of "reception": history is devoid of salvation, and salvation of history. However false this statement is in its absoluteness, it is still a very meaningful warning and antidote to the equally absolute mediation-chains of history, let alone to the nailing of a living body to history's Cross. Not total determination from behind, but freedom: that is an exaggeration framed to counter an equally exaggerated pre-determinism. For the *Novum* should not be made to forfeit in the course of mediation the radical break that is as proper to it as is the *imprévu* to the wonder of the marvellous.

This is where Marcion opens the door to the further depths of the objectively surprising (without which the simple *historical* break would be merely formal). These are the depths of an *alien territory,* one that is utterly unfamiliar and yet, as our home, utterly familiar. The alien God, innocent of the world and untarnished by it, but merciful towards it, touched this earth only once—in Christ: and even then under a veil. Even in his gospel he is veiled. And yet this transcendent *Absconditum* is, in its very distance, the one thing clear; for the sayable can only distort. Men knew nothing of this separated, alien God until Christ came—nor did the Creator-God himself, whom they worshipped. This statement outbids all dualism and strikes right at the heart of the *Pater-Christus* relationship of the Apostles' Creed. The profound intimacy of this alien realm

194

comes from the deep blue of total distance, to which only the Christian eros can adequately correspond: "Home is where no one was before."

No previous religious outlook could have joined together like this the motifs of flight from the petty constrictions of man's inherited position, and of abduction by a strange traveler from a totally alien land: two motifs bound up together in the idea of our "unveiled countenance" in this uniquely alien yet at the same time not unrelated realm. From the politico-historical point of view, of course, the notion of the totally unmediated Absolutely-new, Absolutely-alien is a lot of Jacobin nonsense. But in the early Christian sense, seen against the light of a latter-day soteriology, it was a different matter. Especially as Marcion touched off inside us a streak of expectant yearning which makes it easier to believe in what has not yet come than in what has. So although one cannot speak of historical mediation here, one can perhaps speak of it in a psycho-eschatological sense. Christ, the Son of Man, has no God over him—that is certain. So he has no alien God over him, not even a particularly friendly, grace-ful one. The On-high of Marcion's Christ-phantasm was a simple signal light, beckoning on the *Atopos*.

AUT LOGOS
AUT COSMOS?

30. The Call Before the Door

There is a Within that only broods and dawdles. As if it will
hatch itself out like a hen—nothing more.

But to ponder deeply and genuinely has something of the
search about it: it is a call before the door that leads out into
the open, that comes itself from the open. There is an
Out-there present in it; one that, in its turn, calls—enticingly,
or just waiting for the door to open. One that, like our own
Within, is a state, or preponderantly a state, and not just an
object which might not concern us at all. For an awful lot out
there does concern us deeply. And that gives a certain value
even to self-cultivation.

So however much man's Within may weave its own web, it
cannot, because it is human, be entirely taken up in itself. It
needs Outwardness; it will listen to it and, in the end, will build
there.

196

31. Orpheus

This property so peculiar to man cropped up even when the Out-there only seemed to need it in places. Only in a few things did man want to set himself against the way of the world, or could he do so. And in any case the world went its own way after absorbing into itself with careful moderation the morsel of ego-magic.

One need only think of the legend of Orpheus, above all of Orpheus as the bard of righteousness—though he does admittedly compel his hearers to listen and take note. For even in the legends only isolated things change out-there: only from time to time can a note of self-will be heard to strike against the established order. The resounding ego of Orpheus compels the wild beasts, and even the trees and rivers, to come and listen. And with the power of his calm and gentle but already dying melody he penetrated into the immovable underworld, touching the heart even of the Furies: the Wheel of Ixion stopped, and Eurydice almost stepped up into the light of day again.

If one may say so, the Orphic school honored its legendary master because he was in a position to return from the underworld. The solemn consecrations were concerned with the removal of the fear which comes from an uncertain life and a doubly certain death. This saving flight, or escapist salvation, stood out as very alien in the otherwise so fleshly, worldly Greek milieu. And Orphic asceticism, with its abstention from this bodily world, was doubly alien to the enduring Greek spirit of this-worldliness, above all with the Dionysian orgy in the background. *Soma* was now equated with *sēma*, body with grave, and the god of drunkenness, liberator of limbs, only had to break the bonds of the bodily grave. It was a question of stopping the Wheel of Ixion, in very truth, the wheel of our continual re-birth into new bodies.

Not that all this deliverance from the world was acosmic. The world from which the follower of Orpheus escapes

197

resumes its path at least in its On-high, as light; and the sun itself (although again in a figurative sense) stands still in "pagan" stillness. And yet the Orphic body-grave equation disturbed the Greek sense of this-worldliness literally like a foreign body—far more than Plato did. Indeed Plato was, for that very reason as well for reasons connected with Apollo, not very well disposed towards the Orphic consecrations. Though his Ideas, too, with their outward show, left this world just as far behind, only to intensify it twofold high above, containing it in a "heavenly" way—right up to the point of an Idea of dirt, let alone of light.

In all this the followers of Orpheus were trying out, long before Plato, the late Greek, tentatively Gnostic idea that the world was a prison, a place to be left behind. With the cry *Paue! Paue! Be still! Stop!*—uttered against the Wheel of Ixion, the way of the world. But not in such a way that the Word-which-breaks should die away in an acosmic vacuum. A remnant of the enduringly world-centered Greece is there to see to that; or rather, one that is of even remoter, pagan-oriental, *astro-mythical* inheritance. And in that enchanted circle of external nature the human spirit had warmed itself for so long that it no longer wanted to rise out of it—or could.

32. Exodus and Cosmos in the Stoics and in Gnosticism

For quite long enough the Within was wont to retire, purely for its own sake, from the hateful world out-there. Enclosing itself in privacy, with only rare excursions into and against the affairs of men. Wisdom of that sort was seldom persecuted. The Epicureans and, above all, the Stoics, counseled the quiet life, and advised against living in close proximity to circumstances over which one has no control. In its origins that is no passive counsel, but it was often in fact inspired by the cunning that seeks mere peace of mind; the cunning that, in the narrow confines of Stoicism (though not in the *secessio plebis in montem sacrum*), chose the false wisdom of resignation to the far-ranging look. And did so right up to the point of an entirely sham exodus, whose worldliness was already evident in the attitude of courtly Stoic circles that some things in the world gain more recognition from resistance than from conformity.

A different, or at least more problematic matter, is the logos of the genuinely motivated wise man of Stoicism, who could turn far away from the world from which he came—and with which, in the final analysis, by the very violence of his revulsion from it, he wanted to agree; for he sought an "incorrupt" world of "nature," the "city" of a purely pantheistic Zeus. His bearing was upright now and his path was straight, though none the less "natural" for that. Not only did it free him from inner and outer disturbances, but, at long last, it unearthed the logos in the world as well as in single individuals, and was united with it, until its goal was reached in a world-state run by man: a state which could itself only be uncovered in quiet calm; and one that was a consequence of *imitatio naturae rectae.*

This upright bearing was, however, to be achieved not by a radical break, but, in Stoic worldliness, by intensification, by ever more true-to-life "naturalization" of the creature. What that means is this: that the defeat of the intruding world in the free man, with his unshakability, is in no way a step outside the world of nature, but an ever more immanent function of the true World-being, In-the-world-being, of fulfilled nature. And the assertion of this harmony of Stoic freedom with Stoic determinism in the world was even to bring destiny, *Fatum, "Heimarenē"* in line with Stoic freedom, not as a disturbing element but as one that leads—and the more so the deeper this freedom conceives of and asserts itself: *volentem ducunt fata, volentem trahunt.* Here was no Orphic song wanting to pass outside the cosmic harmony of the spheres; and the *logos* achieving self-sufficiency in the wise, sought only to be caught up in close union with the workings of the *cosmos.*

In this way, the human soul seemed in the final analysis to

199

bear a close relationship to some omnipotent *pneuma* in the present, immanent, other-worldless world. The very *"Hege-monikon"* within him which enables the liberated man to walk upright through the world, was taken to be an enduring part of the *"Logos spermatikos,"* the world's seminal Reason itself.

The exodus was the more violent the worse things looked— the more fate was experienced as oppressive and antagonistic. Not that men rebelled; they were just discontented. They felt like prisoners. The soul seemed like a girl in some dreadful whore-house, waiting only to be carried off, and for the way out to be shown her by the priest. Not least of all in the practice of death which, to the Gnostics, was a form of ascent (albeit a perilous one), just as birth into this lower world was a fall.

And the world traversed by the ascending, returning soul was, even in its truly cosmic, planetary heights, everything but the "city of Zeus" propounded by the Stoics. On the contrary, it was ruled by the Planet-spirits as by evil "archons," real "cosmocrators," and by a Fate that was no longer the friendly one of the Stoa. It was even advisable for the departing soul to have a password ready for its "heavenly journey," so that it could get safely past the evil planets who rule the world—the founts of cosmic trouble and of *"Heimarmenē"* itself. And this *"Heimarmenē"* has now become the inimical spirit of the dark astral myth; no longer is there room in the cosmos for the benign "nature" of the Stoa, or for a Stoic "homology with nature." "Not only the planets, but also the twelve constellations of the zodiac, were reckoned among the demons of destruction; the whole firmament was a devil's harness, the whole universe a tyranny. Sun, moon and stars are together the sphere of fate, *Heimarmenē;* and the devil is regent of the world" (The Principle of Hope, p. 1315). Hence the *Paue! Paue! Stop! Stop!* in the face of determinism, right up to the point of a Gnostic Paul and his "shaking the bars of this world of death." Right up to the point of his word-for-word allusion to the hostile astro-demons of Gnosticism: "For we are not contending against flesh and blood, but against the principalities, against the powers, against the world rulers *(kosmokratoras)* of this present darkness, against the spiritual hosts of wickedness in the heavenly places" (Eph. 6. 12). And the same cry reaches even to Augustine, whose Jesus (a Christian-Gnostic figure) turns away the head of the evil archons so that they can no longer look on man: "Christianity is superior to pagan philosophy in that it bans the evil spirits to the heavens and frees the soul from them" (*De civ. Dei*, X).

Farewell, then, to the world, Nature is burst asunder by transcendence, both inside and out—or at least so it seems in Gnosticism. And yet in the last analysis even this doctrine, precisely as all-transcending, could not leave the *old topos of earth and heaven* behind. For the ascent of the soul (being that of the Gnostic logos so to speak) remained here, both from the point of view of evolution and from that of emanation, paralyzed, or at least confined to the categories of a highly mythical nature. This was so from Valentine right through to Jakob Böhme and Franz Baader—with a higher degree of *"Physica sacra"* than the worldly Stoa with its Zeus-nature had ever seen. For in this doctrine the moon and the sun lift the light of the soul out of this world, not just like demons, but like a sort of excavating machine pulling them up on high. And a particularly nature-oriented element of Gnosticism was the doctrine of emanations from the primordial Light down into the world. This was tied up with the two sexes; and it pointed the way of ascent back to the primordial Light, for it contained the moon and the sun, the female and male, coupled in constant "syzygies" at the various stages in the stream of light which poured out through the world.

But none of this sun and moon magic, filling the heavens above a still diabolical *Heimarmenē*, went beyond the bounds of astral myth, notwithstanding all its *Sursum corda*—indeed, in the end, because of this. And when an even greater astral myth appeared on the scene, one which was transposed beyond the cosmos, it still did not bring anything really new:

the sun and moon stayed where they were. For now, in fact, a new spring was really burgeoning: a spring that came not from any inner light, but from these very same astral regions themselves.

33. Astral Myth in the Bible

For a long time all paths looked outwards, like the one who walked them. Men were hurt, and helped, by powers that were to a great extent inhuman. They themselves played only a tiny part in the channeling of nature out there. Instead, their lot was fear of lightning and thunder, with nothing to call on in the face of failing crops, nor any credit for fat harvest. Man faded into Pan. And Pan's great being was ghostly as well as oppressive, sucking men into a world where no man could call himself in question—could call himself his own.

The primitive and ubiquitous practice of magic in no way contradicts this, any more than does the primitive animistic picture of an all-enlivening World. The magic-maker, too, needs the cooperation of pan-spirits; he takes on their image and likeness—not by using his head, but by means of animal and devil masks over his head. Even though these cults do need their human henchmen, their shamans, none of them, not even the great religions of the nature-myth, can show a real personal founder; all they have are the matriarchal or patriarchal societies of moon and sun. Not even the nature-religions of the Egyptian or the Babylonian state have founder-figures remotely comparable with Moses or Mohammed or, above all, Jesus. And it is even embarrassing to ask about the "founder" of one of the "pagan" religions of Europe: the question is senseless. Even in the person of the hypothetical first story-teller of the nature myth the human element has faded into Pan, to become the whispering of Erda in the cavernous earth, or the sun-giant Gilgamesh, or Thot, the writer of wise sayings, who is none other than the moon-god.

Far more important than any differences between these

primordial figures, all of them superfluous to man was the difference in the nature myth between the matriarchal and the patriarchal, between the rule of earth and moon and that of sun. The nature-idol, as Bachofen discovered, was feminine, matriarchal; it paid homage to narrowness rather than breadth, to cavernousness rather than height, to night rather than day, to Ge-Luna rather than to Sol. Echoes of this can be found in all "chthonian" cults; it is there too in the womb-like *pietas* of Antigone, and even more so in the glory of Mother-Cybele, Astarte, Isis, Demeter—till we come to the crescent-moon under the feet of Mary. The male, patriarchal principle, on the other hand, pays homage only to the sun, as the cosmomorphic principle of lordly majesty. This is the realm of breadth and constructiveness, of a ladder of light coming down and going up to heaven, of planetary towers and stepped pyramids rather than caves. This is where the geometrical pyramids and temples of Babylon and Egypt belong, built strictly to a cosmo-astronomic model, so that they might be the real "house" of the solar god whose path they follow. And the cupola of Chaldea belongs here, too, the reflected image of the dome of heaven: it can still be seen quite clearly in the Pantheon with its planetary decorations, and in Hagia Sophia with its almost unchanged Christian Firmament-figure.

All this *imitatio caeli* which is apt to occur in the house of God reaches back to the deep "paganism" of the astral myth, above all to its post-matriarchal element of sun-primacy. This is where the Out-there is for the first time in full command; the depth of space has unfolded itself completely, stretching from the matriarchal cave right up into the heights; Ge has gone along with Uranus, but in the end Uranus is on top. The astro-mythical outlook penetrated not only the Stoa and Gnosis but also, paradoxically, the Exodus-myth itself—the Bible's own myth of logos withdrawing from nature. Here its effect was to cloud the issues even more, to make things even harder for the myth, without any compensation either; or at any rate to throw up a non-human space around it from the Book of Job right through to the Apocalypse—a space that even from the mythical point of view, precisely from this point of view, could not be thought of as final.

Custom dies hard. Foreign material from Canaan and from remoter, loftier circles forced its way into the "spirituality" of the Scriptures. Pre-Israelitic Canaan had been a colony of Babylon; it was full of soil-cults and stone-cults; Yahweh-worship had a long battle with the local Baalim. Nor was Egypt remembered only for its flesh-pots: there was also Ptah, the creator who molded from clay. Of course, as is often the case with new discoveries, the Asian influence on the Bible (especially the Babylonian, which was strongest) was heavily exaggerated in about 1900. Delitzsch, Winckler and Jeremias produced the "Babel-Bible" complex, which attributed to the Babylonian sagas not only the Ten Commandments and the Fall, the Deluge and the Tower of Babel before them, but also the Patriarchs and the story of Joseph; and, to a great extent that of Moses, too. Finally Jesus himself was reduced entirely to the level of the Asian vegetation-god of the year (cf. Arthur Drews, *The Christ Myth*), his life being traced back accordingly to patterns in the calendar and zodiac. There was so much analogy in all this that a parody of it arose in the question: Was there a Napoleon? The saga-theory was used to deny it, with Napoleon as Apollo, Laetitia as Leda, Corsica as Crete, the twelve marshals as the signs of the zodiac around Napoleon, who was the Apollo-Sun-God, and St. Helena as the Western land where the sun goes down.

All this has its place, but there can still be no doubt about the importance of the astro-mythical influence in the Bible, even when it does not do away with what is proper to the Bible, or nullify its historicity. Though that is not how the "Pan-Babylonians" would put it—not even Alfred Jeremias, the most Bible-centered of them. He made a distinction between the Canaanite myths, which he saw as having a purely "ornamental" impact, and real historical happenings, written-up in the Bible in its own special sense. The Pan-Babylonians even derived the biblical "Hallelujah" entirely from *hilal,* the ancient Semitic name for the new moon; but that sort of thing is just etymological word-gutting. Some words of Jeremias put it in perspective: "Mythological motifs in the story do not in themselves prove anything against the historicity of the whole ... In this context one cannot exclude the possibility of an historical foundation for even such figures as Samson, whose story is said to be pure myth" (his hair was thought of as the rays of the sun and hence as his strength) "and whose very name is proposed as a proof of his (astro-) mythical character" (Samson = little sun) (*Das Alte Testament im Lichte des alten Orients*, 1906, pp. 73 ff.). One might add that even the story of William Tell and Gessler comes from an ancient Scandinavian sun-saga, applied now to the folk hero and the sinister provincial governor without disproving the existence of either of them or of the Swiss revolt. There is here, too, however, a purely astro-mythical motif—in the apple Tell shoots from his son's head, with Gessler as Fenris-wolf, the Winter-giant who wants to kill the youthful sun. The motif has its parallel in the Bible, where it occurs at two decisive points: the child-massacre by Pharaoh in Egypt and by Herod in Bethlehem. Sun-myth is in its turn intertwined with earth-myth in the story of Joseph in the pit, in the Phoenician Attis and the Babylonian Tammuz (hellenized as Adonis), and in the cult of the death and resurrection of Christ: the vegetation-god who dies and rises again is united here with the solar god of the year. Winter burial and Easter Day are two closely interrelated elements of fate in the course run by the calendar-god when he sinks down into the underworld and then rises to new life, as is clearest of all in the Babylonian festivals of Tammuz.

This stereotype of a solemn course, with its festivals every winter and every spring, was, however, open to interruption and *new configuration*, through its division into the twelve *zodiac periods*—an astro-mythical concept if there ever was one. According to this cycle, the sun's spring rising-point changed every three thousand years; and the signs of the zodiac had a special significance for each of these periods, or world-aeons, which they governed. Putting aside for the moment the number twelve (twelve sons of Jacob, twelve apostles, twelve gates and twelve foundations in the Heavenly Jerusalem—Rev. 21. 12 ff.), the delvings of the Babylonians, the all-too-pan-Babylonians, were certainly justified in seeing the zodiac mythology as providing a sign for each new aeon in the Bible. From about 3000, the calendar no longer corresponded with the sun's spring rising-point (the equinox). It moved into the sign of the Bull, the sign of "Apis," and the "golden calf" of Egypt and Babylon. And at about the time of Christ's birth it moved decisively into the next sign, the Ram, in the house of Arnion (= little ram), which marked the ascendancy of the "Lamb." To this extent the sign of Christ had its home in a cosmic fresco, the sign of meekness its roots in an astral myth.

The astro-mythical complex took over the non-biblical festivals completely, and left its mark on the biblical ones as well, in the form of a Christmas that was part solstice and an Easter that was part sacred spring, the *ver sacrum* of nature. And an adequate interpretation of all this was provided by the influence of Asiatic calendar-religions, with their subjection of the man-pneuma-logos line to terrestrial and celestial cycles. This at least gives a more straightforward explanation of the nature-myth elements in Christmas and Easter than is provided by the alternative theory of a simply superior pneuma, according to which nature just lies at our feet and follows us: it is of no value in itself, but merely "celebrates the Christian mysteries unawares." The astro-mythical influence, even on the Bible, would be unthinkable if it did not in fact contain—amid all the undeniable superstition and fantasy—a vast and in no way devalued conception of nature; of a nature that cannot for one moment be reduced to the level of an unconscious preamble, an unoriginal ante-room to man. Nature is not just chaff, or, at best, raw material for the house of man; humankind is not the sole proprietor of products which it has elevated to form an all-embracing *topos* of spirit, spirit, and still more spirit. The immortal Arcadian (indeed micro-macrocosmic) phrase *retourner á la nature* shows this if nothing else, setting itself against any "superior" absolutizing of the words: Let man make the earth his *underling.*

And in any case, does the Out-there, with its material element, exist in vain? Even if sun, moon and stars did fill a place that was not apocalyptically their own, surely they enshrined the Menetekel of this *topos,* its more than purely spiritual "space." These are the ultimate problems still kept alive by the one-time impact of the astral myth on the human race's logos-centered, biblical understanding of itself. They are problems of metaphysics as well as of history. *Aut Logos aut Kosmos* is not, therefore, a simple Either-or like the antithesis *Aut Caesar aut Christus.* It does not exclude the possibility of change in the world, made available to us in and by the cosmos in deep-reaching memories which still enable nature to be seen not just as a cold shoulder, or a source of terror, or a mere receptacle for the past, but as a fount of silent stillness and ever-widening grandeur—homologous to the life of nature around us, which is earthly and Arcadian in the beauty of its silent stillness, while being at the same time under the lofty sway and grandeur of the Great Pair, the moon-sun syzygy.

That, then, is the seductive lure of "paganism." The Bible does not just shrug it off, but breaks it down and goes beyond it.

34. Logos-Myth Again: Man and Spirit, Feuerbach, Christian Mysticism

THE HUMAN SPARK STILL GLIMMERS

In order to move out there must be a Within. If this is weak and smoldering, it can hardly distinguish itself from the Outside around it. If this Outside-us impinges too powerfully the only thing to do is comply and yield oneself up, giving up the infant drive to be oneself, which at this stage finds it even harder to disengage from the clan-environment than from the pressure of being.

A so-called savage, when told about the soul, could find no sign of it inside him, for, among other things, it was invisible. But he pointed to a bird that was flying past, perhaps his tribal bird, and said that that was his soul. This was ego-less in a friendly way; or rather it was the abduction of an unnoticed Within. But there was no friendliness in the way man was assaulted from out there by lightning, thunder, storm and wild beasts.

A spark of truly human enterprise glimmered, however, even here: a life-giving spark, for evil or for good, and one that could not be found in thunder and night, or even in light, without man. For man made magic from his earliest days—magic that could smolder on and glow afresh in prayer. He had, from the very first, called out into the Outside round about him not just Something that could be addressed, but Something whose speech had magic powers. And he had done this despite the poor grasp he had of his own Within; indeed that is the very reason why his own role was so long overlooked.

But this call of his had also been directly into an Up-there; although the spirits outside might well have seemed to dwell already in sufficiently starry heights. Imaginations both feared and loved bore fruit in a field which could not otherwise be called religious. And if that is true of the first feelings of piety which accompanied an upward glance to sun or moon, how much truer is it of all that is humanly measurable in the realm of the Uncommon. The words to the shepherds, for instance: *Do not fear.* That is a real apology for an overdose of other-worldly light. When things have gone that far, there is no holding back the human role in the upward glance.

FEUERBACH AND THE "ANTHROPOLOGICAL"

The In-there which gets itself up like this, and starts to join in, is filled above all with desires. It is not true here that a bird in the hand is worth two in the bush. Even when the sort of need that called for the dream-food of manna is no longer there, a farther-reaching hunger remains: a hunger that projects into the distance what it does not have near at hand, and makes itself ready to receive it. The pictures it paints are of course in the colors of the lords and banquets which the badly-off observed, so to a great extent they serve as a decoy, leading away from poverty *here* to consolation *there* in the Beyond. But the element of religious excess in these superimposed pictures must have been molded in the privations and burning desires of a Within; otherwise it could not have been so totally transposed into an Over-there where it certainly does not occur. Poverty alone is by no means the outward splendor of the Within, but there must be a splendid fantasy at work there—in the objective absence of all splendor—for the Beyond to be decked out in such wasteful terms. That is the whole *raison d'être* of Hegel's youthful words in *Die Positivität der christlichen Religion,* when he says—with so much feeling for *subjective logos*—: "Leaving aside early attempts, it has remained primarily the task of our day to vindicate, at least in theory, as the property of man, the treasures which have been squandered on heaven. But what age will have the strength to enforce this right and really take possession?"

Many stages below this, but very persistently, there followed Feuerbach's attempt to return the heavenly world to man—admittedly to a man conceived of as already present. This was the "anthropological critique of religion," of the creation of the gods; for man should regain possession of the world, his own world, which he has given up to them. The gods are nothing but reflected men, transposed hypostases, the product of desires which presuppose the division of mankind from its "essence" as much as they want mythically—all too mythically—to end it. God is always made in the image and likeness of his worshipper: cruel or benign . . . as unlimited as possible . . . whispering earth or radiant sun . . . immortal . . . remote from the fickle turns of fortune. Hence Feuerbach's desire to bring the Church-God back to man, the human subject, and his implicit demythologization of the pure Up-there of astral myth. Hence his words: "Man believes in gods not only because he possesses fantasy and feeling, but also because he possesses an instinctual drive towards

209

happiness . . .; a god is the satisfaction of this drive in the realm of fantasy" *(The Essence of Religion).*

Noteworthy here is the fact that Feuerbach's predilection for Christianity marks out the Christian "treasures" in the Beyond as preferable to the considerably less human ones of paganism, which was for the most part a matter of star-cults. Even in Feuerbach's "anthropologization of religion," these are much harder to trace back to a "drive towards happiness," let alone to the "essential drive of One's-self." Consequently, most of his heaven-clearing activity is directed at the essence of Christianity, and not at star-cults (only later did the anthropologist turn to these). Even the "sultry dew of love" (Marx) apparent in his humanism could scarcely have been stolen from Marduk's god-emporium, let alone from *Eritis sicut deus.*

It is also noticeable that, for all his return into himself, man is very quiet, very still. Feuerbach does not yet think in social terms about our estrangement from our essence; the economic roots of this alienation remain untouched. And, for the same reason, "man" is still a common—and a static—genus; he has not yet adopted the form of an "ensemble of up to now highly variable social relationships" (Marx). The term "man" is certainly not exhausted by Marx's definition, but Feuerbach does not enrich it by his breaking open of its other-worldly hypostases. All his wishful, this-worldly, idealistic talk about bringing the gods at long last down to earth does not get *homo homini homo* much further than a readily available ensemble of liberal desires. The only thing is this, that no one has made a more concerted effort than he did to turn the flow of human ideals away from the Beyond and back to man whom these ideals reflect. One can even say, with some exaggeration, that no one, so far as *method* was concerned, was as indebted as he to the radically human line in Christianity. Which is why his mere genus "man" is outdone in his own work by the solemnity he accords to the *subject:* here the human dimension he retrieved from the Beyond no longer looks so much like the common man, no longer has such a naturalistic, this-worldly air.

A theory of religion based on *wish ipso facto* passes over into another, Utopian dimension, which does not cease to exist in the subject even when the illusion of an hypostasized Beyond is shattered. Indeed the subject, aware of itself now, and powerful, gains in stature from it, till it stands above nature itself. The idealism reflected in the now pulverized Other-world is revealed as the fruit of purely human powers of transcending which, far from going beyond nature, operate within it. Hence Feuerbach's words: "Belief in the Beyond is belief in the freedom of subjectivity from the limitations of nature—it is, therefore, man's own belief in himself" *(The Essence of Religion);* and, going even further: "The mystery of religion is the mystery of the essence of man."

With that, Feuerbach, for all his supposedly static genus-man, almost enters the realms of *homo absconditus*—the man who has never seen himself face to face. Which undoubtedly throws a special light on his atheism, as well as on his subjectivity—a light that would have been impossible but for the Christianity he criticized so "anthropologically." The disillusioned, liberated reality he proposes is not any simple Nothing-but; it is not a Nothing-but-nature. On the contrary: man only invented the Beyond because a reality of Nothing-but-nature was simply insufficient, and above all because his own essence still had no reality.

Feuerbach's atheism, then, aimed both to destroy a strength-sapping illusion, and to fan the transforming flames which would change the theologically created infinity of man back into a truly human one. Feuerbach equals Enlightenment in that he wanted men to be students of the Here-and-now rather than candidates for the Beyond. But the Beyond should at the same time form candidates for a better Here-and-now: it can, after all, be a "kingdom of freedom"—of the children of God—in more than a merely chimerical sense.

One can see that there is much less room here for the astral myth than for the Christian one, with its Son of Man—despite all the solemnity given to the opting for this world of nature.

211

STRANGE MEETING OF ANTHROPOLOGY
AND MYSTICISM

To persecute is to follow. But it is not always hatred that makes the two poles alike: there are well-known opposites, for instance, which meet when each is pushed as far as it will go. The meeting point in question here, however, is different from both of these. Feuerbach and mysticism, contrary to their avowed intentions, have a Christian root in common.

However much Feuerbach's thought may drift away at times into an abstract genus man, or sink into naturalism, it is still animated by the idea of a subject reclaimed from the realms of God and from the mere Outside-us of the world, and established in a new, and by no means merely cosmic, immanence. His words ring out from the heart of the mechanistic materialism of his day: "My first thought was God; my second was the world; my third and last was man." And this means that the contemporary critique of religion was not just scientific, it was also anthropological, picking the real, live flowers from the theological illusion. There is clear agreement here, *qua* subject, with heretical mysticism—an agreement which goes beyond Feuerbach himself. For if, as he said, the mystery of religion is the mystery of man, then the ideal of man takes on the clear form of an ensemble of *Utopian* relationships. But that dawn has not yet come.

THE "FREEDOM AND POWER OF THE SPIRIT"
IN THE OBJECTIVE INTENTIONS
OF CHRISTIAN MYSTICISM

It is a bad thing to blind oneself to the world. Especially when things out there are bad themselves—when they are going badly. The word "mystic" comes from *"myein,"* to shut the eyes. The question is: what to? Christian mysticism from the fourteenth century onwards by no means shut its eyes to the intolerable world around it with all the oppression from on high; on the contrary, it was the child of a highly contentious, rebellious lay movement, a real popular movement in which the mystics played an increasingly important part. Indeed, they were often denounced as political as well as religious heretics—it was hard to tell the difference. The Lollards, the Béguines, the "Brothers of the Freedom, Power and Fullness of the Spirit," and then the Anabaptists and the Hussites—all were utterly opposed to authority; and all handed on their spirit and their witness without recompense.

Myein: to shut the eyes . . . Here, where Christian mysticism is prepared for battle, it means: to awaken a new sense—a different sense from the one that can register and thoroughly reject the misery out there and the powers up there which maintain it. If the eyes were shut now to the Lord God it was because—to the newly awakened human subject—he was no longer strange: no longer an object held above us, but the very depths of our own subjective Self. He was the inmost *state* (not object) of our own misery, our own wandering, our own suppressed glory. That is the teaching of the mystic Sebastian Franck; and to this teaching Thomas Münzer remained true, dangerously true, even after he had met his end: "God is a great sigh lying unspeakable in the depths of the soul."

The glory striven for, but not attained, lay in the *yearning* of the subject, in the *uttermost depths* of longing, and there alone. These were the same *indivisible depths between man and God* which Meister Eckhart had previously called the "tiny spark, and tower, and castle" of the man-God, the God-man. Or, again, they were the depths of *"synteresis"* (of true self-observation) where the "unveiled face" of man-God and God-man were exchanged, each of them finding there his own Selfness, Self-sameness. That is what Eckhart meant in his "Sermon on the Eternal Birth," when, speaking about the Christ-Logos, the *hidden* Word which came down at midnight, when *all things were silent;* he said: "It is hidden, and for this very reason one must follow it. When St. Paul was caught up into the third heaven and God was made known to him and he saw all things, he forgot none of it on his return; it was buried so deeply within him that his reason could not reach it. It was utterly and completely within him, not outside, but right inside. It was because he knew this that he said: *I am convinced that neither death nor tribulation can separate me from what I find within me.* And on this subject a pagan master has spoken well to another master: I am aware of something within me, shining within my reason. I know well that it is something, but what it is I cannot grasp. It only seems to me that if I were to grasp it I should know all truth. To this the other replied: Then keep well to it! For if you were to grasp it you would find there the quintessence of all goodness, and you would have eternal life. St. Augustine speaks in this sense, too, when he says: I am aware of something within me, playing before my soul and illuminating it. If it could only come to fulfillment and permanence within me, it could not but be eternal life." All of this is, of course, full of the purest logos-myth. Its Within does not remain inside itself, but moves out-there among the still-astral heavens in order to participate, purely by itself, in the Great Man.

The best of Christian mysticism is like that. It can grip one powerfully with the *newness of its topos and its undying spark of utopianism*—a spark struck by something very near to us indeed, but something which has not yet fully shown itself. For, hidden within this subject, is the Moment of our own Selves: the long overdue, and now really present, Here-and-now, the *"Nunc stans"* (Augustine), of the being into which we are ourselves being transformed. The difference between this world-sundering spark and the world-conforming astral myth is very great—the Christian Founder had the face of a man, not of the sun. Though there were still a few relics of the High-above there. Even in Eckhart there is mention of the "God above the gods"—as if the nearness of mysticism had suddenly become very distant, and its depths become the lofty depths of space, instead of the inward depths of the *still hidden Moment* of time which was only just maturing into time. In fact, however, Eckhart's "God above the gods," this "highest darkness where light dwells," was nothing other than the hidden depths of man's own Inwardness, the stable where the Word was born. Christ was the Word of salvation from the Father-Lord, from the starry mantle of heaven, from Fate on high. Eckhart's Logos was received into the deepest warmth of man and human growth—not into the cosmos. It became small. It entered man, as well as being made flesh: "What the heavens could not contain lies now in Mary's womb."

That, then, is how these Christians were taught about the Son of Man: as the rising dawn of their own subjectivity, but, at the same time, as the bursting-asunder of their heaven, and its descent on earth. *Et lux aeterna luceat eis:* the spark of mysticism was struck on this inner transcending without any outer transcendence—*contra omnia saecula saeculorum.*

35. Further Consequences of the Logos-Myth: Pentecost: Veni Creator Spiritus, Not Nature But Kingdom

ANCESTOR AND GOAL

To stand upright is to hold one's head up high. The man who does this is free to look around him: freer, anyway, than if the weight of his body merely dragged him down and bound him to his close environment. Even the circumstances of a long-inherited milieu are less binding on the man who stands up straight. He can, after all, use his hands to tackle them—he no longer needs them for walking.

When he works to provide himself with food and shelter, instead of just collecting what is already there, he frees himself step by step from the loyalties which bind him to inherited tradition, until he finally gains freedom from the *Where-from* of this tradition itself, completing—or breaking—the picture in the form of a freshly thought-out *Where-to*. Ancestors and their doddery, backward-bending cult are increasingly re-placed by a thoroughly forward-looking attitude and goal, and by a cult which does not beg the spirits but commands. A cult, in other words, which frees itself from the accepted customs, and is therefore really more like cultivation . . . building . . . new building. One which makes it possible, then, not only for the great tribal Parent to retreat, but for all his works, which form, or should have formed, past history, to do so too. The Beginning that established all things (or released them) retreats now in the face of a history which has broken free and moves forward: a history that is no longer established, but *be-comes*. Not that the here-and-present world is thereby broken open or abandoned: it is, rather, seen as a river—but one that is still circular, still returning to its source. Only the first faint indications of an outlet or a break-through—even one that is purely the work of man, with no pre-existent goal—are present in the turning away from what is old-established. There is no absolute exclusion of traditional ways. Right in the midst of age-old Pan there is the Heraclitan awareness that all is flux. Fire flows, too (though that also stands upright), and devours the great Ancestor, the primordially established Once-and-for-all of World.

There is no real goal here either, inasmuch as everything returns whence it came. But what would a river be if it did not flow out into another river, different from itself? So there is still room for the Where-to. Static room admittedly, and long the preserve of the Where-from: but *something* can still develop, leaving behind the unconcern of the Beginning. Something can still be seen as open to future development.

FIRST STAGES IN THE TENSION BETWEEN BEGINNING, WAY AND END

When the Primordial-One which is the Beginning is thought of as creative, what comes after it must thereby seem smaller. To proceed from so lofty a source is *ipso facto* to diminish.

The Neo-Platonists, and later on the Gnostics, did not believe in creation by a primordial Father but in emanation from a primordial Light. These emanations, however, were at the same time downward falls; the farther they receded from the Light, the weaker they became, and their only goal was to climb back through the world to their source. This Alpha-stress goes back to Plato, though already in the earlier Academy Speusippos had reversed matters, with his evolutionary stress on the Way which leads away. Right from Aristotle to Leibnitz and Hegel, then, emanation was opposed by evolution, which saw the Primordial-One in all its perfection as the end-product and not the starting-point of development. The *beginnings* of growth took place, on the contrary, in a very vague and imperfect realm indeed: one which stood closer to Plato's questing Eros than to a perfect world of Ideas beyond all growth.

This tension in Greek philosophy between the Beginning, the Way and the End—between the concept of emanation and of evolution—was quite independent of the Bible. And, *sub specie evolutionis,* the Beginning of all things was by no means perfect. But even in Gnosis, where the emanation doctrine was so essential, this Beginning was (especially in the work of Basilides) called the seminal, not the fully-existing God. Even the Gnostics, then, thought not only cosmo-gonically but also theo-gonically: in terms of development to an Omega. The thorny problem of reconciling a primordially existing state of perfection with one that could only be reached in the Eschaton was present even in these ancient schools, where futuristic, let alone Messianic thought was practically unheard of.

It was present all the more in the Bible, where the Alpha-Way-Omega tension reached its climax in the opposition between the principle of creation and that of salvation. Here *creation* took the place of *emanation,* and instead of (or at least as well as) *evolution* there was a break-through, an *Exodus* into the Utterly-new. In this scheme of things, however, the one who created the world cannot be the same as the one who leads out of it again: even the serpent-scapegoat did not relieve the mythical Creator of responsibility for his work. On the contrary, neither the serpent, nor the *Numen* which said, "I will be what I will be," nor the *Novum* of the Prophets and the New Testament are in any way compatible with a Father-God, or with the reversion of the Omega of hope into the hypostasis of a *Deus creator*. It is significant in this context that every element of dissatisfaction in the Bible, every anticipatory demand pushing "Canaan" further and further into the unredeemed Not-yet, either does not know the creation-myth at all, or rates it literally in the last place, behind the idea of an apocalyptic breakthrough into the Utopia of salvation.

If one now turns again to Bible-criticism, this time with a metaphysical end in view, it becomes apparent that the Alpha-element itself is not part of the original tradition: the futuristic element, especially the account of the Exodus from Egypt, is far earlier than the creation-story, both in its text and in its implications. Israel's primitive faith is in Yahweh, who led it out of Egypt; the creation theme, as has been established by Noth, "only came down in one of the written documents," essentially the priestly code, "so it is excluded from the whole pre-literary formation of the Pentateuch" (Martin Noth, *Überlieferungsgeschichte des Pentateuch,* 1948, pp. 48 ff.). And in the priestly code, the creation story—which in fact is concerned with a Ptah-Yahweh, and so is of Egyptian rather than Israelite origin—serves as a sort of antiquarian preamble added to quash doubts which had arisen about Yahweh's goodness, and even more about his power. The idea is clear from the Book of Job, where Yahweh sets out to intimidate the "earth-worm" with his creative might: Where was he, when God made heaven and earth? The Prophets were the ones who gradually pushed it aside (cf. Is. 45. 12), when they banished the ancient Father and his successful cosmos in favor of a new, Utopian heaven and earth (Is. 65. 17). The legendary Almighty of the Beginning now gave way to the *intimate humanity* of Messianism—a Messianism which was newly effective in that it saw itself as focused solely on the future. Achieved creation was replaced by unachieved direction towards a goal which was as far above the present world produced by Yahweh as "Canaan" had been above "Egypt." Especially when things were bad, this goal drew men ever forwards, ever on.

On these prophetic, no longer regressive, stepping-stones, a Logos was approaching with quite a different sort of "evolution." And this time not with old wineskins for new wine.

PENTECOST: CREATION AND CREATOR SPIRITUS

There is a remarkable similarity between the descent of the Spirit and frenzy.

They spoke in tongues, but it was so unclear that only the possessed themselves could understand. To the outsider they seemed to be "filled with new wine"; not that of a new aeon, either, but of a very familiar pagan, orgiastic one. Pentecost was, in fact, intimately connected with what Baader has called a simple "spiritual awakening of the nervous system," and consequently with the Pauline stricture that "he who speaks in a tongue edifies himself, but he who prophesies edifies the church" (not that self-edification was entirely frowned on). And, in particular, Pentecost was concerned with the solemn participation in the Holy Spirit himself, whose coming had so long been awaited. And this connects up in a great sweep of tradition, like some sort of unexpected and deceptive rainbow, with Dionysus and the Maenads. "When the day of Pentecost had come, they were all together in one place. And suddenly a sound came from heaven like the rush of a mighty wind [or pneuma] and it filled all the house where they were sitting. And there appeared to them tongues as of fire, distributed and resting on each one of them. And they were all filled with the Holy Spirit and began to speak in other tongues, as the Spirit gave them utterance" (Acts 2. 1-4).

What distinguishes this text from all previous *ek-stases* is that the element of somnambula there is not (as it was at the Sea of Tiberias and on the way to Emmaus) an apparition of

219

Jesus. Instead, faithful to the logos-myth, the text jumps from God-the-Son to God-the-Holy-Spirit, a third person, reminiscent of the "Spirit of Truth" of John 16. 13. This new Pneuma is, in turn, set off in high futuristic relief by Peter's "Pentecost sermon," which follows straight after it. For Peter quotes the words of the prophet Joel: "And in the *last days* it shall be, God declares, that I will pour out my Spirit upon all flesh" (Acts 2. 17). Pentecost was quite different from all previous feasts of frenzy in that it set the real celebration at the "last days," the end of human history: this finally made room for the complete triumph of the Logos in a true "age of the Holy Spirit." Later on, the controversial Church Father Origen could speak in this vein of a *"tertium Evangelium,"* that of the Holy Ghost. And later still Joachim of Floris, in the full spate of revolutionary heresy, could announce the end of the aeon of *sovereign rule* by the "Father," and the beginning of the aeon of *illumination,* proceeding from the state-less and Church-less Logos.

In a different way, Pentecost stirred up the old problem of Beginning and End again: the problem of an infinitely great Creator-Father, the primordial Maker of all things, including the evil which men begged him to redeem—the God who looked jealously on the Prometheus in man, on the Tower of Babel and all that that implied. Not only in the Book of Job rebel man was compared with the pot which contends with the potter; not only there was he considered laughable.

But now, at Pentecost, a new cry rang forth—the cry of a new creation, where no *Pater omnipotens* held sway. Rhabanus Maurus gave it words in his hymn *Veni creator spiritus* (which Mahler made the foundation-stone of his eighth symphony, the Faust symphony). Here the primeval, heavenly category of creation remains, and remains in unison with its opposite, the category of *salvation.* It is rather the *Deus creator* that drops out: true creativity now has the *Spiritus intus docens* as its subject—the Holy Spirit, who pours himself out in our hearts. To put it in modern terms, the *infinite greatness* of a creative Beginning is lost now, with this future-facing *Veni creator spiritus,* in the *infinite smallness* of a Beginning which is no more than a beginning, a state of pure need. Nor is this new Beginning any once-and-for-all, mythical, pre-earthly creation of the universe, leaving room only for beings which are in themselves complete. It is, rather, a simple *X,* an Alpha present in all being. Incomplete and unobjective in itself, it draws man on through the transient darkness of each moment in the Way of the World. It is the *Not-there of each present Moment,* which, still veiled to itself and seeking itself, truly "evolves" into being in and through World-process and its experimental forms, for it is their primary stimulus and driving-force. Its place in human history is at the decisive front of the *Experimentum mundi,* where man lies equally open to everything and nothing, to fulfillment and to ruin, and where the world is in high labor as the *Laboratorium possibilis salutis.* The *topos* of Way—and, even more so, End—is this same endless forward-looking openness, not the closed *topos* of the astral myth with its "eternal, iron laws"; it is the great *topos* of the Future, still full of objective and really available possibilities for birth, development and experimental forms of fulfillment; the *topos* where the *X* of the Beginning runs ever onward in the still immediate, unmediated, unobjectified, unmanifested Here-and-now of each present moment. Here alone, in this closest closeness and most immanent immanence, lies hidden the mystery, hidden even to itself, that there *is* a world, whatever may be its reason and its End.

This Mystery of man's being, along with its still unfulfilled solution, has its place, therefore, not in some distant pre- and supra-earthly transcendence high-above, but in the ferment of the undiscovered moment, in its most immanent immanence. Its unawareness of itself is the driving force which lies behind the phenomenon of the world, and is also the high, Utopian torment in which the matter of the world wells forth—the Fount and Pain and Quality of world-matter. The true world is here still uncreated, it *has its being in newness*—which is quite

221

the opposite of the antiquarian mythology of *Deus creator* and of an utterly complete, fulfilled Beginning. "The real Genesis is not at the Beginning but at the End"; and it is only when the Where-to and the What-for have at last found adequate expression within us that the Where-from begins to flicker into the focus of our sights. "In this way there comes into the world something which casts light on every childhood, somewhere where no one yet has been: it is called Home" *(The Principle of Hope).* Item: *Creatio est exodus, non est restitutio in integrum.*

MORE ABOUT ALPHA MUNDI AS EMPTY WASTE. NEITHER SUN NOR MOON IN THE APOCALYPTIC "REVELATION," BUT THE CHRIST-FIGURE OF THE KINGDOM

There is much that contrasts with a mere Beginning, a simple Has-been. First of all there is the darkness of the present Moment, always impinging but never grasped, never in possession of itself. The darkness which means that every real beginning is a future thing, alive in the past as a foreshadowing of the future. Or, to put it in other words, the veiled presence of the future here-and-now *is* the open-ended darkness of each present Moment, *is* the pregnant state of all that it contains. In this respect Jacob Böhme's insight into the "primeval void" went far deeper than the massive ancestor-cult and the deified six-days'-work of the priestly code.

The same minimalizing train of thought was taken up by Schelling, who, in his Munich lectures on the history of modern philosophy, said: "The subject, in its pure, essential nothingness, is utterly empty of all qualities. It is still only itself: it is utterly empty of, and in respect to, all being. But it cannot avoid attracting itself—putting on itself . . . The subject can never gain possession of itself simply as that which it is, for in its very attraction for itself it *becomes another . . .;* no longer is it unfettered with being, as before: it has fettered itself with being. It experiences this being as something it has drawn to itself quite by chance. The first *existing being,* the *primum existens* as I have called it, is also, therefore, the primeval chance. This whole construction begins with the first Chance, the first being that is different from itself: it begins with *dissonance,* and it *must* begin like that . . ." What a difference there is between this Alpha and the Ptah-like World-creator of the priestly code.

In Hegel's thought the problem of the Beginning was somewhat foreshortened, but it is significant that even he half-rejected the remnants of the Creator-God. Instead he posited an "Absolute," so small in its beginnings as to be like nothing, but soon containing the whole of creation *ante rem.* This Absolute "resolved to release itself" into nature as the form of Otherness. Now although "resolving" and "releasing" are not at all the same as creating, they do still imply the age-old, almighty Alpha of *Deus creator,* and the high majesty of his ready-made plan for the world; there is no question here of being "empty of all qualities." They imply the infinite power which, even though it does not now create with *Fiat,* can still create categories of emanation—those of "resolving" and "releasing"—which betray all too easily their royal blood.

The Exodus-sign of the *Novum* is a very different matter. Here it is man that is important, and the idea of being on-the-way from an Alpha of simple deficiency to a state of full development. The ready-made cosmos, with its eternal, iron laws, is brought to nought, and songs of cosmic jubilee, from Behold-it-was-very-good to the pagan astral myth, are silenced. The logos-myth has come into command once more, in a very special, *chiliastic* way. The astral myth may, with its zodiac, have governed and controlled the course of time, *but the logos-myth introduced to the world the idea of real historical movement:* the idea of a *Novum that does not come down from on high among the eternal, immutable stars.* The *concept* of World-history and its Eschaton began for the first time with Augustine, the philosopher of a wandering *civitas Christi,* but the most radical and highly colored appearance of this Eschaton was in the Apocalypse of John, the ultimate End-book itself.

"The former things have passed away" (Rev. 21. 4). This cry

223

of liberation refers first of all to death, but also to the old heaven and earth, of which death was a part. The logos-myth has taken on a depth of fantasy, but also of explosive force, to break through into the new, apocalyptic Day. A day where the Lamb will replace the shining of the sun, and a static nature will pass over into the Eschaton, the Kingdom.

36. This-Worldliness in the Astral-Myth

Fullness has often come about by the creation of emptiness behind it. And light has often been dearly bought by the over-hasty diminution and darkening of what came before. So it was when nature, which was at least implicit in the astral myth, suddenly disappeared altogether from the milieu of man.

Superstitious, pagan magic of mountain and valley, of storm and clear blue sky is now passé: it has drifted away in the face of the Bible's spiritual breeze. But nature has also drifted away from its place in the world around us; it has been consigned to the past as a preliminary step which life and man have essentially already taken. The decisive plus of the pure logos-myth has undoubtedly contributed to the creation of this vacuum—or at least this removal of the "sticks and stones" to the lowest level of being—with its easily exaggerated slogan about man making the earth his "underling." For the natural thing then is to treat nature like a servant; or at best to look on it as no more than potting-earth for our roots.

The moon and the sun are ordained from the very first to shine on other "creatures" loftier than themselves; the sun illumines earthly life by day and the moon by night. Of themselves they are nothing; but they may even, eventually, have something of their own to say, outside human history. Nature which does not anthropomorphically serve the pre-ordained purposes of other strata, however, is not in the least demythologized by an ecclesiastically superimposed logos-myth, though the Church asserts in all seriousness that it is, oblivious of the fact that the first mechanistic theory of a nature free from spirits came from a semi-astro-mythical Ananke (physical necessity), and that that was the work of Democritus, not Thomas. The upshot of this was that the cosmos which lay beneath and beyond the rule of the Logos did not appear, in the eyes of the Church, as demythologized, but on the contrary, as fully demonized: as an open gateway to perdition with its ghosts and wild hunters. It is understandable, then, that Christian philosophers like Roger Bacon and Albertus Magnus who also applied themselves to nature, were viewed in the Middle Ages with suspicion. Galileo himself was not received as a demythologizer, and Kepler's place was in an *Harmonia mundi*, a *Mysterium cosmographicum*, not with the transcendent Logos.

This is not to say that there were no exceptions to the transcendence which came with the simple break-through of the logos system. The Bible is full of nature-images (they are there in the New Testament, too), and many parables are based on the beauty—even on the nobility—of purely material things. The Fathers of the Church, too, were consistent in their opposition to the Gnostics, with their fanatical, abstract hatred of nature and flesh. Thomas, in his turn, is familiar (from Aristotle) with a concept of matter whose entelechy can carry the Idea *(forma)* right up to the point of man himself. Only when the order of angels, and the rest of fictitious transcendence beyond them, is reached, does matter (and with it nature) cease to play a part. Up till then there are only *formae inhaerentes,* materialized forms, not *formae separatae.* Thomas was well aware of the apocalyptic dimension, but he could still write the significant words: *"Gratia naturam non tollit, sed perficit"* (Grace does not destroy nature, but perfects it).

Here too, though, no way is left open for human finality actually to *realize* itself in the cosmic dimension—to come down to earth there, so to speak—not even in the *absconditum* of the cosmos. Nowhere does nature so much as cast its shadow over man's concerns, as it does in the astral myths—especially in those which are so strangely transparent. Nature

225

here is a thing of the past, a preparatory step. Or, at the very most, it may be admitted at Christmas and Easter to the lowest rung of being, where it can "celebrate the Christological mysteries unawares."

The attitude taken here by later thinkers becomes clear when one observes their calm unconcern for the Out-there and all its magic. This is primarily a matter of aesthetics, vis-a-vis the beautiful in the forms of nature. These belong to the Non-ego, and consequently *Fichte*, with his complete rethinking of the primacy of man, had no time for them at all. *Kant*, on the other hand, though he would not allow an Out-there independent of consciousness, was equivocal when it came to feelings about beauty and nobility. Beauty came to man not so much from the positive realm of his "spiritual" constructs, but from "landscape" and the "beauty of nature." The artist was therefore a man of genius when he "worked as nature works," not when he followed rules, or even when he enjoyed the "favor of the gods" or of a logos-like spirit of inspiration. Nature, rather than art, is the measure of beauty; but this does not lead back to the old attitude to the stars. The nobility of storm, sea and mountain lies in their ability to crush us down and at the same time raise us up; for in doing so they give us a "foretaste of our future liberty." So the beauty of nature leads back to a moral logos-element in man, while at the same time remaining true to its roots in nature itself.

All this was changed round again by *Hegel*, with his radical pan-logos attitude. The nature-spirit relationship fell back into its biblical state, with repercussions far beyond the aesthetic sphere. Art stood squarely above nature, which was no more than a "bacchanalian god, unbridled and uncontrolled, except in death." And the earth lay "like a giant on his death-bed at our feet," felled by the "breath of the spirit," and utterly future-less. Hegel even goes so far as to say in one place that "the only truth about matter is that it has no truth"—in comparison, that is, with the subjective spirit of the soul: in the realm of objective, absolute spirit the contrast was even greater. This is not to deny, of course, that his *World-structure* was an entirely immanent affair: a structure not of pure spirit but of *World*-spirit, of the spirit of *this* world. And in this respect the ostensible idealist became on the one hand a sort of retail dealer, and on the other hand (the wholesale side of things, so to speak) a devotee of *Spinoza*, the greatest cosmic thinker of the modern age. Hence the way in which he could cross Fichte's subjectivity with Spinoza's Pan, and mix the direct impact of "freedom" with an all-embracing, universal "substance."

Spinoza himself was the last European thinker to come under the influence of the astral myth—or what was left of it, often in cabbalistic dress. There is no sign in his thought of the biblical Other-world, beyond nature; its goodness and evil with respect to man might have been the mere product of false or inadequate affectivity and ideas. Nature takes on the form of an impersonal, coolly sovereign, absolute Fate, and it is driven back into God, where it has no cause beyond itself, and no finality. For finality is a matter of history and of logos and apocalypse, which are excluded from the *amor fati* of the philosopher of nature, and from the calm repose *sub specie aeternitatis* which alone is adequate for him. "Substance" is the last of the names by which the World-sun has been called—now the sun stands at its zenith and casts no shadows. For Spinoza's pantheism is an everlasting *sequi ex* of Euclidian regularity: the astral emanation, as it were, of substantial space into the particular, derived forms of its world. In short, all motion here is equally repose. A cosmos of unparalleled proportions has ousted even the thought of an Exodus-logos, swamping it in the absolute space of a Universe-God, who is timeless and who stretches infinitely through the already over-filled dimensions of Pan—of a Pan whose place is the still supremely astral sphere of the Around-us, not one that is simply another "attribute" of the universal substance. Spinoza's doctrine, then, gives a new lease of life to the cosmic system in its opposition to open-ended time and to the Exodus-logos which comes from, and ends in, man. Nowhere, in the polarity between Eschaton and world, is the Eschaton so remote.

There is still room here, however, for discussion about the topos of nature in pneuma, and above all about pneuma in the *final state* of nature: in short, about the *Kingdom of a logos that is by no means exclusively caught up in itself.* The problem arises of an *entirely re-converted* sort of nature-substance, open to an eschatological logos-kingdom: of a substance no longer drifting blindly without place or space in some "noo-logical" stratosphere, and one which takes the place of an empty idealism built on the mere idea of an idea. One, finally, whose realized being would not be confined to the Around-us of nature, for it would be the actual World-substance itself. Nature, in its profound disparity within human finality, right down to the remotest hidden tendencies of man, unquestion-ably takes up an unwarranted place in the world around us. For human finality is not content to aim haphazardly at the astral regions; it wants to make contact with more than pure Pan. Despite this, however, the world outside and independent of man is far from being *toto caelo* disparate from him, especially in his depths. Long before any question of "humanizing nature" can arise, the straightforward existence of workable raw-material, and the far more breath-taking phenomenon of natural beauty and nobility (which involve an element of response), shows a side of things which differs radically from the cold-shoulder (if it can even be called that) of disparity. A consequence of this is that Goethe, following Spinoza, could evolve a pantheism entirely unaware of its own Utopian depths; one that could rejoice in the humanizing of its univer-sal nature as though *Natura sive deus* were already realized.

The physical processes and structures of the world, as well as the history of man, can undoubtedly be seen as thoroughly experimental, when account is taken of the element of dis-parity always present there. And, when that is done, the raw-material of matter is no longer a dead lump of stuff, but is open to the more genuine Aristotelian definition of matter as the substratum of *"dynamei on,"* of "being-in-possibility"—a definition which is by no means the ultimate in speculation. The eschatological logos, too, the logos that is not concerned with this world at all, actually places the Utopia of new heaven and new earth in this world—despite all its dallying with a purely spiritual un-worldliness. It places it in a mythically and apocalyptically exploded world, but one which, unlike its predecessor, belongs in the realm of nature, and one whose topos has remained within the fully logos-mythical but also meta-*physical* framework of an Eschaton of New Jerusalem. There is no moon or sun there, that is true—the Son of Man is the only lamp in that city; but it is a city built on the territory, in the firmament, of a "nature" that has been both annihilated to form the "Kingdom" and unveiled in all the splendor of its eschatological truth.

That is the *final non-alternative between cosmos and logos* proposed by the new, antithetical, Exodus-revealing *Genesis images* of the Apocalypse. And yet, on this very different plane, *Natura sive deus* seems at last to find its home here too—the home where it is realized and achieves "perfection." One can say in fact without any undertone of myth that the *world as Home* has come: that state which realizes both the heritage of the world around us and the *Novum* of Home, whose subjects are the assembled company of the unveiled countenance. The voice on Patmos may seem exceedingly remote, and its Apocalypse very much confined to human space. The elements of raving fantasy there may seem to mix strangely with those other elements which bore fruit in the *Urbs christiana* (rather than in the cosmos). But nowhere is the Omega of Christian utopianism so untranscendent and at the same time so all-transcending, as in the "New Jerusalem" of Revelations 21. 23.

Religion is full of utopianism, as is evident above all in the Omega which lies at its heart: the Omega of a "free nation on free land"—of *Civitas Christi in natura ut illae civitatis extensio*. This is a realm where the Docetism of pure spirit cannot live, and where the world is *totally* transformed, so that man is no longer burdened with it as with a stranger.

37. The Strange, Strictly Non-Parallel Breakthrough of Both Man-Centered and Materialistic Systems into the "Divine Transcendence," which They Replace

The Within, also known as the soul, is often taken up with its own concerns. It is certainly connected intimately with the body, but not in such a way that its invisible life takes visible, bodily form. It has often been set in contrast to the tangible world outside, as something whose presence lies within itself, as opposed to something that is strewn spatially around man in the world out there. Idealism sees the Way as leading mysteriously within; materialism sees it as a path free from mystery, under the exclusive guiding light of the Out-there, and leading back to the mechanical roots of being.

But Feuerbach did not want to remain an idealist—on the contrary, he was already on his way to the words "Man is what he is"—when he said that his first thought had been God, his second spirit, and his third and last man. This could hardly be considered the clear explanation of a materialist; rather, it was itself in need of the light of mechanics. Marx, too, under the influence of Feuerbach, gave pride of place historically to man and human explanations: "To be radical is to grasp things at their roots. But the root of all things is man." And even later on, when he educed this motto from the mere abstract genus "man," and reduced this genus to an "ensemble of social relationships," human perspectives by no means disappeared from the materialism which then arose on the wider socio-economic plane. Historical materialism succeeded the purely scientific variety, and a dialectics of human productivity grew up alongside that of purely mechanical movements and forces.

But to go further—the juxtaposition of the anthropological

and the materialistic (of "soul" and external matter) may well give rise to astonishment even when the concept of matter is not the common bourgeois one of a mechanistic lump: a concept which, despite the later acknowledgement of sub-atomic energy, cannot even be deemed a relic of the astral myth—except inasmuch as it rules out the presence and activity of man, let alone of the Son of Man, in matter. The history of materialism has, however, brought other concepts of matter to light, besides the "dead," unqualitative, mechanistic ones. Democritus himself taught that the "soul" was composed of special "fire-atoms," and Epicurus qualified Democritus' mechanical "determinism" with a "free fall of atoms"—a deviation from the "straight-line fall" of mechanics, based, so to speak, on free will. Aristotle brought out the crucial idea, only recently understood again, of real, objective possibility, according to which matter, apart from being the mechanical condition for phenomena to arise *kata to dynaton* ("according to possibility"), was also, above all, the *dynamei on,* the "being-in-possibility" itself. Unfortunately, this was still thought of in passive terms: matter was as undefined as a lump of wax, and the "active, formative idea" impressed the particular form into it like a seal. Very soon, however, an "Aristotelian left-wing" arose, discarding the passive notion of matter and replacing it with the active element of the in-forming idea. Matter thus became the *mater-ia,* the Mother of all things: the absolute, self-fructifying, self-sufficient *natura naturans* of the whole *natura naturata* that was the world. The Arabian Aristotelians, Avicenna and Averroës, were especially clear on this point. Their basic tenet was that development is simply *eductio formarum ex materia:* the eduction of forms from a nature that is no longer passive and unqualitative, but is also almost *free from the need for a transcendent Father God.*

This was the point of origin of the idea of a completely immanent World-substance, whose "life" stretched from Paracelsus, Giordano Bruno and Spinoza to Goethe: a substance which was by no means alien to man, but was the cosmic counterpart of him who for Bruno was *uomo eroico* and for Paracelsus *vulcanus interior;* one, finally, which could penetrate into the former realms of a discarded transcendence, and at least polemically (through pan-theism) participate in them. Hence Goethe's words: "What sort of God would that be who merely gives the world a push from outside . . . it is fitting for him to contain nature within himself and himself within nature." This use of the term "nature" is as much as to say that whoever sees *natura naturans* sees the Father, for this nature and the Father are one. And there is also a *subject* here, moving the world from within—a subject of *nature*, not stated in anthropological terms, but certainly in terms free from transcendence.

The great right-wing Aristotelian Thomas Aquinas entirely rejected the idea that matter could have a place in creative form. Instead, he taught that *forma inhaerens* (informed matter), being a "remnant of earth," is found only up to the level of man, who is still a creature of earth, a unity of soul and body. The angels, lying between men and God, are already pure *formae separatae;* and as for "that which men call God," The Lord of heaven, he is utterly free from matter: it cannot, even as *natura naturans,* penetrate his autocratic transcendence. It cannot do so even as Spinoza's Pan which, while being no Son of Man, could almost say: I stand in the place of the Father, *sub specie substantiae.*

But, long before this, Plotinus, the radical transcendentalist, had posited a *hylē noētikē,* a spiritual matter, reaching up to the level of the highest *ousia* or essence. And the Spanish Jew, Avicebron, in the tradition stretching from this paradoxical Neo-Platonism to Giordano Bruno, held to the existence of earthly spirits even higher than the angels, which were themselves by no means exclusively supra-terrestrial beings; he would even have given matter a place in God if that had been possible. In these shadowy echoes of a non-mechanistic materialism, then, "soul" and the allegedly unqualitative Out-there of matter are no longer simple alternatives. At least with Avicenna and Averroës, logos and cosmos occasionally exchange their respectively anthropological and pansophist faces, in their *antithesis to transcendence.* And the Stoa had, long before, incorporated a *"logos spermatikos"* into its crypto-materialism, as a life and direction-giving principle. Though when it took on Christian dress, the logos could no longer allow of an Omega in the shape of the present cosmos, for only the astral myth paid absolute homage to that; and such an idea would also rule out any cosmic *apocalypse.*

The Utopian memories and yearnings conjured up by the notion of the Son of Man naturally introduced in a more radical way than ever the idea of a *Utopian Pan* into the hypostasis of transcendence. For these memories were deeply rooted in subjectivity: in a light which crossed all frontiers of status, and could burn its way even through *natura sive deus.* Rebellious atheism, however, has achieved far wider recognition in the form of *non Deus sed Pan* than in the form of heretically genuine, subject-laden Christianity. The only thing is this—that the last word, literally, in the not unconnected field of anti-transcendence and emancipation, has never in fact gone to Spinoza with his solution of *amor fati* as opposed to that of *Behold, I make all things new.* For this last logos-solution stands far and away above any *natura naturans* or any "subject of nature," and far above all the determinisms and dependencies of the ancient astral myth.

SOURCES
OF LIFE-FORCE

38. The Only Safe Handhold: Openness

Weakness wavers to and fro. Close to it stands cowardice, always evasive, lest once it be held to its word. And sheer soft-headedness is not necessarily very far away—the soft-headed are always unaccountable. Next in line are those who always want to know the score, and will only act when there is nothing to risk. They simply fail the test when things are not quite safe. For some things do demand commitment: some things present a threat, and a challenge, by the very fact of their incompleteness. And that makes them particularly unpalatable to the cowardly—to those who are always ready to bask in the warmth of other men's convictions, no matter whose.

There are times when the waverer stops wavering. He needs something to hold on to, and thinks he has found it. But when his prop and stay is not that of firm completeness he is lost, like a man who has accepted payment in a coin he cannot cash. Then, when times change and the market drops, he turns his back very quickly on his already tottering loyalties. Something that can easily and comfortably be believed in, and learned blindly off by heart, is all the more readily ditched when even a part of it fails. The safe stronghold then seems too shaky for any more than lip-service. The conventional prop of regulations is a variation on this same theme. "It is written . . ."; "The Party is never wrong . . ."; "a gentleman's word is his bond . . .": none of it will stand up to a single jolt, above all to a jolt of thought. The prop that is made in one piece, without core and outer cladding, will break in one piece when the pressure becomes too great.

The only thing one can really hold on to is the search for a handhold—the constant feeling that one is on the way to finding it, and the faithful following of the signs. Only that can stand up to disappointment—indeed it needs it if it is to grow in truth. There is no place for children here; they need ready-cooked food from on high. On this road discontent lasts best; its hope is in itself a handhold for the hoper. The best things must be left to simmer slowly, in anticipation, if their promise is ever to be enjoyed.

There is something there still open to us in the distance. But the gap has not yet been closed, and to fill it falsely is to provide a treacherous handhold that will lead to an even greater fall—that will lead one to one's knees, gambling on a false and fabricated trust, only to have one's hopes shattered along with one's ready-made faith. As if somewhere, somehow, things could be good in themselves, without the constant, ever-undecided struggle. Undecided, that is, except for its all the more decisive determination to stay, despite everything, in open ferment: its determination to remain an open, traversible Way, foreshadowing the future. Out of the future shadows on this Way there comes a continuous call; but no more faith is needed than faith in discontented hope. Such hope is active: it contains the seeds of a conscious, outward-reaching pact with the objective pole of *tendency.*

This is admittedly less than being in really good, safe hands; but it is more than any prescribed (and therefore false) handhold can provide, and it has a far higher view of man. It is

235

better, too, than any of those ready-made, pre-flavored foods
that only go to ruin one's real appetite—the appetite for more.

39. True Enlightenment Is Neither Trivial Nor Shallow

The thinking man will not be taken in. He will always break
away and begin afresh, laying aside the ghost of old ideas,
rejecting the bonds of custom and taboo and the hypocrisy of
the good old days which were really not good at all. The bonds
of faith are well-known in this context for gathering moss, and
for binding men to obsolete forms of rule.

It is another matter when these still extant forms and
structures are seen as unsettled debts. Then they wait for us in
the future rather than bind us to the past. Certain aspects of
Christianity can in this way seem paradoxically familiar to the
emancipated man. He seems to meet them anew and encounter
their binding force afresh rather than merely remember them
as a constant feature of the past. And then it is the turn neither
of history, nor of the arrears of semi-disillusionment, but of his
emancipation itself to show its Christological and Messianic
paces. There is no question here of a mere heritage, like that of
some great cultural achievement whose power and depth is
tied up with a surfeit of religious ideology. The re-encounter
we are speaking of is simply autochthonous: not even freedom
can help finding within itself images taken from the Exodus, or
from the destruction of Babylon, or from the "Kingdom" of
the free. Lenin was certainly right when he attacked the
semi-disillusioned, not to mention the smugglers of reactionary
contraband, in the following terms: "It is one thing if an
agitator speaks like this [that is, in traditional religious lan-
guage] in order to be understood more easily; in order to find a
starting point for his argument, and a mode of expression
familiar to the under-developed masses, so that his views may
make more impact. But it is quite another if a writer actually
starts preaching the 'construction of God,' or a 'God-

constructing' socialism . . . In the former case the thesis 'socialism is religion' serves as a bridge from religion to socialism; in the latter it passes from socialism to religion" (*On the Relation of the Workers' Party to Religion*, 1909). The truth of these words lies in their accurate appraisal of the Marxist fellow-traveler—a breed which resembles a hen with egg-shell still stuck to it, or a half-grown centaur with fore and aft of Church and Party joined only in perpetual "dialog." It is a very different matter, in fact, when real, genuine disillusionment encounters the ancient rebellious archetypes of religion, and does so precisely at the level of godlessness. That can be a very significant encounter, for the disillusionment will lift these archetypes out of the quagmire of oppressive myth and open them up, associating them with its own disruptive essence. Not that the Church of the ruling classes gains thereby; on the contrary, she has always burned heretics quite as willingly, if not more so, than atheists. Which is understandable in view of the fact that heretics have often taken their stand on the early Church—on the good soil of those days and the bad conscience now built on it—and that endangers the Church at its core. The Holy Synod of Russia was far less troubled by the importation of Haeckel's "world riddle" than by Tolstoy's rebellious recollections of the early Church of Dostoevsky's Prince Myshkin, for these attacked the Church on her own ground and pulled down her inner bastions. Marxism, on the other hand, although it has shared very widely in the sort of distortion that accompanied the transformation of Christianity into the religion of the Roman state, actually achieves the fullness of its *Totum* when it encounters the archetypes, already implicit in itself, of "freedom," "Kingdom" and "mastered fate." Nineteenth-century positivism and naturalism did not help it here, for though they excluded transcendence they also excluded one of the life-principles of Marxism: its forward-looking *transcendere,* its *process.* This process can be described as the possible liberation and identification of the history-making subject, and, as such, it contains *archetypes of freedom* more ultimate than the old re-

237

ligious ones; or, rather, these same religious archetypes are now the really ultimate ones, but in a different sense—that of the ultimate *aim* they can now reflect.

They are the product of men free from all delusions, even happy ones. Lip-serving Christians would be useless here: "What do you think? A man had two sons; and he went to the first and said, 'Son, go and work in the vineyard today.' And he answered, 'I will not'; but afterwards he repented and went. And he went to the second and said the same; and he answered, 'I go, sir,' but did not go" (Matt. 21. 28 ff.). This was a parable Jesus spoke to the High Priest and to the elders of the Church; and he added the gloss: "The tax collectors and the harlots go into the kingdom of God before you." In another place he said: "You will know them by their fruits . . . On that day many will say to me, 'Lord, Lord, did we not do many mighty works in your name?' And then will I declare to them, 'I never knew you; depart from me, you evildoers'" (Matt. 7. 20 ff.). The chief fruits by which, today as always, the good news can be known are those of genuine socialist upheaval. But not even the tree which bears that fruit need nowadays grow on the traditional religious ground. It grows, rather, in the garden of the Nay-sayer, in the land of atheism, where the subject lives who has thrown out of his house not only the fear but the whole chimera of transcendence, including its hypostasized patriarchalism.

That does not mean, however, that the tree in question now grows in the soil of *triviality,* which so often follows from a fixed and static enlightenment. Nor does it tower up into a sky of *nihilism* rather than one of transcendence—the sort of nihilism which can spread so dangerously from an atheism that has no implications, no contact with the freedom movement among men and its fundamental stake in the realm of hope. Triviality is the miserable result, and nihilism the diabolical one, when a disillusioned transcendence at the same time removes the *transcendere* that is grounded in the Utopian depths of man and world. Triviality can do away with fear, but only at the price of general atrophy—and with nihilism the

price is the even higher one of despair. *Concrete* disillusionment, however, ends more in bewilderment than in triviality:
bewilderment before the Not-yet-being of what no man has
seen or understood. And, rather than in nihilism, it ends up in
the not unfounded hope that that particular philosophy will not
have the last word after all. Nihilism was an infection of the
decaying bourgeoisie, but apart from possessing the reflexes of
that downfall it undoubtedly had premisses in the cosmological
purposelessness of mechanistic materialism. Being is senseless, however, if it is merely the circular motion of matter;
the very absoluteness of this form of disillusionment brings it
to its knees in a heap of atoms. As opposed to nihilism,
dialectical materialism (with the notice above its door: No
mechanists allowed) admits into its system a whole series of
starting-points and factors in human productivity, apart from
purely physico-chemical ones: cells, for instance, and individual productivity, and the thoroughly qualitative interlock-
ing of infra-structure and super-structure. When it comes to
explaining the world in terms of the world, it can call on the
process of a continuous shift from quantity to quality. And
above all it is aware of the effective *problem* of a Kingdom of
Freedom that is qualified as human. All of this is an antidote to
triviality and nihilism; it is the activation of religion's non-
opiate, non-oppressive elements. For when dialectical materialism hears and grasps the import of the mighty voice of
tendency in this world which it has made its own, and when it
calls on men to work for the goal revealed by that voice, it
shows decisively that it has taken hold of the living soul of a
dead religion, the *transcendere* without transcendence, the
subject-object of a well-founded hope. That is what lives on
when the opium, the fool's paradise of the Other-world, has
been burnt away to ashes. That remains as a call, signalling the
way to the fulfilled This-world of a new earth.

And when the gods of taboo and fear have been abolished
there is room for the advent of a mystery that is *adequate to
the fearless man*. Respect before this mystery now takes the
place of fear: respect, so foreign to triviality and nihilism,

239

reflecting within itself the fearless acceptance of the strange and sinister, the fully human acceptance of the unthinkable. With respect there also comes nobility, bringing with it a first breath of future freedom. For nobility is proper to a *transcendere* in which there is no self-alienation, and to its correlative, the latent power of a hoped-for resurrection. There is no refuge here for fear and ignorance—this is the territory of hope and of its strong will and ability to know. *Messianism is the burning mystery of all revolutionary, all fulfilled enlightenment.* When man is called upon to act morally, heaven becomes an empty, distant thing—even in its capacity as guaranty-fund for the reward of otherwise motiveless good deeds. If he is to maintain his grip on the only enduring *Summum bonum* of human finality, man must be able to see the Kingdom of heavenly freedom as his *geo*-graphical Utopia too. Atheism is the presupposition of any concrete Utopia, but concrete Utopia is also the remorseless consequence of atheism. Atheism-with-concrete-Utopia is at one and the same time the annihilation of religion and the realization of its heretical hope, now set on human feet. Concrete Utopia is in its turn the philosophy and praxis of the *tendency* latent in the world— latent in matter which has been qualified with ultimate direction. This is small enough to allow no room for self-alienation and large enough—Omega enough—to give some remote sense of possible this-worldly reality to the boldest of Utopian schemes.

These ideas belong to the frontiers of Messianism but, rightly understood, they imply the drive to surpass itself and achieve totality which is immanent in the work of human liberation.

40. *Enlightenment and Atheism Do Not Overthrow the "Satanic" with the God-Hypostasis*

In early times evil was not seen as weak. Primitive life was too deeply threatened by it, even in its ghostly manifestations.

That all changed, however, when man gained confidence and no longer looked on the Out-there as quite so dangerous. He gave up his childish ways and dared to use his mind.

This is above all true of those times which we call "enlightened"—the very word means to make clear, to dissipate the fog. And of all these periods the Enlightenment of the eighteenth century was the most self-possessed. It was the fruit of the struggle of the bourgeois will to break free from the long ages of stultifying and oppressive gloom and to reach for the light. On the whole, at that time, life seemed pleasant and friendly. When the people broke free from the lying grasp of prince and priest the scales fell *en masse* from their eyes. Obvious evil in the form of poverty, illness, wickedness and the occult was viewed either as a delusion or, at the very most, as a relic of medievalism. This resulted in a very salutary devaluation of the general fear of ghosts, and in an easing-off of the horrors of witch-hunts, which were still a very real evil. In these matters enlightenment was the sworn enemy of the monsters of night, and the wise man was called on to put aside its "fearful temptations." The Lisbon earthquake of 1755 broke into this best of all possible worlds with a wave of revulsion: evil could no longer be the mere absence of good. But only the old, despotic Bible, so strongly rejected by the Enlightenment, could provide an explanation: this great rift in the peaceful order of nature was a punishment decreed by an otherwise gentle heavenly Father.

But the Lisbon earthquake receded, albeit rather slowly, from the scene, and a general mood of optimism prevailed up to and beyond the French Revolution, as the tribute paid by an enlightenment *à tout prix* to the rulers' need for peace. So although the so-called satanic element did not fall out of literary fashion, it did to a great extent (more than its theistic counterpart) fall out of philosophical use. For this philosophical enlightenment did not really go in for the technique of denunciation—the technique of high-lighting the Anti-light in order the better to grapple with it. The optimism of the day saw evil rather as something small and weak, a mere blemish on the beauty of an otherwise perfect world. Even concepts like hallucination and aggressive drive, however, proposed from the *subjective* point of view as grappling points in man's basic struggle with evil, and concepts like oppression and war or the inhumanity of class-controlled means of production and trade, proposed from the *objective,* social point of view—even these farther-reaching ideas are fundamentally inadequate in the face of a phenomenon like Auschwitz. They can neither explain it causally, nor enable it to be assumed *post factum* into human speech. Schopenhauer was the only thinker of the nineteenth century to undertake the transposition of his "Thing-in-itself," the will-to-live, into thoroughly diabolical terms; but even he could not, in his description of the night of terror into which the World-as-will was plunged, achieve quite the same consistent pitch of speechless, eloquent horror that Dante, and Dante alone, had reached with his "Abandon hope, all ye who enter here," inscribed on the portals of his inferno. Even Schopenhauer thought he could banish the misery of the world to the realm of pure appearances by virtue of a merely individual denial of the will to live.

It is, in fact, a common occurrence that the generation which strives for light should show its hatred of the darkness by reducing its dimensions, or passing it over, or at least relativizing it to such an extent that one might be led to think the Enlightenment had already been achieved—*toto inferno* as well as *toto caelo.* A special case of this is the fairy tale—that early example of an enlightenment which could reduce evil to the Evil One, a devil whose very stupidity was calculated to be a source of encouragement. On another plane it was also due to the Enlightenment that, in the great works of literature and philosophy which followed it, the figure of the Adversary should be treated as undualistically and unmanicheistically as possible, being reduced and relativized to a broken, defeated collaborator in a final, pre-arranged victory.

In this almost universal glow of optimism, the undefeated "Behold, it was very good" of biblical theocracy rang out into an atmosphere of purely world-centered good-naturedness, for

Hegel, following the Enlightenment, had localized goodness as entirely immanent in the world. But even apart from all this secularization (which in itself was alien to its spirit), the Enlightenment had no room in its immediate scheme of things—not even a reserve place—for the sort of evil that could appear at Lisbon or Auschwitz. It was, then, almost automatic that the growing disbelief in God should be accompanied by a growing disbelief in his adversary—and there lay the problem. Even Voltaire's Candide found it easier after the Lisbon disaster to attribute real existence to demons than to consider realistic the enlightened optimism which could see the world as pure day. However, this reduction of the Evil One to the point of invisibility did not by any means put him out of work. For the satanic is a far firmer plank than the theistic, when angels are seldom seen and the God of all creation is simply undetectable.

Light that brings nothing but beauty can deceive. It is certainly a good antidote, however, to the grumbling and grousing that just want to assert their own wretchedness. The Enlightenment was a very salutary and human thing, though far from being either comforting or beautifying, when it quenched the funeral pyres with water which did not come from weeping, and put a stop to all the devilish deceit and superstition of the day. Revulsion was consigned to the realm of stupidity, as were the priests who preyed on the stupid masses, and in every quarter of the sky the clear light of day broke through. Yet in all this there was a very short-sighted confidence: there was the optimistic notion that man was good and nature perfect wherever corruption and torment could be kept at bay. This notion served as a sort of protective enclosure for all it touched. The world seemed idyllic, and its carefree harmony was reflected in the *dolce vita* of the aristocracy. Leibnitz, with his great and energetic mind, had conceived of the present world as no more than the best of all *possible* worlds, but Shaftesbury, the simple optimist, saw things differently: the world was a constant harmonious interplay of things in continual ascent to higher forms of finality.

243

This unmitigated faith in progress ran on into the last century, a far less noble age, blinding men all the while to the countless manifestations of disruption and emptiness whose negativity was itself by no means immediately negated. It trampled on over flattened, barren cornfields, over wars that were far from suddenly becoming "locomotive forces of world history," and over a whole world of such things as Auschwitz, where no sign of redeemer or savior showed.

But evil had already made it clear that it was not in its interests to make much noise. It was content, while still on the way, to appear in the harmless guise given it by the Enlightenment. "You see a man like other men"—Mephisto's words are quite harmless and quite within the law; there is no sign of the cloven hoof or of the apparatus of witchcraft, no hint of taboo or of the sort of ritual that accompanied God's gala-appearance in the thornbush—"Do not come near; put off your shoes from your feet, for the place on which you are standing is holy ground" (Ex. 3. 5). Faust's meeting with Mephistopheles differs from Moses' meeting with Yahweh: the ceremonial of Satan is very different from that of God. The term "diabolical" has found vogue again in recent literature and history. Here one can clarify its meaning phenomenologically: this pasteboard figure is most successful when it appears for what it is, without making any metaphysical demands at all. For the "diabolical," in its "essence," does not "want" one to believe in it at all, and in this it is opposed to the "divine," which even in its polytheistic, let alone its monotheistic manifestations, "demands" implicit faith—and needs it. For the so-called "divine" is entirely ordered to faith, whereas for evil there is as much empirical evidence as (and more than) one needs. Even in terms of *concrete phenomenology*, let alone of a mere *eidetic* survey, it has no need of faith—quite the opposite, in fact.

How, then, did this dilemma affect the *a-theism* of the Enlightenment, its most brilliant blow for freedom? Blind fear was now, for the first time, deposed, and with it went all the scandalous obscurantism which had served the divinely established authorities of feudalism so well. The Lord-God hypostasis was over-thrown, and men could now see and criticize their own immaturity and their self-alienation. This humanistic, de-theocratizing function of atheism was so far-reaching and clear, and so different from the equally staggering potentialities of optimism when it comes to the emancipation of the satanic, that even when, as with Nietzsche, the atheist became confused with the Antichrist, the innate power of atheism to break all encapsulating boundaries, including those of the inferno, could still force its way to the top. The result of this, in Nietzsche, was an atheism whose bold Utopian tone was due precisely to the death of faith in God: "We are, perhaps, still too close to the *immediate consequences* of this event—and, contrary to what one might think, these consequences, its consequences for us, are not at all sad and gloomy. They are, in fact, like a new sort of light that is difficult to describe; they are like a new sort of happiness, relief, light-heartedness, encouragement, dawn . . . In the event, we philosophers and 'free spirits' feel ourselves bathed in the warm rays of a new dawn; when we hear the news that 'the old God is dead' our hearts overflow with thankfulness and astonishment, with premonition and expectation. The horizon may not be bright, but it does at last seem free; our ships can sail out again to face danger; every risk of knowledge is now once more allowed; the *sea*, our *sea* lies open before us again—perhaps there has never been such an 'open sea' before" (Nietzsche, *The Joyful Wisdom*).

But, with this statement, Nietzsche (and even more so all abstract atheism) shows to an astonishing, thought-provoking extent, something of the same precarious minimalization which characterized the Enlightenment's attitude to everything it wanted to deny—whether this was hanging on to the satanic or to the theistic plank, or had jumped from one to the other. For where in this simple eradication of the God-hypostasis was there still room for its use as an apologia for every sort of tutelage, every sort of hierarchy, every sort of static master-serf relationship? And where, above all, was

245

there still room for the great Opponent, the Zeus-archetype of lordship who, though veiled in transcendence and myth, was never thought of as a merely optional extra, for without him Prometheus (and, *mutatis mutandis,* Job) would never have been able to make his archetypal rebellion at all. It is in fact quite clear that the simple, optimistic denial of evil in the world can find a ready-made refuge in a certain type of atheism—the atheism that will also place beyond all discussion (not just beyond purely mythological discussion) the question of evil within the concept of God and its transcendent hypostasization.

The result of this is a general loss of depth on the part of the Negative, even in *metaphysics.* And metaphysics, far from having any interests in myth (or its hypostasization), goes straight to the foundations of fear and salvation which lie in the *depths* behind and beyond the world. There is no room here for any exaggeration or isolation in the treatment of evil, as was the fashion in the all too elevated cult of despair, or in Adorno's jargon about the "non-actuality of the good." And metaphysics also goes much further than the mere grumbling and grousing we have spoken about, with its purely negative dialectics which both Marx and Hegel were forced to relativize, so far removed was it from the real class-struggle, so remote from being so much as an "algebra of revolution." *Personified despair* is useless here, but so is its opposite, the *personified trust* purveyed throughout the ages by authority both ecclesiastical and civil, with its thoroughly conformist "Be comforted." The power of this pre-ordained confidence manifests itself within the clerical apparatus in the hierarchy of ownership and the ownership of the hierarchy, and this has precisely the same effects as defeatism—the revolution is suppressed. Neither of the two exaggerations, however—the one stemming from idle negativity, the other from guaranteed positivity, leaves the narrow confines of a space which, for Nietzsche, had been burst asunder by atheism. In fact the contrary is true, even when all static systems are verbally rejected. And although both despair and confidence are prepared to pay verbal homage to the openness of a hope that is dedicated to the struggle, they view it on the one hand as a mere decoration, a sort of weak but delicate perfume, and on the other hand as a sort of gilt-edged picture of providence tacked for purely contemplative purposes to the end of the traditional sermon. In contrast with this, and because it does not see its premises as already agreed with (as do both depair and confidence), hope itself concentrates its attention on the realm of the Not-yet-achieved, on the Not-yet of the achieved, and does so precisely for the sake of the struggle—for the sake of winning the historical process. All really *tested hope,* therefore, and all really *militant optimism,* must go through the ever more searching and destructive experience of the historical process, brought about by the powers of anti-Utopia ranged against those of the Utopia of light. And the darkly pondering, ever-searching earth joins forces here with our non-contemplative activity in the constant quest for salvation.

In view of the fact that evil does not want men to believe in it, it might be useful here, and important for the real fight against its mythical hypostasis (more so, at any rate, than the usual loss of depth, the usual reduction of its dimensions), to take note of some words from *The Spirit of Utopia:* "The principle holding us here in its bungling and vengeful hand, restricting us, persecuting us, blinding us: the spider; the eating and being eaten; the poisonous scorpion; the visiting angel; the demon of chance, misfortune, death; the stench of murdered humanity; the homelessness of sense and meaning; the banal, impenetrable wall separating us from any sign of providence; the Magician of 'pious' pan-logism—this principle *cannot* be the same one that at one moment proclaims itself our future judge, and at the next presents itself as one who has long guarded us in the ways of unfathomable, supra-rational reason, and who, despite our sinful pride which caused the world to 'fall,' has long cherished us in his heart." To speak unmythologically, the Negative is present at the heart of Process-as-such, motivating it as a process of healing salvation; for there would be no process at all if there were not something there

247

that should not be there, something to serve as a constant threat. What would become of the militant dialectical primacy of the principle of hope if there were not a highly actual (though not as yet decisive) presence of Nothing (that is, of possible total defeat) to set it off as the *postulate* of All (that is, of possible total fulfillment)? Or again, meta-religious enlightenment (the enlightenment of the *object itself, not just of awareness of the object)* also implicitly involves the presence of evil behind it and around it and ahead of it; for it is not content just to be enlightened in itself, but seeks to banish darkness altogether in a struggle which defies comparison. And this struggle will be just as much frustrated by any attempt to make an absolute of the Negative as of the Positive—as if the historical process of "naturalizing man and humanizing nature" were somehow already lost or already won.

In fact, however, there is enormous Utopian potentiality in the world: potentiality for an Optimum educed from an undefeated Negative. When atheism drove out the hypostasized reality of Lord and Master from the *topos* of the 'divine," it opened up this *topos* to receive the one and only final mystery, the pure mystery of man. In Christianity, and even *post Christum,* this mystery is called: our Kingdom.

41. Moral, and Final, Sources of Life-Force

That which lives and moves will begin over and over again—will begin from out of itself. For it has a pulse even if it does not yet have a heart. And in this constant pulsing rhythm, now, now, always now, the day flows by as if it knew no interruption. The healthy man, above all the healthy man, will then live his day in a single carefree stream of life, not stopping and starting, but bearing its burdens calmly.

Outside his body, however, many factors stop and start at will, and prevent him from living calmly, as his body does, from day to day. So there is no question really of a constant stream of momentless uninterruption. Nor is it any good to say that one lives because one lives, not in order to live. Shock after shock wells up from a no longer gently flowing (or, more likely, entirely submerged) Where-to and What-for, breaking in on one's consciousness and suddenly demanding real life-force, real courage, which must come from sources that can no longer be taken for granted. This can happen even to the healthy man when the normally friendly but quite unpredictable run of life suddenly fails him in a crisis.

When this happens in capitalist society, the have-nots have to take the consequences of never being any more than unmarketable goods—the goods called "labor force," which they constitute, and which, in hard times, are no longer in demand. And even in prosperous times, when the labor force is used, this reduction of the exploited to saleable goods leads to such self-alienation, to such a waste-land of human existence, that a very special life-force is called for if the oppressive, crippling daily round is to be endured. —Standing every morning half asleep in front of the factory gates; leaving it every evening, exhausted and fed up with stereotyped, subalternated profit-making. And doing so just for a wage, a mere fraction of what the workers have produced, and one whose sole function is to produce more labor for the following day. The crippling work-circle is never left behind—it just grows tighter.

Even the better-off are alienated from themselves—Marx pointed that out. The difference is that in this alienation the capitalist feels himself confirmed as a capitalist and that alone: the loss of self, the waste-land is, so to speak, of a higher sort. Life can seem a poor, worthless thing even in the higher strata; the boredom of the man who is shielded from need and from being a mere cog can be just another form of long protracted death.

And, at the end of life, however "fulfilled" or "unfulfilled" it may be according to the sordid standards of class-distinction, there is the certainty of death (the American saying is: Hangmen also die . . .)—a highly inadequate end, generally breaking, only very rarely rounding off, the human life. Not even the suicide has turned his back on the will-for-more which lies at the heart of life; he seeks, rather, to liberate life from all its unfulfilled ideals and goals. As Schopenhauer said, he by no means contradicts the will to live a really *better* life, but, paradoxically, continues to affirm it; what he rejects is simply the conditions under which he has himself had to live. Apart from the suicide, however, perhaps even greater strength is needed to face up to the ordinary sort of death, in all its unchosen inevitability.

And even within the sheltered confines and shallower insights of daily life a leaden melancholy can arise, and then many people are in sore need of the so-called wings of life-force, the wings of energy and courage. For not all ages and all societies are so bursting with dissatisfaction and concrete plans for change that the laboring masses can take some clear, perhaps even spirited, steps to struggle up out of the oppression of a dull and grueling life. In fact, in order to forestall these outbreaks of the courage-to-contradict, every age in which dullness was the order of the day had had at least to make gestures towards providing a fleeting substitute for life-force in the form of circuses, a rubber-stamped sort of entertainment whose phantom figures really only served to bring more boredom. The idea being, of course, to come to rest in the bourgeois *juste milieu,* however crippling that might be—or also, perhaps, to provide a substitute for the "spiritual consolations" which no longer drew the crowds. But the real result of this was simply to bury the true sources of life-force in this *juste milieu,* however unforgettable they might remain in their urge to break through, and, above all, however unswerving might be the path by which they bear the moral In-spite-of to its summit, along with the final In-memory-of which surely carries no marshal's staff or bishop's crozier in its kit-bag, but rather the opposite: the invariant factor of a kingdom of rational beings which is more than just intelligible. Instead of this, however, one hears on every hand the false, capitulating tones of a morning prayer which, even to pious souls, can only really sound like Wilhelm Raabe's pungent travesty: "Lord, give me this day my daily illusion." But even then, though thoroughly beaten down, life-force stands not at the "Sisyphus" but at the "Waiting for Godot" level—that of waiting for an illusion. And in this very waiting, in the missing out on what would not be illusionary, there are surely still some signs of a life-force which must find the paradox of the In-spite-of not paradoxical but quite natural, quite understandable—along with the *Plus ultra* which in the present condition of the world is quite indispensable. In short, when life-force is not a pleasure it is a duty; and when it is not a duty it is the pleasure taken on earth in the still remote and absent goal to which life has started moving.

Whatever lives, lives out of itself, surpasses itself. The individual ego, aware only of itself, must not take itself too seriously—it will, anyway, die more than once in life, like the things that stand around it. The ego is no exception to that rule. The enduring element within us, the element which is not (in either sense of the word) in vain, does not adhere to our precious ego but comes from our still veiled and hidden depths—not from something taken as seriously as a private bank account. But this does not mean that the in-turned ego takes up residence within itself, as a higher form of being-just-so, a substitute for authentic frontier-existence. No mishap can destroy that altogether. So the *first real trickle* of life-force comes from that principle within us which makes us *stand up straight,* whether this is understood in an organic or a political or a moral way.

The Stoics recognized this principle and called it the capacity for independence. Not that there was any real fight for independence and openness in those times—but the principle still persevered through thick and thin, in the face of oppression and misfortune, as the *Hegemonikon,* the seat of manliness and resolution—*Impavidum ferient ruinae.* The Stoa did certainly tend to declaim a bit about all this, but still, the first stirrings of a moral life-force, the first signs of real spirit, have their source in the simple, age-old directive to lead an upright life. This did not do away with death, but neither did it capitulate in the face of failure, or of the axe, or fate. It did not yet point beyond imperturbability to the wings of indestructibility. But it did point to an utter scorn for death which in its Stoic form called for no fanaticism but rather simply refused to be disturbed in its depths of moral dignity. There was, of course, no deep-seated rebelliousness here, for the Stoa did not for a moment want to transcend the given world of man and nature. On the one hand this world was the "perfect city of Zeus," but on the other hand the wise man could really only put on a thick skin against its trials. Only with *Christianity* did the subject begin to become a thing of mystery—and then the outer world became a thing of darkness: the city of Zeus was laid in ruins and its good providence turned back into a demonic one, inimical to man. Christianity brought with it a resurgence of the attitude that no longer expects anything from the world, and did so despite its notion that man had been crippled by sin and was therefore unable any more to stand upright. It brought in a *transcendere* that was more than just internal, blasting a great hole through the famous Stoic constancy in life and death, and making way for the beating wings of a glory which, though still hidden within us, was, in the intentional order, entirely indestructible.

With that, *finality* came to join morality as a *second* source of life-force: the finality which lay in the courage to break free from this devil's guesthouse, this world. Nor was this courage inspired purely by the mythical wish-*mysterium* of Christ's ascension to a transcendent On-high; *mystical* sources were called on too; for example the words of Augustine, as Eckhart quotes them: "I am aware of something within me, playing before my soul and illuminating it. If it could only come to fulfillment and permanence within me it could not but be eternal life." Even if this category of "eternal life" does not, for modern, non-mystical man, shine right through death and break its force, it does imply the deep presence of something that has not yet appeared on the surface of him who is, as it were, the Inside of the world. For the deep core of man, the level with which Augustine and Eckhart were concerned, is extra-territorial to any previous category of human appearance—or, therefore, *disappearance.* And in its "playing" and its "illuminating," its *foreshadowing of itself without appearing,* it points to the same end as the deepest life-force—the centrally important insight, foresight, of *Spero ergo ero.* This is the real Utopian source of a finality which does not destroy, but inaugurates our true, essential being.

The "playing" and "illuminating," however, also contain an impulse which has never been content to remain hidden among the foundations: an impulse which first appeared in olden times with the advent of Christianity, when it replaced the immobile Stoic concept of *ataraxia.* Its presence can be felt, "playing before the soul and illuminating it," even when it is not by any means the great *perfectum* or *plusquamperfectum* of *amor fati* or *amor dei,* whose glory is all too ready-made and complete. Instead of this sort of confidence in the already-defined and its *definitivum* there is hope: the hope that stays with us in the midst of doubt and stormy waters, inspired by that light whose *being,* even with Augustine and Eckhart, is the total *future* in which we come forth from the Deep-within of upright stance.

The form in which this *last,* this really *"final"* sort of life-force found expression was no longer medieval, so it remained untouched by secularization. In fact, secularization set it for the first time on really human feet. And, in the absence of this praxis, the dream of a better life has kept the life-force open to Utopia. This dream could sometimes be illusionary, but when it steered clear of rashness it was wide open to the dawning of a better world. Nor was this by reason of any empirical *adaequatio intellectus ad rem,* but precisely by reason of a creative *inadaequatio* of mind and the factual (though by no means satisfactory or enlightening) world. Some words of Kant are relevant here, coming as they do from this same region of empirically open but humanly veiled evidence. In his *Dreams of a Ghost-seer* (which he certainly was *not*) he deals with the question of final life-force, providing an antidote to the saying "Much wisdom brings much grief;" the passage runs: "It is not my opinion that any predisposition or any inclination which may have slipped in before the moment of scrutiny would be able to deprive my spirit of its ability to be led in whatsoever direction should be taken by the reasons for or by those against, with one exception. For the weighing scale of the mind is not entirely unpartisan, and one of its arms, bearing the inscription *Future hope,* has a mechanical advantage which so operates that even when light reasons fall into the pan attached to it, they lift up on high the weightier speculations on the other side. This is the only inaccuracy that I am not well able to remove, and that, in the event, I shall never want to remove." And in fact the "weightier speculations" fall more easily into the scale-pan of hope than into its opposite. For they are the speculations of that ultimate thought-full recollection of the one thing that makes it worth living, and being organized, and having time, and having not only knowledge but conscience too. With the Bible providing the most ultimate of ultimate intentions, leading the speculations, making them the "weightier" ones even here. And with the meaning of life (and of nature) flowing always from hope in the one thing necessary, whose home is the *Experimentum vitae et mundi,* the Man on the front, the profoundly laboring *Laboratorium possibilis salutis* which men call history. Until their eschatological harvest is ready, either as the failure of life in retreat and a world in entropy, or as something that is in the process of transcending all life-force, something that plays even before the meta-religious recollection and illuminates it—something that, as the Omega of all that is matter-for-being, bears upon its forehead the unsolved cypher, and possesses for itself the ability to be-for itself which is the Kingdom. The far from simple, but unfortunately now somewhat common-or-garden paradox of concrete Utopia taken from my *The Principle of Hope,* is rooted not only in the force exerted by a distant goal and by the conditions governing the way to that goal, but, even more, in the manner in which that *distant* goal is involved in every *proximate* goal, making it a real goal and not just another more or less simple reproduction of past life. It is a paradox whose home is the future horizon, a paradox of utter finality, impregnated with the idea of a "perfection" which, far from one day becoming bankrupt, will one day be able to earn its designation as our "unveiled countenance." And the *Chorus mysticum* of this Omega is the same one that heralds the advent of Christ with its simple solution of a finally free *Humanum*. It may well be that Christ's advent is the last un-seen-through myth, but it is also the ultimate cipher, the last number that will only show on some final balance-sheet where man stands as "everlasting joy" and nature is gathered up into the final unity of the "heavenly Jerusalem."

Everywhere one looks, the Messianic is the last handhold of life and the ultimate resultant of the light of Utopian truth. To the clever that is folly, to the pious it is a pre-fabricated house, but to the wise the sense of Utopia is the most real and pressing problem of an unsolved world. It follows that life itself has sense inasmuch—precisely inasmuch—as it forms itself in dissatisfaction, in work, in rejection of the inadequate and in prophetic premonition of the adequate. Man does not lose himself in these heights; he surpasses himself.

42. *Sources of Possible Death-Force: Departure*

Dying is not the same as death: it is just a pallid sort of life, a very this-worldly affair, however closely connected with the death which follows. It is an act, and even the act of extinction is very different from the resultant state. There is room in it for a fear and a courage different from those which face death. Signs of pain are, after all, signs of life. However deadly they may be, they point forward to a danger rather than to an already present reality. Nevertheless the pungent scent of death is certainly present in what precedes it, and the fear of dying is surpassed by the horror of death as like by like, for dying is a living departure. We cannot experience death in our own bodies, and that makes it so much the less disturbing to have a preview of it in others—a preview of a reckoning that is quite sure to come, as the epitaph says: "What you are, I once was; what I am, you will one day be." The strength necessary to pass through this is quite different from the strength needed for living and dying, however hard or however shallow those experiences might be.

The dying ego has always before it that pulverizing, annihilating dread so peculiar to man, for animals fear dying, not death. They have no self-conscious ego that can foresee its own annihilation, and can fear the plain and final fact of death even more than it fears the act of dying. Where then can man find strength to face this outright and immediate devaluation? Where can he find courage to face the most democratic, and most hostile, of human levelers? One can appeal, of course, to the encouraging picture of death as a peaceful rest—the Greeks saw it as the brother of sleep, and the Bible as the repose taken after the evening meal at the end of the day's work: Abraham died an old man and full of years. There is a lot of truth in this too, at least when death comes in old age as the cool of night after the heat of day—so much so that courage might seem unnecessary. But the Greek picture of death as sleep did not last long. Homer's attitude to the shades was one of pity, and late antiquity experienced an unparalleled outbreak of the fear of death, which no Phaedo-dialogue of the dying Socrates could still. In the Bible, too, where earthly well-being had long seemed all-sufficient, and had long submerged the fear of death, the Book of Ecclesiastes struck a bitterly dispirited note: as the beasts die, so dies man; death is just the same, whether he rebels against it or not. There is, of course, ostensibly another side to this picture: there is the full acceptance of death on the Cross, a particularly terrible end, presented by the Bible as the irresistible source of a really death-conquering force. Baptism is entry into the *death of Christ* as the *guarantee of resurrection,* and it was this inherent finality, not any moral content, that appealed to the fear of

256

death in late antiquity. Though of course the ruling classes in the Roman Empire found the so-called patience of the Cross a splendid ideology when it came to supporting their own interests: Christianity appealed to them on very different grounds.

Among the so-called last words of the Redeemer, however, there is one phrase which stands out even in the Synoptic redaction as particularly contrary in spirit to the patience of the Lamb and the resigned acceptance of death from Yahweh's hand. The anguish of Gethsemane already shows that Jesus knew nothing of Paul's theology of sacrificial death, and by no means accepted subjectively the much-vaunted necessity of his end. The catastrophic proportions of the abandonment he felt on the Cross and the utter blankness of a death which certainly looked forward to no Easter are epitomized in the despair and accusation of words which stand out like an Aramaic signpost from the Greek of the rest of the New Testament: *"Eli, Eli, lama asabthani!* My God, my God, why hast thou forsaken me?"* The *locus classicus* of these words is *here,* not Psalm 22. 2 from which they are quoted; for here alone do they lash out against the hardest of all forms of oppression—annihilation. And far from softening the antithesis, the Job-like tone makes it sharper, for it is here that the avowed Messiah, the Son of Man, summons up the last sources of his courage to reject God and bring him down along with himself, calling him the God of abandonment—which means the God of death. Though admittedly the wish-myth of resurrection, thanks to the wish-*mysterium* it contains, had to turn round against this in the very next breath and fill with its astounding "revelation" the gap left by the most utter of all abandonments. Religion, right from the Greek notion of death being the brother of sleep to the Christian faith in Easter, has always tried to provide a form of courage that simply refuses to take death as true. But the *Credo quia absurdum* has not in fact lasted, however much its miraculous Utopia may stand as an *intermissio regulae* in the face of common fear and equally common banality, in the face of the sheer dimensionlessness

257

of death, asserting the open-ended problem of the Future—a problem which centers on death, and one that is of constant relevance even in the meta-religious sphere. Which means, finally, that our transcending without transcendence in no way has to demolish this explosive courage against death. For even without pre-fabricating any dwelling in another world, an incomplete This-world should be able to make room for the unquenchable spirit whose roots lie in the remarkable and the miraculous. But again, not as a final solution.

In the midst of life death crowds in from all sides; how shall we face it? It is so near, and yet at the same time so far, whether in the brief moment of an accident or in the longer days and years of sickness. In the common span that we call daily life no massive shock disturbs the normal house. But it is quite another matter when incurable illness walls one up in a hospital. That is a frontier situation, and one which often brings with it the first stirrings of metaphysics. The *facies hippocratica* of the soul, sealed with the great black mark, then looks, strangely enough, for the most part back across the past; if it looks forward into the Beyond it only does so conventionally. Nowadays not even pious souls experience the fear and the superstitious certainty of former times regarding what comes *after* death; for them the encounter is simply a "catechism," one with things which might or might not come. The terrors of hell and the joys of heaven are, at best, something met with in preparation for confirmation. But it was different in the days when ghosts appeared at every turn and death seemed a mere show, not at all a descent into nothingness. Or when, at the opposite end of things, St. Catherine could draw the attention of her confessor to the roses God had sent her the night before her death, and when he failed to see them could reply: "But of course—God only sent them for me." This sort of thing is no longer with us (apart, perhaps, from some pockets of anachronism in peasant quarters), but it is still strange that most candidates for death are so preoccupied with their past, and lack even the most sceptical, objectless curiosity about their coming end. Even the precious private ego, often so selfish and narrow, is concerned only to show a fine concern for the fate of his family or business once he is gone, however much he may himself really fear death. The very most that is allowed is that the moment of death should see a highly concentrated review of the whole of life—but even in that fable there is no question of any fore-taste of an individually tailored, and, in the final analysis, substantial future state. Brecht does enlarge the picture somewhat with the idea that an individual of moral worth should think, not of entering some new world, but of leaving a better world behind him. But even this looks back at something that is complete, and although there are echoes here of the old quest for immortality in one's works, the precondition of having something to bequeath is, in present-day society, seldom verified. In any case, none of this looks forward to the possibility of really new experience for the particular individual, for the particular concrete intensification, formed-intensity, of the continually forward-going being of mankind. None of it looks forward to the *Novum*.

In these circumstances the more modern attitude of deep curiosity in death as in a departure might well seem a great improvement, for all its rarity. Death, in the words of the sceptic Montaigne, was *"le grand Peut-être"*—which went against not only the positive dogmatism of the religious tradition, but the equally dogmatic negativity of pure mechanism with its opposite sort of rashness. The only scientific answer to these two dogmatisms was *"Non liquet,"* for the evidence was simply insufficient to provide more than a *Peut-être* for either the continuance or the non-continuance of life. With the difference, noted scientifically by Kant in *Dreams of a Ghost-seer*, that the smallest sign of immortality would be enough to save that whole structure, whereas the mere absence of such a sign is not enough to justify its dogmatic denial. In addition to this forward-looking curiosity, however, there was the far from purely scientific interest in

259

death of the post-Renaissance bourgeoisie (cf., for example, Pomponazzi, *De immortalitate animae,* 1516). The intention here was to do away with the debilitating fear of death among the lower classes and at the same time to abolish the power of the Keys of Rome. In this context, too, the words of Ecclesiastes were revived: as the beasts die, so dies man. But the revolutionary spirit of freedom underlying the deep (and not even deep) pessimism of these words was kept out of sight, for reasons of state, along with the devaluation which not only (quite rightly) removed the terrors of the Other-world, but also any idea of making sense of death at all. And which, going far beyond the annihilation of the individual, reduced the whole work of mankind to lonely, meaningless futility against a background of cosmic entropy or, in earlier times, of atomic decay and death. There was no cause here for rejoicing in a purely mechanical defense of death, but there were grounds for summoning up all one's courage to utter a final, open, undogmatic *Non omnis confundar, non omnia confunduntur:* I shall not altogether be confounded, all things will not be confounded. Grounds too for a by no means obsolete fundamental attitude to oneself such as one has towards those one loves, and above all towards the woman, Beatrice. This being, this aura, these images cannot pass away; they shine through death, whether it be past or yet to come. Or, to be more masculine, the formed-intensity that is My-own-self reaches its high point phenomenologically when it breaks out in search of more light, more room, and Home. There is no accidental over-steeping of the boundaries here, no mere chance shaking-out of one's wings, but rather something that lies close to the words put by the young Goethe on the lips of his Moses of the Koran: "Lord, make room for me in my narrow breast." Something, therefore, that is simply not touched by the departure and the downfall of this narrow breast itself.

All this makes for a new understanding of the unthinkable, shocking wish, the meta-religious, hereditarily Utopian wish-*modus* present in the resurrection of Christ: *De te homo, nondum naturans, supernaturans, fabula narratur.* The *"fab-ula"* in question tells of what man is really about, and tells it for the first time—the intense core of his intentionally-directed being has only ever appeared in small hints, in attempts at hope and at the formation of resurrection-Utopias. For at the inmost kernel of our being we are *homo absconditus,* and that alone: we are the one authentic mystery of our own most immediate immediacy, and that mystery has never objectified itself. So, never having really come to be, it can never really pass away. The *homo intensivus sed absconditus,* the still infolded closest closeness of our deepest depths, is, *by virtue of being Not-yet-being,* utterly and completely extra-territorial to the great destroyer of being called death. No one can claim to have made the journey to the heart of the fire of our existence, so, not having been found, it must remain unquenched. Not even the departure into death can pull the X down into nothingness, so long as the world still involves a journey, and a process, and the material for that process—so long as the world still *is* those things. So long as *natura naturans,* and even *supernaturans,* in its turn, is imperfect and incomplete, full of real, objective possibility for future forms, future identities, future realizations. Here there is room to move; room for the *Non omnis confundar* of each man's, and then mankind's true being, as it waits, extra-territorially, in the wings. Kant remarked pointedly enough, in a passage still full of the old religious, "Idea" of another world (though not now of this Other-world as object), that our place there and our fate would presumably depend largely on how we had performed our office in the present world. However that may be, one might at least think that the good and the beautiful, the noble and the profound, which operate, albeit disjointedly and remotely, in our present precarious existence, would be able to strengthen our spirits to face death by calling into play the emotive force of expectation, and even that of surprise at the non-completeness of things. For our still undiscovered essence is in very truth the *topos* of the expectant, non-capitulating search—the *topos,*

261

inaccessible as yet to all that comes to be and passes away, where, even in the dark face of night, that search can find an enduring meta-religious—and therefore all the more meta-physical—dwelling-place.

Death will most certainly catch up with the man who just stands around and thinks about all this. And when his corpse is finished and done with, flushed away almost, there are still the flowers—they have to be put somewhere. Flesh corrupts; and if there is, or was, a soul, it has certainly flown now. Only stones remain, and they are untouched by the fact that the late lamented no longer sees them, for they are lifeless. One of the world's whims, so it seems from the death bed, is to refuse to show itself to the dead; but to the great anorganic giant of the Around-us that is no whim at all.

At this unexpected, but particularly appropriate, juncture, the old, still persistent alternative *aut Kosmos aut Logos* comes back into focus as a burning existential issue. On the one hand the question is of returning to *Gē*, the mother earth, or else of being shot off into the universe; on the other hand it is one of resurrection and new life. The alternatives of astral-myth and logos-myth have a sort of secularized re-union here with death—is man to be like a stone or to be like a spirit? Or, to go even further, which of the two remains, human history or extra-human nature—nature not just in its capacity as a preamble to human history, for in that function the logos breaks into it and surpasses it? Or is it the great vault of the anorganic cosmos around us that remains, as the context enshrining even death? If that were so, the logos-like "spirit" of human history would be only an episode, with no substantial significance at all. It is, of course, quite right to say that even though myth may be the foundation of art it cannot be the foundation of philosophy, above all of scientific philosophy. And yet the history of science can quote evidence of the astral-myth at work in a secularized form in Bruno and

Spinoza's primacy of nature, and that of French naturalism, and evidence of logos-myth at work in the primacy of human consciousness as found not only in Leibnitz and Hegel, but, above all, in pre-Christian idealism. But, to bring this back to the question of death—the freedom-spirit of the logos works against any ultimately static envelopment in cosmic speculation, and the non-transcendent immanence of the cosmos works against the ultimate topos-lessness of the never more than approximate liberation implicit in logos-speculation. (Which gives added relevance, *sub specie mortis,* to Lenin's words: "Intelligent idealism is closer to intelligent materialism than stupid materialism is.")

However, just as human history to date is simply prehistory, so too the place occupied by cosmic nature does not belong to it. That is the point behind the Eschaton element in the logos-myth, with its symbol of the New Jerusalem, for that is the final, explosive liberation of the Christian Thing: a liberation operating neither high-above nor deep-within, but in a transformed *world* of total friendship: a world of Home. It is significant here that the Arch-*humanum* of this city of fantasy and speculation is thought of as existing in the cosmos, in "space," albeit in an a-topical, apocalyptic space. And "death has now passed away" for this very reason, that the liberation here is of a new earth, not of any a-spatial realm of spirits. Although it is undoubtedly the most high-flown, not to mention mythological, of all treatises on Utopia, the Apocalypse of John has, more than any other book, stirred up the earth-bound breast to bathe not so much in the red rays of transcendence as in the dawn of a better world on earth, a world "prepared as a bride" for the "souls" of the saved—for it is they who are thought of as remaining.

But enough of this religious imagery. At the core of every man there is an element of extra-territoriality to the disappearance and demise of what he simply has not yet become, and the name of this element's true territory is: *Spero ergo ero*—not-undiscovered identity.

263

43. Hunger, "Something in a Dream," "God of Hope," Thing-For-Us

> Just as an elastic body contains its greater
> dimension only by striving after it, so
> a monad contains its future state . . . One can
> say that in the soul, as in everything else,
> the present is pregnant with the future.
> *Leibnitz, Letter to Bayle* (1702)

Man's whole *raison d'être*, the What-for of all life's work and, ultimately, of the life-force itself, can easily fall prey to fierce questioning when, despite a plentiful supply of daily bread, the other bread of life, the concrete "What" of What-for and Where-to, begins to dwindle.

These questions will not, of course, be raised in the slums and hovels of stifling poverty, nor, at the other end of the scale, in those quarters where the profit race (still largely based on a more or less exotic poverty) provides its own ready-made answers, and where life is led by the bourgeoisie who cannot in any case (according to Marx) see beyond the end of their corporate nose. Money makes for sensuality; cash can laugh.

The other hunger, the unassuaged, explosive hunger of the life-force, presents itself as the continual Not-yet of true human possession. It is an aspect of the quest for meaning, and, far from drugging the hunger for meaning (and with it the non-meaning of death) with any opium of the people in the form of dreamed-up compensation in another world, it fills it with the food of restless labor, working away, unswerving and incorrupt, to gain a true awareness and genuine satisfaction of man's Utopian needs. Only in this way—not in the ideological apologias of any ruling class, nor in the remorseless morality and finality of the Utopia of missing expectations which echoes through the pages of a homeless, twisted history—only in this way can that other dream come into being: the radical, subversive dream of the Bible which, far from being rooted in a haze of opium, stems from a profound wakefulness to the future, to the great dimension of light with which the world is pregnant. This dream can make the future present even in the past. It harbors no crippling historicism and no over-abrupt Jacobinism, but simply the irrepressible sense of the awakening of meaning. In Marx's words: "It will then become evident that the world possesses something in a dream of which it need only become aware to possess it in truth" (*Letter to Ruge,* 1843).

The "something" in this dream, and the awareness which brings it to reality are, even in Marx, neither more nor less than the anticipated presence of the Kingdom of Freedom, kept alive in the hope of those who walk with the laborers and heavy-laden, the degraded and despised, and available only to those who can stand up on their own two feet. The "something in a dream" was, and is in its avowed utopianism, nothing to do with the acquisition of profits and the mis-appropriation of values which only laugh on one side of their face, nor with the subjectively lonely world of illusion, so alien to all ideas of tendency. The ultimate concrete awareness of all true hunger, and its concrete activity, is directed towards possession of this "something" in its Not-yet-being. But the really paradoxical element in all this is that Utopia does not end with its final, concrete realization—it begins there. That is the meaning of Marx's words. For the "something in a dream" is, after all, *rebus fluentibus,* in some way an *objective, concrete "something";* it is something in a state of process, something *still pending in latent hope,* drawn on to its vanishing point in the perspective of meaning, drawn to the gravitational center of an as yet unrealized At-all, which men used to call God; but which a-theism sees as the Utopian Omega of the fulfilled Moment, the Eschaton of our immanence, the illumination of our incognito.

The forward-look has replaced the upward-look. Feelings of humility and obeisance vis-à-vis the prince and lord are no more than a memory, as are prayers of supplication and all the rest of the baptized beggary. Even the Bible's ownmost emotion of hope is unworthy of us whenever it makes man a servile retainer, waiting only for manna from on high. Hope cannot at the same time raise itself from the ground in a transcending sweep and bow down humbly to take alms, conscious only of the so-called Fall behind it as the symbol of human nullity, and of the imperious, unmerited (if you follow Luther) realm of grace above it. Where there is hope there is religion, but where there is religion there is not always hope: not the hope built up from beneath, undisturbed by ideology.

What then is the goal of this hope? It is not only the theocratic sections of the Bible that give the ever-open reply to those whose nature is pure enough to receive it: "and everlasting joy will dwell upon them"—the unveiled light of Utopian joy, the light of man, welling up *de profundis,* from his depths, not his lowliness. It is the final apocalyptic result of the "dream," the utmost limit of Utopia where that "dream" would pass over from its proper dimension of hope (at the worst a dimension full of fantasy) into the most alien and heteronomous of hope-dimensions—the point where the real newness of the Bible, with its Exodus and Kingdom, would give way to the On-high, where there is no room for man.

This being so, hope is able to inherit those features of religion which do not perish with the death of God. There are such features—for, contrary to all pure facticity, the *Futurum* of hope was thought of as a property of God's being, and one which distinguished him from all other gods. The Thing-for-us, the world-for-us in the "dream" of something-without-God but with the hope that is his essence. This world has one perspective only; it is the perspective of the front . . . openness . . . *Novum* . . . the ultimate matter for being . . . to be . . . Utopia. And no secret is at the same time so remote and so near as that of *homo absconditus* in the midst of this world which has its own mystery and its own problem to bear, in the how and the why and the wherefore of its being. These questions remain at their deepest level unsolved, waiting for the answer that will bring identity; and they do so not only

266

where we men are concerned, not only where our knowledge of the world is concerned, but also with respect to the world itself in its ownmost process.

44. Conclusion: Marx and the End of Alienation

"Come to your senses!" An appeal at once very old and very new. Give up being used—misused—for other men's gain. Give up being a beast for other men's burden. Give up being made to fight your own flesh and blood, and dying for those who are not your flesh and blood at all—while our Sunday-men, one moment worldly, the next moment spiritual, but always loyal to their lord, stand by and give their blessing.

The pastors paid willing homage to the power which had crucified the first Christian heretic—it was, after all, often their own power. But to the poor and the exploited and the deprived they preached patient tolerance, not force. They were not, of course, disturbed when the oppressors used force, whether it was the constant intimidation of daily life or the unmasked brutality which countered all outbreaks of impatience down below. In those circumstances gas and pistol were called means of defense, and rebellion, however justified, was terror. The power of the On-high was draped in ideology, and songs of praise were ready even for the loaded revolver. "They deck out the altars, and the poor suffer bitter hunger"—Amos's words have always been relevant, and generally in vain. Even the "decking out" of art and philosophy, apart from "giving expression to their age in thought," has often in fact put up an apologetic mask in front of it, gilding the fog of false con-science, spinning a thick web of words.

But prescinding now from all this whitewashing, the ideolo-gy of late capitalism contains a special element of the class-conditioned alienation of man from himself, an element first brought to the light of day by Marx. This ever-intensified form of alienation can be seen most clearly in the society governed by monopoly capitalism, where both man and material things

267

are reduced to the status of goods, and where a thoroughly misguided consciousness has brought with it the most astonishing self-alienation and wasteful self-sacrifice to empty, false and alien interests. Not without reason has the anthropological and religious critique of gods and goddery come down to earth from heaven. Not without reason did Marx speak of the "fetishistic" character of commodities, and of the "illusions" of ideology, until in the end, thanks to economics, these somewhat less transcendent scales also fell from men's eyes. Significantly enough, in fact, the whole analysis of alienation and the attempt to restore the alienated factors to the human subject began with the critique of religion: with the young Hegel's statement about the "treasures squandered on heaven," and the anthropological insights added forcefully—if not very profoundly—by Feuerbach. It was again from books that the fire broke out when Marx publicized the fact that a mythical heaven had stolen and alienated the ultra-earthly phenomenon of goods, along with their producer, whom it had reduced to a personified work-force, a mere commodity. One must never forget here that Marx's critique of alienation and goods would hardly have arisen at all if it had not been for his previous involvement in, and critique of, religion. Unlike Feuerbach, however, he was not content to see man's treasures squandered on heaven simply in order to bring them back from alienation to some abstract species man. Instead of that, he put the whole ideology of the On-high on a par with heaven, and denounced not the condition of abstract man but the actual, given ensemble of capitalist relations and, above all, its victims, the laborers and the heavy-laden. For they are the most alienated of all (whether they know it or not); and they are at one and the same time a possible lever towards the downfall of those relations which hold man in abandoned slavery, and the immediate heir to that fall.

This detective glance at history, seeing through it and its ideologies, undoubtedly belongs to the cold current in Marxist thought. But the What-for, the distant goal of this penetrating glance, belongs to the warm current evident in the beginnings of Marxism, for it is unquestionably rooted in the originally Christian ground-plan for the "Kingdom of Freedom" itself. It is the *cold current,* however, that brings the statement, relevant to most of our past history, that "when ideas and interests meet it is always the ideas that capitulate." And it is the cold current that says of the revolution, which at long last is objective and not a mere figment of abstract Utopia, that "the working class does not have to implement ideals, but [has] to liberate the tendencies towards those ideals which are already present in society." In the same way, too, Engels (quite rightly) gave one of his books the very cooling title: "The progress of socialism from Utopia to science"; though sometimes, as the *warm current,* and the results of its absence, proclaim, this particular progress can be overdone. And then the warm current needs science, not as somehow non-Utopian, but as the concrete realization, at last, of Utopia.

Far from being a contradiction in terms, concrete Utopia is the firmest of handholds, and by no means only where the propaganda and implementation of socialism is concerned. The whole *surplus force* of culture finds its salvation there, and these forces are becoming more and more relevant to us all the time—above all, the wealth of artistic allegories and religious symbols, whose day is not yet done when the ideology which bore them disappears. An old sage once said that man is easier to save than to feed. The coming age of socialism will find, when everyone has sat down to the meal, that the conventional reversal of this paradox is very indigestible indeed: that man is easier to feed than to save. Taking everything into consideration, that is—ourselves and socialism and death, and the crucial secret that there is in fact a world at all to be set straight. For the really enduring sort of self-alienation is not so dependent on the false society that it will go when that society goes: its sources lie deeper than that. Marx said: "To be radical is to grasp things at their roots. But the root of all (viz. social) things is man." The first letter of John (3. 2) also takes man as the root, but rather as being on the way to something than as being a real cause: "It does not yet appear what we shall be,

269

but we know that when he appears we shall be like him, for we shall see him as he is. And every one who thus hopes in him purifies himself as he is pure." The "he" admittedly refers to the so-called Father in heaven, but it is the Son of Man, of one essence with the Father, that is really meant: he is our own, true, radical identity, appearing at the end of history. If these two tests had ever come face to face, the encounter would have shed a searching Utopian light on the problem of universal alienation and its possible cure. From the Christian point of view, "that which men call God" would have become man at last; from the philosophical point of view, Hegelian phenomenology would have been left high and dry by the idea that substance is now subject.

It would be a strange meeting—but then, why not? The meeting is strange even when it occurs at far less remote places than the root-point of man, the root which has not yet flowered. Or, if it has flowered, then only in such a way that the bloom always has to bear an alien blight. Only at its deepest moments (and they were not deep) did the nineteenth century see the end of all metaphysics as the consequence of such strange atheistic systems as those concerned with the dissolution of alienation *(Dieu et létat)*. The vulgar Marxists can be left out of the reckoning here, let alone the transcendence conservationists. *Hic rhodus, hic salta*—daring to dance, to leap, to explore the new, without any sort of catechism.

There is a passage in the *Economic and Philosophic Manuscripts of 1844* in which Marx reaches out in an astounding piece of speculation, constructing a chiasmus that in recent years has become so well known as to be almost unknown again. He goes so far as to speak of the "resurrection of nature," and to do so with a certain humor, a mysterious lightness of touch, which makes the break with the past all the easier, and even more so the break with the oppression of the moment, in which this supremely Utopian chiasmus must seem both scandal and folly. His words are well known: "Naturalization of man, humanization of nature"—an ultimate, teleo-logical solution of a sort very rare in Marx. The warm current is at work here in the complete reversal of alienation. But it would be banal to see the naturalization as no more than *mens sana in corpore sano*, and the humanization as a mere domesti-cation of nature in an improved late-Arcadian key. This is, in fact, a really penetrating phrase; there are a lot of them latent in Marxism, but too few ever get actually said. It is a phrase whose two halves could have come from Jacob Böhme and Franz Baader respectively, with on the one hand their well-springs of fresh water and on the other their Sun-man or Man-sun.

Marx himself did not need such an encounter, but Marxism in its reduced form certainly does. And, so far as Christianity is concerned, how else, apart from the chiasmic interchange of man and nature with its real, crucial secret, can it hope to get away from the transcendence it has just seen through? Natu-ralization of man—that would mean his incorporation into the community, his final this-wordly awakening, so that, free from all alienation, we could really control our *hic et nunc*. Humani-zation of nature—that would mean the opening-up of the cosmos, still closed to itself, to be our Home: the Home once expressed in the mystical fantasy of new heaven and new earth, and echoing on through the beauty and quality of nature as these have found expression in painting and poetry, with the great leap out of the realm of necessity drawing ever closer to man. Not to mention that out-and-out qualitative, all-shattering horizon of *apocalypsis cum figuris* kept open not in antiquity but in the Christianity of Dürer's day, at least in the realm of fantasy.

The effort to turn such far-flung images as these into a more concrete form of Utopia is, of course, only thinkable in terms of a leap of memory; at the foreshadowing-point of imminent earthly liberation and freedom there is more than enough for man to do if he is to make anything more solid. The only thing is that no humanism would be tolerable if it did not implicitly possess these far-flung but profoundly happy images of the

Where-to, the What-for and the At-all to complement its morality. And the freedom of these images lies in the extension of the as yet unextended *homo absconditus* in the world—in the experiment of the world. In that experiment the human dimension is quite open enough to utter destruction, and there is more than enough disparate universe surrounding a now-dead world. If that were all there was, the whole Prometheus-dimension, and the realm of the freedom-seeker would provide at the very most an element of beauty, but with no sign of a movement towards meaning. However, the whole world to date, the world of mere facts with their openness to annihilation, is untrue. The only true things are the process found in the world, and the voice of that rebel who said to Pilate, with a very different party-allegiance in mind, allegiance to the *Novum:* "Every one who is of the truth hears my voice." And then their place is the struggle, the point of resolution, the warm current, with the cry of mankind in their ears, and the memory of that cry, out on the front of world-process.

Non omnis confundar: I shall not altogether be confounded; that holds good for our humanized nature even in its extra-territoriality. It is, of course, not a proximate goal; one cannot live from it, and our human history is a far more day-to-day affair than this distant aim at a final goal. All the more reason, then, why the ideologies and illusions, the mythologies and theocracies of ecclesiastical Christianity should by now have run their day, along with the fixed, transcendent, stationary In-the-highest of a world beyond all cares. True Marxism has no time for all that, but takes true Christianity seriously—too seriously for just another grey and compromising dialog. When Christians are really concerned with the emancipation of those who labor and are heavy-laden, and when Marxists retain the depths of the Kingdom of Freedom as the real content of revolutionary consciousness on the road to becoming true substance, the alliance between revolution and Christianity founded in the Peasant Wars may live again—this time with success. Florian Geyer, the great fighter of those wars, is reputed to have had the words *"Nulla crux, nulla corona"*

272

scratched on the blade of his sword. That could be the motto of a Christianity free, at last, from alienation. And the far-reaching, inexhaustible depths of emancipation in those words could also serve as a motto for a Marxism aware of its depths.

Vivant sequentes. Marxism, and the dream of the unconditioned, follow the same path and the same plan of campaign. A *Humanum* free from alienation, and a World into which it could fit—a world as yet still undiscovered, but already somehow sensed: both these things are definitively present in the experiment of the Future, the experiment of the World.